# THE SCOTS WEEK-END

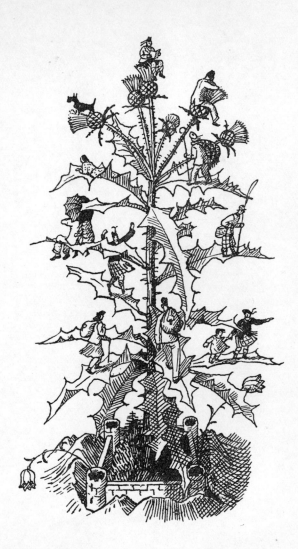

# THE SCOTS WEEK-END

*AND*

*CALEDONIAN VADE-MECUM*

*FOR*

*HOST, GUEST AND WAYFARER*

LONDON

GEORGE ROUTLEDGE & SONS, LTD.

68-74 CARTER LANE, E.C.

1936

PRINTED IN GREAT BRITAIN
BY R. & R. CLARK, LIMITED, EDINBURGH

TO
# LORD TWEEDSMUIR
### A KINDLY SCOT

Thir a that suigeartach ceolar
Ceannaich-sa mo leabhar oran
Theag' g'un deam e feum ri'd' bheo dhut
Ged nach mor a phris.

James MacGregor

# CONTENTS

# ACKNOWLEDGEMENTS

WE have to thank the following for their courtesy in permitting us to quote from copyright works:

(1) *Prose and verse extracts*: Lord Tweedsmuir [John Buchan], Mr C. M. Grieve [Hugh MacDiarmid], Dr. Charles Murray and Messrs Constable & Co., Ltd. (for "Ay, Fegs" from *In the Country Places*); Professor James Moffatt, D.D., and Messrs Hodder & Stoughton (for the extracts from the former's translation of the Old Testament); Mr Edwin Muir, Dr. J. M. Bulloch, Mrs Joyce Maxtone-Graham [Jan Struther], Miss Helen B. Cruickshank, Captain G. G. Macfarlane [Patrick Miller], Mr R. Farquharson Sharp (for extracts from the works of William Sharp); the Executors of Roger Quin the younger, Messrs W. C. Henderson, Ltd., St. Andrews (for the poems from *The Scarlet Gown*, by R. F. Murray); Messrs William Hodge & Co., Ltd. (for poems by Robert Browning (Scotus), J. R. Christie, T. L. Douglas, George Fletcher and A. S. Wallace from *University Verses*); Messrs Hodder & Stoughton (for extracts from *Tobersnorey*, by Sir James Cameron Lees, D.D.); Messrs Jackson, Son & Co., Glasgow (for extracts from *A Heretic*, by Walter C. Smith, D.D.); Messrs Oliver & Boyd, Edinburgh) for "Blessing on the Kindling" from *Carmina Gadelica*); the Moray Press, Edinburgh (for the epigram by William Soutar); the Porpoise Press (for poems by Alexander Gray, Roderick Watson Kerr, William Ogilvy and George Malcolm Thomson); and the proprietors of the *Glasgow Herald* (for "The Best-dressed Highlander" by D. M. Mackay).

(2) *Songs*: Mr David Stephen and Mr Ian Whyte (for the original rounds); Dr. Millar Patrick (for some of the precentor's rhymes); Mr Duncan Morison and Mr Malcolm MacInnes (for island airs); Mr Hector

MacIver (for the words of the Lewis Bridal Song);
Mr H. M. Willsher and Dr. R. C. Buist (for "If the
Kirk wad let me be"); Dr. David Rorie (for "The
Lum Hat wantin' the Croon"); Mr Moultrie Kelsall
(for bothy ballads); Mr William Kemp (for "I dinna
like McFarlane); Messrs Boosey & Co. (for "An
Eriskay Love-lilt" and "The Road to the Isles"); and
Paterson's Publications, Ltd. (for "Flat-footed Jean").

While we believe the foregoing to be a complete
statement of our indebtedness, it is possible that there
are a few omissions, in which case we offer our apologies
to those to whom they are due. It also may be that by
inadvertence we have included one or two copyright
items, for it is not always easy in the case of long-
deceased authors to ascertain whether copyright still
subsists or to trace the present owners of it. Here again,
if we have offended we hope we may be forgiven.

# PREFACE

In the common form of preface acknowledgements of assistance, if made at all, are put last. This is a shabby practice at best, and in the present circumstances would be inexcusable, for without the generous collaboration of many friends our project of *The Scots Week-End* could never have been carried out. Our first duty, therefore, is to thank "JAMES BRIDIE" for his demonstration of the heather-bedside manner; ERIC LINKLATER for his sage guidance in the delicate matter of holiday friendships which he has refused to have entitled "Don Juan in Caledonia"; DAVID CLEGHORN THOMSON for bearing the main burden of the musical section; ROBERT HURD for his illustrated notes on Scottish architecture; and a lad we daurna name, owing to the etiquette of Parliament House, for the learned and lively opinion he has given on the law of Scotland as it affects the holiday-maker. With the main literary contributors we must join EVELYN DUNBAR, to whose witty and accomplished pencil we owe the decorations.

These have been our chief coadjutors, but there are many more to whom we are indebted—so many, indeed, that it would be no mere phrase to say that they are too numerous to mention. Yet a few must be mentioned. Thus we must thank Dr. J. M. Bulloch, whose authority on the subject is undisputed, for the notes on Scottish regimental tartans, which embody information not to be found in any other book; Mr Edward Scouller, who has put at our disposal his copious and curious learning on Scottish children's games; Miss F. Marian MacNeill and Mr George Malcolm Thomson for help in the meat-and-drink section; and Mrs Robert Ornsby for expert advice on our native breeds of dog.

Nor is this all by a long way, as we cannot even claim much originality of conception for our miscellany. Obviously there would have been no *Scots Week-End* if Mr and Mrs Francis Meynell had not previously thought of *The Week-End Book*, which has delighted the English-speaking world for these dozen years and is likely to go on doing so for another generation. To the Scot, however, the appeal of *The Week-End Book* is limited by what is its very charm—its essential Englishness, the spirit of the English countryside that it breathes, and the peculiarly English allusiveness of its literary quality. On particular points, too, such as flora and fauna, law and architecture, its information is largely inapplicable north of the Tweed. Yet, rightly or wrongly, for good or ill, Scotland has some reputation as a holiday country, and it is only reasonable that it should have its own holiday book. *The Scots Week-End* is our attempt to supply that. Of its imperfections we are well aware, but we do not beg to be excused on account of them. We would even make a virtue of them, because they are largely characteristic of the national genius. Further, in selecting their material the editors of *The Week-End Book* were limited only by the boundaries of the ample term "English"—that is to say, they could include anything from a Burns lyric to a negro spiritual. We of *The Scots Week-End*, on the other hand, have, with a few exceptions, been confined to native writers and singers. In these narrow circumstances our wonder is that we have so much to show.

Some criticisms of the anthological parts had better be anticipated. Let it be said in the first place that personal caprice has had a large share in the business of selection. That may be forgiven if the net result is amusing. Caprice, however, has been qualified by two serious considerations. Generally speaking, Scottish anthologies are apt to be both hackneyed and solemn. The masterpieces of the old "makars" and the ver-

nacular poets of a later day are paraded again and
again as if their merits could not be over-emphasised.
It also happens somehow that these prime favourites
are apt to be concerned with the more sombre emo-
tions. Why this should be is not clear. The Scots are
not an exceptionally dismal race. On the contrary, in
comparison with (say) the Irish, they are cheerful and
easy-going. One can but surmise that they feel there
may be something not quite right in the sight of
heaven about their natural good spirits, and so "wi'
pains they put a Sunday face on". Conventional Burns-
worship, which regards mainly the less robust aspects
of the poet, has likewise done much mischief. There
was good Scots verse before Burns, and there has been
some since his day that is not to be despised. Not the
least of the many services that Lord Tweedsmuir has
rendered to Scottish letters is that in *The Northern
Muse* he has shown the present generation of Scotsmen
how much richer and more varied is their inheritance
of lyric poetry than they had been led to believe.

Our little anthology was conceived in something of
the same spirit, subject to the limitations of a book that
is professedly for lighter moments. Like the Vicar of
Wakefield's first sermon in prison, it is calculated to
amuse rather than to edify. It includes very few old
favourites, for these, as we have said, have been more
than sufficiently rehearsed. Burns figures little in it,
and even so mainly as an epigrammatist; but Hogg
gets, if not his due, at least more generous treatment
than is usually accorded him. He was a great man,
who at his best could rival Burns in lyric poetry and
excel Scott in prose. Stevenson is not represented at all.
His experiments in Scots verse are juvenilia, and, when
one comes to consider them, not very good ones. On
the other hand, the Victorian age produced Scottish
practitioners of the art of light verse who are not
remembered as they deserve to be. Lord Neaves, perhaps, is no more than a ready and rollicking versifier,

but George Outram is an accomplished wit, and Robert Fuller Murray a disciple of Calverley who might well have rivalled his master had death not taken him while still in his pupilage. We have also drawn upon the considerable body of fugitive light verse that may be found, if one has the patience to look for it, in the files of Scottish newspapers and university magazines since the beginning of the century. The poets of our so-called Renascence have presented a more difficult problem, because in the nature of the case their work so far consists more of experiment than of achievement. "Nae doot themsels they ken it weel", for the general response of those we approached with permission to quote was a courteous but sardonic consent. "Use what you like", was the substance of it, "and much good may it do you." Well, it has done us the good of enabling us to give poems by "Hugh MacDiarmid" and Edwin Muir, to mention no others. But admittedly our selection of the moderns is not in any sense representative.

Of the rest of the anthology not much need be said; but we hope the section called "Unlucky Numbers" may serve to refute the charge made by "Hugh Mac-Diarmid" in a recent work that Scotland has not quality enough to produce truly "good" bad poetry, and that the hoot of the Stuffed Owl is seldom heard on our side of the Border. Praise of Scotland we found difficult to fill from non-Scottish writers, while Dispraise of Scotland revealed an embarrassing wealth of material. Paradoxically the Sabbath section proved the most intractable of all. The Scottish Sabbath is a subject apparently that foreign writers can hardly bring themselves to speak of, while the eulogies of the native writers are either ludicrous or manifestly insincere. It is perhaps significant that the National Bard is silent on the painful topic.

A word on the song section and we have done. Here, as in the anthology, the aim has been to avoid as far as possible the beaten track, but as it is the essence of the section to provide songs that for the most part can be sung in chorus round the fire, a certain regard has had to be paid to old favourites. Consideration has also been had for local sentiment. Thus, in addition to Aberdeen's "Where Gadie rins", which is in many popular collections, we have given Angus's "Lum Hat wantin' the Croon" and Hawick's "Pawkie Paiterson", which are not so generally known. There are also some snatches of street ballads and other odds and ends which have never appeared in print before.

DONALD CARSWELL
CATHERINE CARSWELL
*Editors*

# PROEM

## THE SUM OF WISDOM

*Sweet is the light of life, and pleasant is it for the eyes to see the sun. If a man live many years, let him have joy throughout them all; let him remember that the dark days will be many. All that comes after death is emptiness.*

*But be sure that for all this God will bring you to account.*
*But remember your Creator in the flower of your age.*

So rejoice in your youth, young man,
be blithe in the flower of your age;
follow your heart's desire
    and all that attracts you.
Banish all worries from your mind,
    and keep your body free from pain
(for youth and manhood will not last)
ere evil days come on,
and years approach when you shall say,
    "I have no joy in them";
ere the sun grows dark,
    and the light goes from moon and stars,
and the clouds gather after rain;
when the guards tremble in the house of Life,
    when its upholders bow,
when the maids that grind are few and fail,
    and ladies at the lattice lose their lustre,
when the doors to the street are shut,
    and the sound of the mill runs low,
when the twitter of birds is faint,
    and dull the daughters of song,
when old age fears a height,
    and even a walk has its terrors,
when his hair is almond white,
    and he drags his limbs along,
    and the spirit flags and fades.
So man goes to his long, long home,
    and mourners pass along the street,
on the day when the silver cord is snapped,
    and the golden lamp drops broken,
when the pitcher breaks at the fountain,
    the wheel breaks at the cistern,
when the dust returns to earth once more,
    and the spirit to God who gave it.

*Ecclesiastes (Dr. Moffatt's Version)*

# HERE'S TAE US!

## OR

### *IN PRAISE OF SCOTLAND*

THERE'S TAE US!

OR

IN PRAISE OF SCOTLAND

*Caledonia! Caledonia! What recollections, what impressions in the name of the first poetical country, whose brilliant inspirations, the direction of my studies permitted me to learn! Here, all is natural, grand, sublime, all bears the character of solemn, unalterable antiquity. The manners of this people, their dress, their language even, are like themselves pure from mixture; and (a remark without exception) wherever the original, or at least the immemorial language has been preserved, there is still a nation, because a nation is a language.*

CHARLES NODIER

*In all my travels I never met with any one Scotchman but what was a man of sense.*

F. LOCKEN, D.D. (1667–1740)

# SCOTIA AND THE SCOTS

THE londe Scotia hathe the name of Scottes that [there] dwelle. The men are lyght of harte, fiers and couragious on theyr enmyes. They love nyghe as well death as thraldome, and they account it for slouth to dye in bed, and a great worshyppe and vertue to deye in a felde fyghtynge agaynst enmyes. The men ben of scarsey lyvyng, and many suffre hungre longe tyme and eate selde tofore the sonne goynge downe, and use fleshe, mylke meates, fyshe and fruites more than Brytons: and use to eate the lasse brede: and though the men bene semely ynough of fygure and of shape, and fayre of face generally by kind, yet theyr owne scottyshe clothynge dysfygure them full moche. And scottes be sayd in theyre owne tonge of bodyes painted, as it were kytte and slytte. For in olde tyme they were marked with divers fygures and shape on theyr fleshe and skyn, made with yren prickes, as Isidore saith, [in his] "de Vocabulis Gentium".—*Bartholomew's De Proprietatibus Rerum, c.* 1250.

Thereunto we finde them to be couragious and hardy, offering themselves often unto the uttermost perils with great assurance, so that a man may pronunce nothing to be over harde or past their power to performe.—*Holinshed's Description of Scotland.*

# THE NATIONAL PARADOX

Quhen that I had ouersene this Regioun,
　The quilk, of nature, is both gude and fair
I did propone ane lytill questioun,
　Beseikand hir the same for to declare.
　Quhat is the cause our boundis bene so bair?

3

Quod I: or quhat dois muve our miserie?
Or quhareof dois proceid our povertie?

For, throw the supporte of your hie prudence,
    Of Scotland I persave the properteis,
And als considderis, be experience,
    Of this countre the gret commodities:
    Firste the aboundance of fyschis in our seis,
And fructuall mountanis for our bestiall,
And, for our cornis, mony lusty vaill:

The ryche ryveris, pleasand and profitabyll;
    The lustie lochs, with fysche of sindry kyndis;
Hantyng, hawking, for nobyllis conveyabyll;
    Forestis full of da, ra, hartis & hyndis;
    The fresche fontanis, quhose holesum cristall
        strandis
Refreschis so tha fair fluriste grene medis,
So lak we no thyng that to Nature nedis.

Of every metal, we have the ryche mynis
    Baith gold, sylver, & stonis precious,
Howbeit we want the spyces and the wynis
    Or uther strange fructis delycious,
    We have als gude, and more neidfull for us.
Meit, drynk, fyre, clathis, thar mycht be gart
        abound,
Quilkis als is nocht in al the Mapamound.

More fairer peple, nor of gretar ingyne,
    Nor of more strenth, gret dedis till indure.
Quharefor, I pray you that he wald define
    The principall cause quharefor we ar so pure;[1]
For I marvell gretlie, I yow assure,
    Considerand the peple, and the ground,
    That ryches suld nocht in this Realme redound.

                                    *Sir David Lyndsay*

[1] *I.e.* poor, not pure, which would be going too far.

## O SI SIC OMNES!

So that night he brought me to a place called Cockburnspath, where we lodged at an inn, the like of which I dare say, is not in any of his Majesty's dominions. And for to show my thankfulness to Master William Arnot and his wife, the owners thereof, I must explain their bountiful entertainment of guests, which is this:

Suppose ten, fifteen, or twenty men and horses come to lodge at their house, the men shall have flesh, tame and wild fowl, fish with all variety of good cheer, good lodging, and welcome; and the horses shall want neither hay or provender; and at the morning at their departure, the reckoning is just nothing. This is this worthy gentleman's use, his chief delight being only to give strangers entertainment gratis; and I am sure, that in Scotland beyond Edinburgh, I have been at houses like castles for building; the master of the house his beaver being his blue bonnet, one that will wear no other shirts, but of the flax that grows in his own ground, and of his wife's, daughters', or servants' spinning; that hath his stockings, hose, and jerkin of the wool of his own sheeps' backs; that never by his pride of apparel caused mercer, draper, silk-man, embroiderer, or haberdasher to break and turn bankrupt. And yet this plain home-spun fellow keeps and maintains thirty, forty, fifty, servants, or, perhaps, more every day relieving three or fourscore poor people at his gate; and besides all this, can give noble entertainment for four or five days together to five or six earls and lords, besides knights, gentlemen, and their followers if they be three or four hundred men, and horse of them, where they shall not only feed but feast, and not feast but banquet, this is a man that desires to know nothing so much, as his duty to God and his King, whose greatest cares are to practise the works of piety, charity, and hospitality; he never studies the consuming art of fashionless fashions, he never tries his strength to bear four or five hundred acres on his back at once, his legs are always at liberty, not being fettered with golden garters, and manacled with artificial roses, whose weight, sometime, is the last reliques of some decayed Lordship. Many of these worthy housekeepers there are in Scotland, amongst some of them I was entertained, from whence I did truly gather these aforesaid observations.—*John Taylor* (*The Water Poet*).

## COME TO SCOTLAND

Now as for the Nobility and Gentry of the Kingdome: certainely, as they are generous, manly, and full of courage: so are they courteous, discreet, learned Schollers, well read in best Histories, delicately linguished, the most part of them being brought up in France or Italy: That for a generall compleat worthinesse, I never found their matches amongst the best people of forrane Nations: being also good housekeepers, affable to strangers, and full of Hospitality.

And in a word the Seas of Scotland and the Iles abound plentifully in all kind of Fishes, the Rivers are ingorged with Salmond, the high-landish mountains overcled with Firre-trees, infinite Deere, and all sorts of other Bestiall, the Valleyes full of Pasture, and Wild Fowle: the low layd Playnes inriched with beds of grayne: Justice all where administered, Lawes obeyed, malefactors punished, Oppressors curbed, the Clergy religious, the people sincere Professors and the Country peaceable to all men.—*William Lithgow* (1632).

## "LAT THEM SAY..."

"Our neighbour nation will say of us, poor Scotland! beggarly Scotland! scabbed Scotland! Lousy Scotland!

yea, but Covenanted Scotland! that makes amends for all".—*Robert Calder, Scots Presbyterian Eloquence Displayed.*

## THE DIVINE PATRIMONY

One Mr John Hepburn, lecturing on the second psalm, told "That there was a dialogue betwixt the Father and the Son in heaven. The Son said, Father, will you give me my portion now? Your portion, Son, says the Father, indeed shall you; thou hast been a dutiful son to me, thou never angered me in thy days; what portion will you have, Son? Will you give me poor Scotland, saith the Son? Scotland, said the Father, truly thou shall get poor Scotland, and he proved that it was Scotland he sought, from ver. 8. I shall give thee the outmost part of the earth for a possession. Now, Sirs, Scotland is the outmost part of the earth, and therefore it was given to the Son for a patrimony."[1]  *Idem.*

## PRISTINA VIRTUS

A manly surliness, with Temper mix'd
Is on their meanest Countenances fix'd
An awful Frown sits on their threatning Brow,
And yet the Soul's all smooth, and Calm below;
Thinking in Temper, rather grave than Gay,
Fitted to govern, able to obey.
Nor are their spirits very soon enflam'd
And if provoked, not very soon reclaim'd.
Fierce when resolv'd, and fix'd as Bars of Brass,
And Conquest through their Blood can only pass.
In spight of Coward Cold, the Race is brave,
In Action Daring, and in Council Grave;
Their haughty Souls in Danger always grow,
No man durst lead 'em where they durst not go.

[1] Cf. page 29.

Sedate in Thought, and steady in Resolve,
Polite in manners, and as Years Revolve;
Always secure their largest share of Fame,
And by their Courage keep alive their Name.
*Defoe*

The Scots are as diligent, as industrious, as apt for Labour and Business, and as capable of it, when they are abroad, as any People in the World; and why should they not be so at Home? and, if they had Encouragement, no doubt they would.—*Idem.*

## BELIEVE IT OR NOT . . .

The conclusion of the Abridgement of the Scotch Chronicle is the rare and wonderful things of that Countrey; as in Orkney, their Ews bring forth two Lambs a piece; that in the Northermost of Shetland Islands, about the Summer Solstice, there is no Night; that in the Park of Cumbernaule are White Kine and Oxen; that at Slanes there is a putrifying water in a Cove; that at Aberdeen is a Vitriolin Well, that they say is excellent to dissolve the Stone, and expel Sand from the Reins and Bladder, and good for the Colick, being drunk in July &c. These prodigious wonders in one Countrey are admirable, but these are not half of them. Loughness never freezes; in Lough Lommond are fishes without fins: and 2dly the Waters thereof rage in great waves without wind in calm weather: and thridly and lastly, Therein is a floating Island. In Kyle is a deaf Rock 12 foot every way, yet a Gun discharged on one side of it, shall not be heard to the other. In another place is a Rocking-stone of a reasonable bigness, that if a Man push it with his finger, it will move very lightly, but if he address his whole force, it availeth nothing; with many more marvels of a like nature, which I wou'd rather believe than go thither to disprove.—*The Observator's New Trip to Scotland* (1708).

# GLASGOW

Glasgow is, to outward appearance, the prettiest and most uniform town that I ever saw, and I believe there is nothing like it in Britain. It has a spacious *carrifour*, where stands the cross, and going round it, you have, by turns, the view of four streets, that in regular angles proceed from thence. . . .—*Edward Burt* (*fl.* 1730).

# HIGHLAND AIR FOR HEALTH

The air of the Highlands is pure, and consequently healthy, insomuch that I have known such cures done by it as might be thought next to miracles—I mean in distemper of the lungs, as coughs, consumptions &c.—*Idem.*

# HIGHLAND PRIDE

An English lady . . . told me lately, that seeing a Highlander basking at the foot of a hill in his full dress, while his wife and her mother were hard at work in reaping the oats, she asked the old woman how she could be contented to see her daughter labour in that manner, while her husband was only an idle spectator? And to this the woman answered, that her son-in-law was a *gentleman*, and it would be a disparagement to him to do any such work, and that both she and her daughter too were sufficiently honoured by the alliance.—*Idem.*

A young girl in rags, and only the bastard daughter of a man very poor and employed as a labourer, but of a family so old that, with respect to him and many others, it was quite worn out. This girl was taken in by a corporal's wife, to do any dirty work in an officer's kitchen, and, having been guilty of some fault or neglect, was treated a little roughly, whereupon the neighbouring Highland women loudly clamoured against the cook, saying, "What a monster is that to mal-treat a *gentleman's bairn*!" And the poor wretch's resentment was beyond expression upon that very account.—*Idem*.

The love of kindred, so honourable to the Highland character, procures for *natural children* in that country a kindness and attention which they do not meet with elsewhere. A married lady in the Highlands would consider her children disgraced if their *half-brothers* and *half-sisters* were not suitably provided for in the world.—*Editorial note (R. Jameson) on above*.

## HIGHLAND CARRIAGE

The Highlanders walk nimbly and upright, so that you will never see, among the meanest of them, in the remote parts, the clumsy, stooping gait of the French *paisans*, or my own country-fellows, but, on the contrary, a kind of stateliness in the midst of their poverty. —*Edward Burt*.

The young women of the mountains of Scotland are, in general, remarkably clean, when compared with our peasants. There is a charm in the arrangement of their hair, and an ease and grace in their manner of holding their head. Their short petticoat, commonly of a deep colour, shows off the whiteness of their legs, which are admirably shaped, though large and vigorous. They have the beauty of strength.—*Charles Nodier*.

## HIGHLAND HOSPITALITY

There lives in our neighbourhood, at a house (or castle) called Culloden, a gentleman whose hospitality is almost without bounds. It is the custom of that house, at the first visit or introduction, to take up your freedom by cracking his nut (as he terms it), that is, a cocoa-shell, which holds a pint, filled with champagne, or such other sort of wine as you shall choose. You may guess by the introduction, at the contents of the volume. Few go away sober at any time, and for the greatest part of his guests, in the conclusion, they cannot go at all.—*Edward Burt.*

Much as we had heard of Scots hospitality, we yet did not conceive that it ever could have been carried to the extreme in which we found it. Our first intent was merely to stay a night with our friend; instead of which, the neighbouring gentlemen leaguing themselves together, agreeably detained us a considerable number of days. No sooner had we visited one than another threw in his claim; and thus, loading us with a profusion of unmerited, though most gratifying kindness, they baffled our firmest resolves, and compelled us to enjoy as much satisfaction as enlightened, well-bred, liberal society could afford; and to finish all, some of the principal gentlemen insisted on accompanying us through the Highlands, and actually did so. . . .

But disinterestedness is not exclusively confined to the better sort; the poor even share it in this country, and according to their humble means, are as anxious to shew their hospitality and friendship as those of the amplest extent of fortune. Many Highlanders would be offended at the offer of a reward; accept of their services, appear satisfied, and they are usuriously repaid for everything they can do for you; nay, what is more surprising, this extends itself to many of the lowest servants; one of whom, from Lord Breadalbane, having been pressed to accept of some acknowledgment for the trouble he had been at to oblige us, flew out of the house with all imaginable trepidation, resolutely declining the offer, and seemingly hurt that he should be supposed capable of accepting a pecuniary gratification.—*Richard Joseph Sulivan* (1778).

## THE SCOTTISH TOWNS

The Scottish towns are like none which I ever saw, either in England, Wales, or Ireland: there is such an air of antiquity in them all, and such a peculiar oddness in their manner of building. But we were most surprised at the entertainment we met with in every place, so far different from common report. We had all things good, cheap, in great abundance, and remarkably well dressed.—*John Wesley*.

## THE HAPPY LAND

On the whole, I must say, I think the time we spent there was six weeks of the *densest* happiness I have ever met with in any part of my life; and the agreeable and instructive society there in such plenty has left so pleasing an impression on my memory, that, did not strong connections draw me elsewhere I believe Scotland would be the country I should choose to spend the remainder of my days in.—*Benjamin Franklin*.

## POOR BUT NO PAUPERS

Every Sunday a collection is made in the different congregations for the sick and necessitous, as poor's rates are unknown in Scotland; but as the natives can practice the lesson of being content with little, or are possessed of such a spirit of independence, that they will not submit to the disgrace of asking alms without urgent necessity, the small pittance thus gathered weekly, and placed under the distribution of the minister and elders, has hitherto been found sufficient for every purpose of regular charity. Thus in a country where the greatest number are poor, there are yet very few beggars.—*Thomas Pennant* (1769).

## LIFT UP YOUR EYES TO THE HILLS

I am returned from Scotland charm'd with my expedition: it is of the Highlands I speak: the Lowlands are worth seeing once, but the Mountains are extatic, & ought to be visited in pilgrimage once a year. None but those monstrous creatures of God know how to join so much beauty with so much horror. A fig for your poets, Painters, Gardiners, & Clergymen, that have not been among them: their imagination can be made up of nothing but bowling-greens, flowering shrubs, horse-ponds, Fleet-ditches, shell-grottoes, & Chinee-rails.—*Thomas Gray.*

## HERE ARE LADIES

O cruel & audacious men to blast
The fame of ladies more than Vestals chaste;
Should you go search the globe throughout,
You will find none so pious & devout;
So modest, chaste, so handsome, and so fair,
As our dear Caledonian ladies are.
When awful beauty puts on all her charms,
Nought gives our sex such terrible alarms,
As when the hoop & tartan both combine
To make a virgin like a goddess shine.
Let Quakers cut their clothes unto the quick,
And with severities themselves afflict;
But may the hoop adorn Edina's street,
Till the South Pole shall with the Northern meet.

*James Thomson*

## GRACE BEFORE MEAT

A conversation took place, about saying grace at breakfast (as we do in Scotland) as well as at dinner

13

and supper; in which Dr. Johnson said, "It is enough
if we have stated seasons of prayer; no matter when.
A man may as well pray when he mounts his horse,
or a woman when she milks her cow (which Mr Grant
told us is done in the Highlands) as at meals; and
custom is to be followed."—*Boswell*.

## DINNER AT INVERARAY CASTLE

Towards the end of the dessert the ladies withdrew,
in conformity with the custom of the country. The
toasts then commenced, and a great number was
drank with spirit and vivacity. The English [*sic*]
provide for everything; and if the diuretic influence of
the liquors is felt, there are certain utensils at hand,
which are used without ceremony; and as the ladies
here are extremely delicate, this may be the reason
for their withdrawing before the toasts begin.—*Faujas
de Saint-Fond* (1784).

## GLASGOW WOMEN

In general the women display an elegance and
agility in their gait, and many of them have charming
persons.—*Idem*.

## LOCH LOMOND

Even among the oranges, the myrtles, and the
jasmines of Italy, I shall often meditate on the wild
and romantic beauties of this spot.—*Idem*.

## THE HUSBANDS' PARADISE

Nothing prompts the desire to get married like the
sight of the numerous happy households which are to
be found in this country. I have often said that
Scotland is the husbands' Paradise. These gentlemen,
however, don't appear to appreciate their good

fortune, and take it all as a matter of course.—*The Chevalier de Latocnaye.*

## CLERICAL COURTESY

Then I had to call on a minister fifteen or twenty miles farther on. If in the remote depths of a French province a traveller were to halt at a country clergyman's house he would find, I suppose, a human being, but no more. Here I was received as an honoured guest. My host talked to me on all sorts of topics with the courtesy and address of a man of the world, and in addition gave me some valuable information about my itinerary even to the most distant parts.—*Idem.*

## REELS—EIGHTSOME AND DRINKSOME

I took the opportunity of going several times to the subscription balls given every three weeks at Montrose by the local lairds. I never saw a very large company, but it was perfectly chosen and really brilliant. The Scottish dance, or *reel* is extremely difficult for a foreigner to follow; the time is so fast and so different from the French country-dances, that very few can master it, but the natives dance it very gracefully and nimbly.

Besides, in this excellent country, you drink neat. I several times joined in fairly copious libations, but in particular I can never forget the white Lisbon of a certain doctor who proposed Royalist toasts that I could not possibly refuse to a degree that sent so much loyalty to my head that I was glad there was a wall on my way back to my inn.—*Idem.*

## THE SUTHERLAND CLEARANCES

I have never—not even in Galicia—seen any human habitations so bad as the Highland *black-houses*. . . .

The Irish cabin, I suppose must be such a heap of peat with or without stones, according to the facility of collecting them, or the humour of the maker. But these men-sties are not inhabited, as in Ireland, by a race of ignorant and ferocious barbarians, who can never be civilized till they are regenerated—till their very nature is changed. Here you have a quiet, thoughtful, contented, religious people, susceptible of improvement, and willing to be improved. To transplant these people from their native mountain glens to the sea coast, and require them to become some cultivators, others fishermen, occupations to which they have never been accustomed—to expect a sudden and total change of habits in the existing generation, instead of gradually producing it in their children; to expel them by process of law from their black-houses, and if they demur in obeying the ejectment, to oust them by setting fire to their combustible tenements—this surely is as little defensible on the score of policy as of morals. —*Southey*.

## NORTHERN GODDESSES

The ladies of Edinburgh possess a more graceful deportment than those of London; they are at once slenderer and more fragile. Up to the present time I have found among them fewer laughing Hebes than haughty Junos and stately-walking Dianas. . . . To grace of figure the young ladies of Edinburgh add, for the most part, the charm of some agreeable talents. There are few of them who are not musicians, and who are deficient in extraordinary skill in the labours of the needle; there are few of them also unacquainted with French.—*Amedée Pichot* (1822).

## THE SOUL OF THE GAEL

The Highlanders are a grave and intelligent people, of a turn of mind peculiarly inquisitive, and susceptible of improvement from education. This spirit of curiosity, for which the Highlander is remarkable, and the consequent information which he is generally found to possess with regard to distant places and events, may be partly at least attributed to that expansion of mind which he naturally acquires from a rambling and excursive mode of life, and the daily opportunities he enjoys of contemplating nature on the most extensive scale. To the same circumstances it would seem we are to attribute that slight dash of melancholy with which the Highland character is uniformly tinged. The melancholy of the Highlander being far more morose, and having no tendency to misanthropy, seems rather to be a habit of mind produced by the combined effects of sensibility, solitude, and the habitual contemplation of sublime scenery. Little employed in cultivating the ground, his mind is not fettered by minute attention to a single spot; the range of his excursions is wide, but it is lonely. In tending his flocks he scales the lofty mountains, and traverses the extensive moor or dusky forest, and has occasion from time to time to contemplate the grandest objects in nature—the war of the elements—the impetuous torrent sweeping everything before it—the thunder of heaven, reverberating, in repeated peals, among the mountains—the violence of the winds, rendered furious, by being pent up in a deep and narrow valley— and snow coiled up in heaps, that interrupts for weeks the intercourse of a whole district. All these circumstances, alike unfavourable to frivolousness of thought, are well calculated to fix down the mind to habits of sober thinking, and to impress it with serious meditation on the vicissitudes of human affairs. Notwithstanding this general character of what may be called pensive susceptibility, which belongs to the Highlander, he is in the highest degree alive to joyous feelings. The Highlanders are fond of music and of dancing, with diversions of all kinds. In ancient times, when the hospitality of the chieftain furnished subsistence to his numerous dependants, it is remembered, in the traditions of the generation last passed, that the recitation of ancient Celtic poetry formed their favourite amusement; thus innocently did they twine the garland of poesy around dark Winter's brow.—*Beriah Botfield* (1829).

## OUR VIRTUES

Virtues peculiarly Scotch—of self-denial, submission to severe hardship without repining, education and refinement much beyond their condition, with considerable ambition and aspiring thoughts.—*Mrs Grace Fletcher*.

My impressions of the hospitality, kindness, and superior information of the Scotch, in comparison with those of the same rank in England, were confirmed by my second visit to Scotland.—*Eadem*.

## OUR LOVE

Il y a beaucoup d'amour dans la classe des paysans en Ecosse.—*Stendhal*.

One cannot but be conscious of an underlying melancholy in Scotswomen. This melancholy is peculiarly attractive in the ball-room, where it gives a singular piquancy to the enthusiasm and earnestness that they put into their national dances.—*Idem*.

## THE HIGHLAND SOLDIER

The Highlander is never a smart soldier, but he is always a good soldier, and soon made one, if not too harshly treated.—*Felix MacDonogh*.

# THE HIGHLAND CHIEF

When in one of the Hebrides myself, the whole fortnight was one scene of hunting, shooting, banqueting, dancing, fiddling, and piping; fresh fish was caught daily by the chief's fishermen; game in abundance supplied the table, at which the laird presided with all the dignity of an absolute, petty prince, and what added to the romantic appearance of the mansion and the scenery, was a tower covered with ivy, the ruins of a distant church, a peep at the sea, and the piper's walking in a stately manner up and down before the window.

When my friend came south, I saw him daily in Edinburgh; he walked about town with all the majesty of a scenic king, although he came up to Edinburgh to raise money; for he had so many clansmen and kinsmen, *friends* (connections), foster brothers and dependants, that he was much straitened in his affairs, although this did not appear at home, where he bred and grew everything for his family's consumption, and had nothing to pay for but his liquors and clothing. His person was erect, his complexion fresh, but sunburnt, his eye as keen as a hawk's, his voice loud and authoritative, his manner distant from pride, but warm and kind when in private and entertaining his friends. He complained bitterly of the narrowheartedness of monied men.—*Idem.*

The chief of a Scotch clan, with his poniard and pistols, like a buccaneer, his *cacique* cap, his cloak resembling Grecian drapery, his party-coloured hose, which, like all the stuffs of the country, recall to mind the tatooing of the ancient inhabitants, which they have thrown into oblivion, his club of laburnum bent back as the sign of his command, his savage deminudity, and, with all that, his noble and gentle mien, is a living tradition, perhaps the only one in Europe, of our ages of strength and liberty. Though proud, and very proud of the dazzling beauty of their dress, they do not walk—they fly without looking at anything, without stopping at anything; and traverse towns like lions that have lost their way. In fact they must feel there some painful sentiments. Their inhabitants were once free like themselves, but have precipitated themselves under the yoke of associations and laws, in order to gratify their idleness and their cupidity. I can easily understand that the Highlanders must despise the breeches of the civilized man. Chains come after them.—*Charles Nodier*.

## SAWNEY'S HUMOUR

I muse how any man can say that the Scotch, as a people, are deficient in humour! Why, Sawney has a humour of his own so strong and irrepressible that it broke out all the stronger in spite of worldly thrift, kirk - session, cutty - stool and lectures.—*Hartley Coleridge*.

## GENTLEMEN, THE QUEEN!

All the Highlanders are so amusing, and really pleasant and instructive to talk to—women as well as men—and the latter so gentlemanlike.

We were always in the habit of conversing with the Highlanders—with whom one comes so much in contact in the Highlands. The Prince highly appreciated the good-breeding, simplicity, and intelligence which make it so pleasant, and even instructive to talk to them.—*Queen Victoria*.

## KOSSUTH'S TRIBUTE

If the gratitude which I owe as a man and as a patriot to the people of Great Britain in general allowed me to make any distinction between different places according to the duration of the kindness I received, I should have to say that in Scotland I felt as if in a second home, and that I was received as a son, and never repudiated. . . . The chief national characteristics of the Scotch are constancy and unwearied perseverance. These qualities have made that dreary and barren land a home of prosperity, a flourishing paradise. Those who see with envy that Scotchmen go anywhere, take to anything, are always and everywhere happy, are in the habit of saying that you may bury a Scotchman in the bowels of Vesuvius and he will find a way out. It is meant for irony, but is the greatest compliment that can be paid to a nation. . . . This steady perseverance which has wrought such wonders of material progress (setting an example to those who consider and take counsel for years while slowly carrying out some trivial undertaking!), does not belie itself in respect of political sympathy and faithfulness to principles. When once a Scotchman has become somebody's friend, he steadily remains his friend. When once he has taken up any matter, he does not drop it again through good or evil report. His interest is not like a fire of straw, but like that of the gathering coal which he burns on his hearth.—*Louis Kossuth.*


## JUNE IN THE MOUNTAINS

But it is in June, I think, that the mountain charm is most intoxicating. The airs are lightsome. The hill-mists are seldom heavy, and only on south-wind mornings do the lovely grey-white vapours linger among the climbing corries and overhanging scarps. Many of the slopes are blue as a winter sky, palely blue, aerially delicate, from the incalculable myriad host of the bluebells. The green of the bracken is more wonderful than at any other time. When the wind

plays upon it the rise and fall is as the breathing of the
green seas among the caverns of Mingulay or among
the savage rock-pools of the Seven Hunters or where
the Summer Isles lie in the churn of the Atlantic tides.
Everything is alive in joy. The young broods exult.
The air is vibrant with the eddies of many wings, great
and small. The shadow-grass sways with the passage
of the shrewmouse or the wing's-breath of the darting
swallow. The stillest pool quivers, for among the
shadows of breathless reeds the phantom javelin of the
dragon-fly whirls for a second from silence to silence.
—*William Sharp*.

# WHA'S LIKE US?

## *OR*

## *IN DISPRAISE OF SCOTLAND*

*The vile Scots. . . .*

PETRARCH

*Scotland has had many an ill picture drawn for her in the world; and as she has been represented in False Draughts, no wonder the Injurys she has suffered are intolerable. All the Spies sent hither have carry'd back an ill Report of the Land, and fill'd the World with weak Banters and Clamour at they know not what.*

DEFOE

*Oft have I heard thee mourn the wretched lot
Of the poor, mean, despis'd, insulted Scot,*

CHARLES CHURCHILL

*The Scots cannot endure to hear their country or Countrymen spoken against.*

JOHN RAY

# A POSY OF MISCELLANEOUS ABUSE

SHORTLY to conclude, trust yow no Skott, for they wyll yowse flatteryng wordes, and all is falsholde.— *Andrew Boorde, c.* 1534.

Treacherous Scotland, to no interest true.—*Dryden.*

But after this description of these mountains you may ask, of what use can be such monstrous excrescences?— *Edward Burt.*

Had Cain been Scot, God would have chang'd his
    doom,
Not forced him wander, but confined him home.
                       *John Cleveland.*

There never came a fool out of Scotland: they all stay at home.—*Anon.*

The Scotch are proverbially poor and proud, we know they can remedy their poverty when they set about it. No one is sorry for them.—*Hazlitt.*

A land of meanness, sophistry and lust.—*Byron.*

I have been trying all my life to like Scotchmen, and am obliged to desert from the experiment in despair. . . . The tediousness of these people is certainly provoking. I wonder if they ever tire one another!— *Charles Lamb.*

A Scotsman is one who keeps the Sabbath and every other darned thing he can lay his hands upon.— *American saying.*

After illicit love and flaring drunkenness, nothing appeals so much to Scotch sentiment as having been born in the gutter.—*T. W. H. Crosland.*

There was once a Scotchman—and now there are millions of the bastards.—*Cockney saloon bar jest.*

## THE FLOWERS OF EDINBURGH

FORASMEKLE as the burgh of Edinburgh, quilk is the chief and principall burgh of this kingdome, quhair the soverane and heich courtes of Parliament, his Majesties Privie the Counsall and Colledge of Justice, and the Courtis of Justiciarie and Admiraltie are ordinarilie haldin and keipt, and quhairunto the best pairt of the subjectis of this kingdome, all degreis, rankis, and qualities hes a commoun and frequent resort and repare—is now become so filthie and uncleine, and the streittis, venallis, wyndis, and cloissis thairoff so overlayd with and coverit with middingis, and with the filth and excrement of man and beist, as the noblemen counsellouris servitouris, and utheris, his Majesties subjectis quha ar ludgit within the said burgh, can not have ane cleine and frie passage and entrie to thair ludgeingis, quhairthrow thair ludge-ingis ar becum so lothsume unto thame, as they ar resolvit rather to mak choice of ludgeingis in the Cannongate and Leyth, or some utheris partis about the towne, nor to abyde the sycht of this schamefull uncleinnes and filthiness, quilk is so universall & in such abundance throuch all partis of this burgh, as in the heitt of somer it corruptis the air, and gives greit occasioun of seikness: and forder, this schamefull & beistlie filthiness is most detestable & odious in the sicht of strangeris, quho beholding the same, as con-straynet with reassoun to gif out mony disgracefull speiches aganis this burgh, calling it a most filthie pudle of filth & unclaines, the lyk quhairof is not to be

26

seine in no pairt of the world: quhilk being a greate
discredite to the haill kingdome, that the principall &
heid burgh thairof sould be so void of pollice, civilitie,
ordour, & gude governement, as the hie streittis of the
same cannot be keipit cleine; & the Lords of Secreit
Counsall, understanding perfytlie that the said burgh,
and all the streittis & vennallis thairof may very
easilie, & with litill ado, be keipit and haldin cleine,
gif the people thameselfis wer weill & civillie disposit,
& gif the Magistratis tuk caire to caus thame, and
everie ane of thame, keip the streittis foranentis thair
awin boundis clein, as is done in uther civill, handsome
and weill governit cities: THAIRFOIR the Lordis of
Secreit Counsall commandis and ordanis, be this
presents, &c.—*Act of the Privy Council of Scotland anent
the Burgh of Edinburgh, March 4, 1619.*

Every street shows the nastiness of the Inhabitants, the
excrements lye in heaps, and there is not above one
house of Office in the Town, which may not improper-
ly be call'd a house of Office itself. In a Morning the
Scent was so offensive, that we were forc't to hold our
Noses as we past the streets, and take care where we
trod for fear of disobliging our shoes, and to walk in
the middle at night, for fear of an accident to our
heads. The Lodgings are as nasty as the streets, and
wash't so seldom, that the dirt is thick eno' to be par'd
off with a Shovell. Every room is well scented with a
close stoole, and the Master Mistress and Servants lye
on a flour, like so many Swine in a Hogsty; This with
the rest of their sluttishness, is no doubt the occasion of
the Itch, which is so common amongst them. We had
the best lodgings we could get, for which we paid
31.5s. Scots, being about 10d. a night English, and
yet we went thro' the Master's Bed chamber and the
Kitchin and dark Entry, to our room which look't into
a place they call the close, full of Nastinesse, 'tis a
common thing for a Man or woman to go into these

closes at all times of the day, to ease nature. We were mightily afraid of the Itch the first night, which made us keep on our white thread Stockins, and gloves, but we had the good fortune to escape it.—*Joseph Taylor* (1705).

## THE SCOTTISH PEOPLE

They christen without the cross, marry without the ring. . . . They keep no holy-days, nor acknowledge any saint but St. Andrew. . . . Their Sabbath exercise is a preaching in the forenoon, and a persecuting in the afternoon. . . . They think it impossible to lose the way to Heaven, if they can but leave Rome behind them.

To conclude, the men of old did no more wonder that the great Messias should be born in so poor a town as Bethlem in Judea, then I do wonder that so brave a prince as King James should be born in so stinking a town as Edinburgh in lousy Scotland.—*Sir Anthony Weldon.*

The People are proud, arrogant, vainglorious Boasters, bloody, barbarous, and inhuman Butchers. Cousenage and Theft is in Perfection amongst them, and they are perfect English Haters; they shew their Pride in exalting themselves, and depressing their Neighbours.— *Anon.* (1670).

## ANOTHER POSY OF PLEASANTRIES

I will not deny, but Scotland has formerly given very eminent Scholars to the World; nay, I will go further, there are no finer Gentlemen in the World, than that Nation can justly boast of; but then they are such as have travelled, and are indebted to other Countries for those Accomplishments that render them so esteemed, their own affording only Pedantry, Poverty, Brutality, and Hypocrisy. . . .—*Scotland Characterised* (1701).

Some are of Opinion, that, when the Devil shewed our
Saviour the Kingdoms of the Earth, he laid his thumb
upon Scotland, and that for a twofold Reason: *First*,
Because it was not like to be any Temptation, *Next*,
Being Part of his Mother's Jointure, he could not dis-
pose of it during her Life.—*Ibid*.

Their Women are, if possible, yet worse than the Men,
and carry no Temptations, but what have at Hand
suitable Antidotes. . . . Their Voice is like Thunder,
and will as effectually sowre all the Milk in a Dairy,
or Beer in a Cellar, as forty Drums beating a Prepara-
tive. It is a very Common Thing for a Woman of
Quality to say to her Footman, "Andrew, take a fast
Gripe of my A——, and help me over the Stile. . . ."—
*Ibid*.

They pretend to be descended from one Madam Scota,
Daughter to King Pharaoh; but the best Proof, they
give of it, is their Bringing two of the Plagues of Egypt
along with them, *viz*., Lice and the Itch; which they
have intailed on their Posterity ever since. . . .—*Ibid*.

## IN CHURCH

The Minister made such a prodigious noise in broad
Scotch, and beat his Pulpit so violently, that he
seem'd better qualified for a Drummer than a Parson.
The women were most vail'd with plods, which gave us
but little opportunity of passing our Judgment on the
Scotch beuatyes, but those we saw were very indifferent. There is no other place but the Church to take a
view of them, for in Edenborough the Kirk allows of
no plays, or publick Entertainments, neither are there
any walks for the Ladyes; When any one dyes, the
Bellman gives notice to all faithful brothers and sisters,
and a day or two after acquaints them with his
Funerall. It's very observable, that a poor pedlar, tho'

29

almost eaten up with the Itch and Vermin, wears his
Sword, and has his little Box resembling a Tapp, fill'd
with Mundungoe in his pocket, without which he can't
live, and if he has but a few Baubies, or half pennyes,
about him, he strutts like an Emperour; They talk of
everything in the Superlative degree.—*Joseph Taylor*
(1705).

## AT MOFFAT

We here met with good wine, and some mutton
pretty well drest; but looking into our beds, found
there was no lying in them, so we kept on our cloaths
all night and enjoyed ourselves by a good fire, making
often protestations never to come into that country
again.—*Idem.*

## ADULLAM

Their Countrey is that barren Wilderness
Which Cain did first in banishment possess;
An open-mouth'd Asylum that received
Your broken Debtors, and your Fugitives,
A sure Retreat for Rebels and for Thieves,
A greedy, dark, degenerate place of Sin
For th' Universe to shoot her Rubbish in:
Europe unloads her Offal in a heap,
And gives the Scots those Jakes She will not keep
And Africk, to compleat their Character
Has empty'd all her outcast issue there,
Pimps, Bullies, Traitors, Robbers, 'tis all one,
Scotland, like wide-jaw'd Hell, refuses none.

    ·       ·       ·

The pregnant Roots that in the Garden settles
Are Garlick, Poppies, Artichoks and Nettles;
Potatoes with advantage they can sow
But Honesty's a weed that will not grow.
       —*A Trip lately to Scotland* (1705)

# THE GREEKS HAD A WORD FOR IT

The Plague of Darkness was said to be thick darkness, to be felt, which most undoubtedly there People have a share in, as the word σκοτίη (Darkness) implies; the darkness being appliable to their gross and blockish understandings (as I had it from a Scholar of their own Nation).—*The Observator's New Trip to Scotland* (1708).

If all European Travellers direct their course to Italy, upon the account of its Antiquity, why should Scotland be neglected, whose wronkled surface derives its original from the Chaos? The first Inhabitants were some Straglers of the Fallen Angels, who rested themselves on the Confines, till their Captain Lucifer provided places for them in his own country.—*Ibid.*

# THE CALEDONIAN BORE

There are some people who think they sufficiently acquit themselves, and entertain their company, with relating facts of no consequence, but all out of the road of such common incidents as happen every day; and this I have observed more frequently among the Scots than any other nation, who are very careful not to omit the minutest circumstance of time or place; which kind of discourse, if it were not a little relieved by the uncouth terms and phrases, as well as accent and gesture peculiar to that country, would be hardly tolerable.—*Swift.*

# BRAVE WORDS

A pedling shopkeeper, that sells a pennyworth of thread, is a *merchant*, the person who is sent for that thread has received a *commission*, and, bringing it to

31

the sender, is making a *report*. A bill to let you know there is a single room to be let, is called a *placard*, the doors are *ports*, an enclosed field of two acres is a *park*, and the wife of a laird of fifteen pounds a year is a *lady*, and treated with—your *ladyship*.—*Edward Burt*.

## HIGHLAND HOSPITALITY

One thing I should have told you was intolerable, viz., the number of Highlanders that attended a table, whose feet and foul linen, or woollen, I don't know which, were more than a match for the odour of the dishes.—*Idem*.

## THE FISHING INDUSTRY

The fishermen would not be mentioned but for their remarkable laziness . . . until they are driven out by the last necessity, they will not meddle with salt-water. At low ebb, when their boats lie off at a considerable distance from the shore, for want of depth of water, the women tuck up their garments to an indecent height, and wade to the vessels, where they receive their loads of fish for the market; and when the whole cargo is brought to land they take the fishermen upon their backs, and bring them on shore in the same manner.—*Idem*.

## THE KILT

The common habit of the ordinary Highlander is far from being acceptable to the eye . . . this dress is called the *quelt*; and, for the most part, they wear the petticoat so very short, that in a windy day, going up a hill, or stooping, the indecency of it is plainly discovered.—*Idem*.

# WHISKY

I have been tempted to think that this spirit has in it, by infusion, the seeds of anger, revenge, and murder. This I confess is a little too poetical, but those who drink of it to any degree of excess behave, for the most part, like true barbarians, I think much beyond the effect of other liquors.—*Idem.*

## DISTRESSED AREA

The houses of the Common people here [Deeside] are shocking to humanity, being formed of loose stones and covered with parings of earth, called *devots*; or with heath, broom, or branches of fir. The fare of the inhabitants is equally mean: oatmeal, barley cakes, and potatoes, are their usual food; and their drink, whiskey, sweetened with honey. The men are thin, but strong: idle, because they have nothing to stimulate their industry, and indifferent about what is not absolutely necessary to their existence. The women are remarkably plain, and early acquire an aged look; but they are more industrious than their husbands, and are the principal supporters of their families.— *Thomas Pennant* (1769).

## DR. JOHNSON'S OPINIONS

Their weather is not pleasing, half the year is deluged with rain. From the autumnal to the vernal equinox a dry day is hardly known, except when the showers are suspended by a tempest. . . . Their winter overtakes their summer, and their harvest lies upon the ground drenched with rain.—*Journey to the Hebrides.*

Mr Johnson's hatred of the Scotch is so well known . . . that 'tis perhaps scarcely worth while to write down the conversation between him and a friend of that nation who always resides in London, and who at the return from the Hebrides asked him, with a firm voice, what he thought of his country. "That it is a very vile country to be sure, Sir", (returned for answer Dr. Johnson). Well, Sir! replies the other somewhat mortified, God made it. "Certainly he did (answers Mr Johnson again); but we must always remember that he made it for Scotchmen, and comparisons are odious, Mr S——, but God made Hell".—*Mrs Thrale.*

Sir Allan M'Lean bragged, that Scotland had the advantage of England, by its having more water. Johnson: "Sir, we would not have your water, to take the vile bogs which produce it. You have too much! A man who is drowned has more water than either of us"; and then he laughed.—*Boswell.*

I having said that England was obliged to us for gardeners, almost all their good gardeners being Scotchmen—Johnson: "Why, Sir, that is because gardening is much more necessary amongst you than with us, which makes so many of your people learn it. It is *all* gardening with you. Things which grow wild here, must be cultivated with great care in Scotland.— *Idem.*

Mr Ogilvie was unlucky enough to choose for the topic of his conversation the praises of his native country. He began with saying that there was very rich land around Edinburgh. Goldsmith, who had studied physic there, contradicted this, very untruly, with a sneering laugh. Disconcerted a little by this, Mr. Ogilvie then took a new ground, where, I suppose, he thought himself perfectly safe, for he observed, that Scotland had a great many noble wild prospects. Johnson: "I believe, Sir, you have a great many. Norway, too, has noble wild prospects; and Lapland is

34

remarkable for prodigious, noble, wild prospects. But, Sir, let me tell you, the noblest prospect which a Scotchman ever sees, is the highroad that leads him to England!"—*Idem*.

He defended his remark upon the general insufficiency of education in Scotland, and confirmed to me the authenticity of his witty saying on the learning of the Scotch: "Their learning is like bread in a besieged town: every man gets a little, but no man gets a full meal. There is", said he, "in Scotland, a diffusion of learning, a certain portion of it widely and thinly spread."—*Idem*.

He would not allow Scotland to derive any credit from Lord Mansfield, for he was educated in England. "Much", said he, "may be made of a Scotchman, if he be *caught* young."—*Idem*.

Mr Arthur Lee mentioned some Scotch who had taken possession of a barren part of America, and wondered why they should choose it. Johnson: "Why, Sir, all barrenness is comparative. The *Scotch* would not know it to be barren." Boswell: "You have now been in Scotland, Sir, and say if you did not see meat and drink enough there". Johnson: "Why yes, Sir; meat and drink enough to give the inhabitants sufficient strength to run away from home".—*Idem*.

After musing for some time, he said, "I wonder how I should have any enemies; for I do harm to nobody". Boswell: "In the first place, Sir, you will be pleased to recollect, that you set out with attacking the Scotch; so you got a whole nation for your enemies". Johnson: "Why, I own, that by my definition of *oats* I meant to vex them". Boswell: "Pray, Sir, can you trace the cause of your antipathy to the Scotch?" Johnson: "I cannot, Sir".—*Idem*.

## NEBULAE MALUSQUE JUPPITER

The humid and penetrating atmosphere of Scotland had for some time affected me in a very disagreeable manner, notwithstanding the active life I led. I found that the mists, the frequent rains, the change of winds, the sharpness of the air, and the absence of the sun plunged me into an involuntary melancholy, which I should not long have been able to support.—*Faujas de Saint-Fond.*

## "THE CONSUL'S BROW WAS SAD, AND THE CONSUL'S SPEECH WAS LOW"

Put no faith in aught that bears the name of music while you are in Scotland, he said; you have not a fiddler in France who would not make a Rossini at Edinburgh. In my character of consul it is my duty to protect the subjects of His Most Christian Majesty against all delusive pretences. I was taken in on my first arrival, and all you have to do is to profit by my experience. I was asked to a private concert; I suffered the infliction of several airs with exemplary patience. My host asked me if I were not enchanted. "Very much," I replied, "but I like a little more variety; those mournful ditties shake my nerves." "What mournful ditties! they are nuptial airs." You may conceive how mortified I was, as well as my entertainer: I thought I was listening to funeral chants; as to the bagpipes, they positively put me to the rack.—*Amedée Pichot* (1822).

## "A PARTICULARLY DISAGREEABLE NATION"

Among ourselves, the Scotch, as a nation, are particularly disagreeable. They hate every appearance of comfort themselves and refuse it to others. Their climate, their religion, and their habits are equally averse to pleasure. Their manners are either distinguished by a fawning sycophance (to gain their own ends, and conceal their natural defects), that makes one sick; or by a morose, unbending callousness, that makes one shudder.—*Hazlitt.*

## HATE

There was very little amusement in the room but a Scotchman to hate. Some people you must have observed have a most unpleasant effect upon you when you see them speaking in profile—this Scotchman is the most accomplished fellow in this way I ever met with. The effect was complete. It went down like a dose of bitters, and I hope will improve my digestion. At Taylor's too, there was a Scotchman—not quite so bad for he was as clean as he could get himself.—*Keats.*

## SIR MORGAN O'DOHERTY'S FAREWELL

Farewell, farewell, beggarly Scotland,
 Cold and beggarly poor countrie!
If ever I cross thy border again,
 The muckle deil must carry me.

There's but one tree in a' the land,
 And that's the bonnie gallows tree;
The very nowte look to the south,
 And wish that they had wings to flee.

Farewell, farewell, beggarly Scotland,
 Brose & bannocks, crowdy & kale!
Welcome, welcome, jolly old England,
 Laughing lasses & foaming ale!

'Twas when I came to merry Carlisle,
 That out I laughed loud laughters three:

37

And if I cross the Sark again
　　The muckle deil must carry me.

Farewell, farewell, beggarly Scotland,
　　Kiltit kimmers wi' carroty hair,
Pipers who beg that your honours would buy
　　A bawbee's worth of their famished air.

I'd rather keep Cadwaller's goats,
　　And feed upon toasted cheese and leeks,
Than go back again to the beggarly North
　　To herd 'mang loons wi' bottomless breeks.
　　　　　　　　　　　　　*James Hogg*

## "FREEDOM AND WHISKY GANG THEGITHER"

To be fou' or, as he would put it, to have a drappie in his eye, is the Scotchman's notion of bigness and freedom and manly independence. He is a ranter and roarer in his cups, and on the whole much more distressing to meet drunk than sober—which is saying a great deal.—*T. W. H. Crosland.*

## SCOTTISH RESERVE

The Scots are not easy in conversation. They are more anxious to shine than to please. Everyone wishes to be thought wise, and you shall often see a stupid fellow entrench himself in gravity and preserve a profound silence, from the selfish fear of exposing his ignorance, or risking the little share of reputation he may possess. But see this man in another company where he knows he is surrounded by those more stupid than himself, he shines away and engrosses the whole conversation. His hearers hate him for his superiority; yet they are contented he should shine, rather than that they should run the risk of discomfiture by opposing him. In all companies, where there is an obvious

diversity of talent, is to be observed this submission of
inferior to superior ability; and when persons of equal
colloquial abilities are thrown together, their discourse
is rather disputation than conversation. An excessive
frigidity is the consequence of the want of the frank-
ness, which with us is the heart and soul of social
enjoyment. A cautious reserve appears to pervade the
breast of every Scotsman; he answers a question as if
he were undergoing a cross-examination; the mysteri-
ous habit grows upon him, till he makes a secret of
things which it would do him no manner of harm
although all the world knew them.

An Edinburgh gentleman, who has all the open
straightforwardness of English manner, said to me the
other day, "I cannot endure the selfish reserve of
my countrymen. They become tolerable only when
they are half tipsy."—*An English Commercial Traveller*,
1815.

## "THAT KNUCKLE-END OF ENGLAND"

It requires a surgical operation to get a joke well
into a Scotch understanding. Their only idea of it, or
rather that inferior variety of this electric talent which
prevails occasionally in the North, and which, under
the name of WUT, is so infinitely distressing to people
of good taste, is laughing immoderately at stated
intervals. They are so imbued with metaphysics that
they even make love metaphysically. I overheard a
young lady of my acquaintance, at a dance in
Edinburgh, exclaim, in a sudden pause of the music,
"What you say, my Lord, is very true of love in the
*aibstract*, but——" Here the fiddlers began fiddling
furiously, and the rest was lost. No nation has so large
a stock of benevolence of heart: if you meet with an
accident, half Edinburgh immediately flocks to your
door to inquire after your *pure* hand or your *pure* foot,
and with a degree of interest that convinces you their

whole hearts are in the inquiry. You find they usually arrange their dishes at dinner by the points of the compass; "Sandy, put the gigot of mutton to the south, and move the singet sheep's head a wee bit to the nor-wast". If you knock at the door, you hear a shrill female voice from the fifth flat shriek out, "Wha's chapping at the door?" which is presently opened by a lassie with short petticoats, bare legs, and thick ankles. My Scotch servants bargained they were not to have salmon more than three times a week, and always pulled off their stockings, in spite of my repeated objurgations, the moment my back was turned. Their temper stands anything but an attack on their climate. They would have you even believe they can ripen fruit; and, to be candid, I must own in remarkably warm summers I have tasted peaches that made most excellent pickles; and it is upon record that at the siege of Perth, on one occasion, the ammunition failing, their nectarines made admirable cannon balls. Even the enlightened mind of Jeffrey cannot shake off the illusion that myrtles flourished at Craig Cook. In vain I have represented to him that they are of the genus *Carduus*, and pointed out their prickly peculiarities. In vain I have reminded him that I have seen hackney coaches drawn by four horses in the winter, on account of the snow; that I had rescued a man blown flat against my door by the violence of the winds, and black in the face; that even the experienced Scotch fowls did not venture to cross the streets, but sidled along, tails aloft, without venturing to encounter the gale. Jeffrey sticks to his myrtle illusions, and treats my attacks with as much contempt as if I had been a wild visionary, who had never breathed his caller air, nor lived and suffered under the rigour of his climate, nor spent five years in discussing metaphysics and medicine in that garret of the earth—that knuckle-end of England—that land of Calvin, oat-cakes, and sulphur.—*Sydney Smith*.

# LUCKY NUMBERS

*A SELECTION OF GOOD AND OCCASIONALLY
GODLY BALLADS*

*Take the Muse's servants by the hand.*
BURNS

## ANIMULA, VAGULA, BLANDULA

O besy goste! ay flickering to and fro,
   That never art in quiet nor in rest,
Till thou cum to that place that thou cam fro,
   Quhich is thy first & verray proper nest:
   From day to day so sore here artow drest,
That with thy flesche ay walking art in trouble,
And sleeping eke; of pyne so has thou double.

*James I of Scotland*


## OF THE CHANGES OF LYFE

I seik about this warld onstable
To find a sentence conveniable;
   Bot I can not in all my wit
   Sa trew a sentence find of it,
As say: "It is dissavable".


For yisterday, I did declair
How that the sasoun, soft and fair,
   Come in als fresh as pacock feddir;
   This day it stangis lyke ane eddir,
Concluding all in my contrair.


Yisterday fair sprang the flowris,
This day they are all slane with showris,
   And foulis in forrest that sang cleir,
   Now walkis with ane drerie cheir:
Full cauld are bayth thair beddis and bowris.


So nixt to symmer wynter bene;
Nixt eftir confort, cairis keine;

43

Next eftir mydnycht, the myrthful morrow;
Nixt eftir joy, ay cumis sorrow:
So is this warld, and ay hes bene.

*William Dunbar*

## COVET EARNESTLY THE BEST GIFTS

Come nevir yit may so fresche and grene
Bot Januar come als wod and kene,
Wes nevir sie drouth bot anis come rane:
All erdly joy returnis in pane.

Heir helth returnis in seikness
And mirth returnis in haviness,
Toun in desert, forrest in plane:
All erdly joy returnis in pane.

Sen erdly joy abydis nevir
Wirk for the joy that lestis evir;
For uder joy is all bot vane:
All erdly joy returnis in pane.

*Idem*

## APOSTROPHE

Was nocht gud King Solomon
Ravished in sundry wise
With every lovely paragon
Glistening before his eyes?
If this be true, true as it was, lady, lady,
Should I not serve you, allace, my fair lady.

When Paris was inamorit
Of Helena, dame beauteous speir,
Then Venus first him promisit
To venture on and nought to fear;
What sturdy storms endurit he, lady, lady,
To win her love, or it would be, my deir lady.

44

Know ye not how Troilus
Wanderit and lost his joy,
With fates and fevers marvellous,
For Cresseid fair that dwelt in Troy?
Till pity planted into her breast, lady, lady,
To sleep with him and grant him rest, my deir lady.

I reid sometime how venturous
Leander was his love to please,
Who swam the water perilous
Of Abedon those surging seas,
To come to her there as he lay, lady, lady,
Where he was drownit by the way, my deir lady.

Anaxerete so beautiful
Whom Iphis did behold and see
With sighs and sobbis pitifall,
That paragon long wooit he;
And when he could not win her so, lady, lady,
He went and hangit himself for wo, my deir lady.

If all these wichts of wirdiness
Endurit sic pains to take,
With valiant deeds and sturdiness,
Inventering for their ladies' sake,
Why should not I, pure simple man, lady, lady,
Labour and serve you the best I can, my dear lady.

*Bannatyne MS.*

## THE HAPPY LIFE

Blissit be sempill lyfe withoutin dreid!
    Blissit be sober feist in quyetie!
Quha her aneuch, of na mair hes he neid,
    Thocht it be lytill in-to quantitie.
    Greit abondance and blind prosperitie
Oftymes makis ane evill conclusioun.
    The sweitest lyfe thairfor in this cuntrie
Is sickernes, with small possessioun.

45

O wantoun man, that usis for to feid
   Thy wambe, and makis it ane good to be,
Luik to thyself! I warne thee wele, but dreid:
   The cat cummis and to the mouse hes ee.
Quhat vaillis than they feist and rialtie,
   With dreidful hart and tribulacioun?
Thairfoir best thing in eird, I say, for me,
   Is blyithnes in hart, with small possessioun.

Thy awin fyre, my friend, so it be bot ane gleid,
   It warmis weill, and is worth gold to thee;
And Solomon sayis, if that thow will reid,
   "Under the hevin ut can nocht better be
   Than ay be blyith and leif in honestie".
Quhairfoir I may conclude be this ressoun,
   Of eirthly joy it beiris maist degrie,
Blyithnes in hart, with small possessioun.

Robert Henryson

## HERMES THE PHILOSOPHER

Be mirry, man! and tak nocht far in mynd
   The wavering of this wrechit warld of sorrow;
To God be humill, and to thy freynd be kynd,
   And with thy nychtbouris glaidly len and borrow;
   His chance to nycht it be thyne to morrow.
Be blyth in hairt for ony aventure,
   For oft with wysmen it hes bene said adorrow:
"Without glaidness availis no tresour".

Mak thee gude cheir of it that God thee sendus,
   For warldis wrak but weilfair nocht availis;
Na gude is thyne said only bot thow spendis,
   Remenant all thow brukis bot with bailis;
   Seik to solace when sadness thee assailis,
In dolour lang thy lyfe may nocht indure;
   Whairfoir of confort set up all thy sailis:
Without glaidnes availis no tresour.

46

Follow on petie, fle truble and debait;
   With famous folkis hald thy company,
Be charitabill and humill in thyne estait,
   For warldly honour lestis bot a cry;
   For truble in erd tak no malloncoly;
Be rich in patience, gif thow in gudis be pure;
   Who levis mirry, he levis michtely:
Without glaidnes availis no tresour.


Thou seis thir wrechis set with sorrow and cair,
   To gladdir gudis in all thair lyvis space,
And when their baggis are full, their selfis are bair,
   And of thair richness bot the keping hess;
   Whill othiris come to spend it that hes grace,
Whilk of thy wynning no labour had nor cure;
   Tak thow example, and spend with mirriness:
Without glaidnes availis no tresour.


Thocht all the werk that evir had levand wicht
   Were only thine, no moir thy pairt dois fall,
Bot meit, drynk, clais, and of the laif a sicht,
   Yit to the juge thow sall gif compt of all;
   Ane raknyng rycht cumis of ane ragment small,
Be just and joyous, and do to none injure,
   And trewth sall mak thee strang as ony wall:
Without glaidness availis no tresour.

*Idem*


## THE TWENTY-THIRD PSCHALME

The Lord maist hie
I know will be
 As herd to me;
I cannot lang have stress nor stand in neid;
He makes my lair
In fields maist fair,

47

Quhair I bot care,
Reposing at my pleasure, safely feid.
He sweetly me convoys,
Quhair naething me annoys,
But pleasure brings.
He brings my mynd
Fit to sic kynd,
That fors, or fears of foe cannot me grieve.
He does me leid,
In perfect freid,
And for his name he never will me lieve.
Thoch I wald stray,
Ilk day by day,
In deidly way,
Yet will I not dispair; I fear none ill,
For quhy thy grace
In every place,
Does me embrace,
Thy rod and shepherd's crook me comfort still.
In spite of foes
My tabil grows,
Thou balms my head with joy;
My cup overflows.
Kyndness and grace,
Mercy and peice,
Sall follow me for all my wretched days,
And me convoy,
To endless joy,
In heaven quhair I sall be with thee always.
                                    *Alexander Montgomerie*

## ADVICE TO LOVERS

If you would lufe and luvit be,
In mynd keip weill these thingis three,
And sadly in thy breast imprent;
Be secret, true and patient.

For he that patience cannot leir
He shall displeasance have perqueir,
Though he had all this worldis rent;
Be secret, true, and patient.

For who that secret cannot be,
Him all good fellowship shall flee,
And credence none shall him be lent;
Be secret, true, and patient.

And he that is of heart untrue,
Fra he be rend, farewell, adieu,
Fie on him, fie, his fame is went;
Be secret, true, and patient.

Thus he that wants of the things three
A lover glad may never be,
But ay is something discontent,
Be secret, true, and patient.

Nocht with thy tongue thyself discure
The things that thou hast of nature,
For if thou dois thou should repent;
Be secret, true, and patient.

*Anon.*

## PROVERBIA AMORIS

He that luifis lichtliest
    sall not happen on the best.
He that luivis langest
    sall have rest suirest.
He that luivis all his best
    sall chaunce upon the gudliest.
Quha sa in luif is trew and plaine
    he salbe luifit weill againe.
Men may say quhat ever they pleis
    in mutuall love is mekill eis.

*M. A. Arbuthnot*

## DECLARATION

I wil be plane,
And lufe affane,
For as I mene,
 So take me,
Gif I refrane,
For wo or pane,
Your lufe certane,
 Forsake me.

Gif trew report
To you resort
Of my gud port,
 So take me;
Gif I exort
In eveil sort,
Without confort,
 Forsake me.

Gif diligens
In your presens
Shaw my pretens,
 So take me;
Gif negligens
In my absens
Shaw my offens,
 Forsake me.

Your and no mo,
Whair evir I go;
Gif I so do,
 So take me;
Gif I flee fro,
And dois nocht so,
Evin as your fo,
 Forsake me.

Gif I do prufe
That I you luf
Nixt God abufe,
   So take me;
Gif I remufe
Fra your behufe
Without excuss,
   Forsake me.

Be land or se,
Whair evir I be,
As ye find me,
   So take me;
And gif I le,
And from you fle,
Ay whill I de,
   Forsake me.

It is bot waist
Mo words to taist,
Ye haif my laist,
   So take me;
Gif me our cast,
My lyf is past;
Even at the last
   Forsake me.

My deir, adew,
Most cleir of hew,
Now on me rew,
   And so take me;
Gif I persew,
And beis nocht trew,
Cheris ye ane new,
   And forsake me.
     *Alexander Scott (fl.* 1550)

## CONFESSIO AMANTIS

The thing that may her please
  My body sall fulfil,
Whatever her disease,
  It dois my body ill.
My bird, my bonnie ane,
  My tender babe venust,
My luve, my life alane,
  My liking and my lust.

We interchange our hairtis
  In otheris armis soft;
Spreitless we twa depairtis
  Usand our luvis oft;
We murne when licht day dawis,
  We 'plain the nicht is short,
We curse the cock that crawis,
  That hinderis our disport.

I glowffin up agast
  When I miss her on nicht,
And in my oxter fast
  I find the bowster richt;
Then languor on me lies
  Like Morpheus the mair,
Whilk causes me uprise
  And to my sweet repair:

And then is all the sorrow
  Furth of remembrance
That ever I had a morrow
  In luvis observance.
Thus never do I rest,
  So lusty a life I lead,
When that I list to test
  The well of womanheid.
          *Idem*

52

## A TESTAMENT

I will nae priests for me shall sing,
Nor yet nae bells for me to ring,
But ae Bag-pype to play a spring.
                *Walter Kennedy* (1460–1508)


## THE ATONEMENT

Behold the start that man was in
And also how it he tint throw sin
    And loist the same for ay;
Yet God His promeiss does performe,
Send His Son of the Virgeny borne
    Our ransome for to pay.
To that grit God let us give gloir
    To us has been sae gude,
Quha be His death did us restoir
    Quhairof we weir denude
        Not karing nor sparing
        His body to be rent,
        Redemyng, releiving
            Us wuhen we ar all schent.
            *Sir Richard Maitland* (1496–1586)


## THE MERRY HEART

When I have done consider
    This warldis vanitie,
So brukil and sa slidder,
    So full of miserie;
Then I remember me
That here there is no rest;
    Therefore apparentlie
To be merrie is best.

Let us be blyth and glad,
    My friendis all, I pray.

53

To be pensive and sad
  Na-thing it helps us may.
Therefore put quite away
All heaviness of thocht:
  Thoch we murne nicht and day
It will avail us nocht.

*Idem*


## SUMMER MORNING

The golden globe incontinent
  Sets up his shining head,
And o'er the earth and firmament
  Displays his beams abroad.

For joy the birds with boulden throats,
  Against his visage sheen
Take up their kindly musick notes
  In woods and garden green.

The dew upon the tender crops,
  Like pearlis white and round,
Or like to melted silver drops,
  Refreshis all the ground.

The time so tranquil is and still
  That nowhere shall ye find,
Save on the high and barren hill,
  An air of passing wind.

All trees and simples, great and small,
  That balmy leaf do bear,
Than they were painted on a wall
  No more they move or steir.

Calm is the deep and purple sea,
  Yea, smoother than the sand;
The waves that weltering wont to be
  Are stable like the land.

The cloggit busy humming bees,
   That never think to drone,
On flowers and flourishes of trees
   Collect their liquor brown.

The Sun, most like a speedy post
   With ardent course ascends;
The beauty of the heavenly host
   Up to our zenith tends.

The burning beams down from his face
   So fervently can beat,
That man and beast now seek a place
   To save them from the heat.

The herds beneath some leafy tree
   Amidst the flowers they lie;
The stable ships upon the sea
   Tend up their sails to dry.

With gilded eyes and open wings
   The cock his courage shows;
With claps of joy his breast he dings,
   And twenty times he crows.
         *Alexander Hume* (1560–1609)

## PICNIC

The caller wine in cave is sought
   Men's brothing breists to cule;
The water cauld and cleare is brought,
   And sallets steip't in ule.

Some plucks the honie plum and peare,
   The charie and the peache;
Some likes the reamand London beer,
   The bodie to refresh.
         *Idem*

## THE TWA GODS

Fra bank to bank, fra wood to wood I rin,
  Ourhailit with my feeble fantasie,
  Like til a leaf that fallis from a tree,
Or til a reed ourblawin' with the win'.

Twa gods guides me; the ane of them is blin',
  Yea and a bairn brocht up in vanitie;
  The next a wife ingenrit of the sea,
And lichter nor a dauphin with her fin.

Unhappy is the man for evermair
That tills the sand and sawis in the air;
  But twice unhappier is he, I lairn,
That feedis in his hairt a mad desire,
And follows on a woman thro the fire,
  Led by a blin and techit by a bairn.

*Mark Alexander Boyd*

## AUBADE

Hay! now the day dawis
The jolie cok crawis
Now shroudis the shawis
  Throu Nature anone.
The thissell-cok cryis
On loveris wha lyis,
Now skaillis the skyis,
  The night is neir gone.

The sesone excellis
Thrugh sweetness that smellis;
Now Cupid compellis
  Our heartis eachone.

56

On Venus wha waikis,
To muse on our maikis,
Syn Sing, for their saikis
"The night is neir gone".
*Alexander Montgomerie*

## HYMN ON THE ASCENSION

Bright portalles of the skie
Emboss'd with sparkling starres;
Doores of eternitie
With diamantine barres;
Your Arras rich uphold
Loose all your bolts and Springs,
Ope wyde your Leaves of gold
That in your Roofes may come the
King of kings.

Scarff'd in a rosie Cloud
Hee doth ascend the Aire;
Straight doth the Moone Him shroud
With her resplendent Haire;
The next enchristall'd Light
Submits to him her Beames,
And Hee doth trace the hight
Of that faire Lampe which flames of
beautie streams.

Hee lowers those golden Bounds
Hee did to Sunne bequeath;
The higher wandring Rounds
Are found his Feete beneath.
The Milkie Way comes neare,
Heaven's axell seemes to bend
Above each turning Spheare
That roab'd in Glorie Heaven's King
may ascend.

57

O Well-spring of this all,
   Thy Father's Image vive!
Word, that from nought did call
   What is, doth reason, live;
   The Soul's eternal Foode,
Earth's Joy—Delight of heaven,
   All Truth, Love, Beautie, Good,
To Thee, to Thee, bee praises ever given.


Now each etheriall Gate
   To him hath opened bin;
And Glorie's King in State
   His Palace enter in:
   Now com'd is this High Prest
In the most holie Place,
   Not without blood addres't
With Glorie Heaven, the Earth to crowne
     with Grace.


The Quires of happie Soules,
   Wak't with that Musicke sweete
Whose Desant Care controules
   Their Lord in Triumph meete;
   The spotless Sprights of light
His Trophees doe extole,
   And arch't in Squadrons bright
Greet their great victor in his Capitole.


O glorie of the Heaven!
   O sole Delight of Earth!
To thee all power bee given
God's uncreated birth;
Of Mankind lover true
Indurer of his wrong,
   Who dost the world renew
Still be Thou our Salvation and our Song.

*Drummond of Hawthornden*

58

## PHYLLIS

In Peticote of Greene
Her Haire about her Eine,
Phillis beneath an Oake
Sat milking her faire Flocke:
Among that strained Moysture (rare Delight)
Her Hand seem'd Milke in Milke, it was so white.

*Idem*

## THE STRANGE CONTENTMENT

Faire is my Yoke, though grievous bee my Paines,
Sweet are my Wounds, although they deeply smart.
My bit is Gold, though shortned bee the Raines,
My Bondage brave, though I may not depart:
Although I burne, the Fire which doth impart
Those flames, so sweet reviving Force containes,
That (like Arabia's bird) my wasted Heart,
Made quicke by death, more lively still remaines.
I joye though oft my waking Eyes spend Teares,
I never want Delight, even when I grone.
Best companied when most I am alone;
A Heaven of Hopes I have midst Hells of Feares.
  Thus every Way Contentment strange I finde,
  But most in Her rare Beautie, my rare Minde.

*Idem*

## KNOWLEDGE CONFOUNDED

I know that all beneath the Moone decayes,
And what by mortalles in this World is brought,
In Time's great periods shall returne to nought;
That fairest States have fatal Nights and Dayes;
I know how all the Muse's heavenly lays,
With Toyle of Spright which are so dearly bought,
As idle Sounds, of few or none are sought,
And that nought lighter is than airy praise;

59

I know fraile Beautie like the purple Flowre,
To which one Morne oft Birth and Death affords;
That Love a Jarring is of Mindes' accords,
Where Sense and Will invassall Reason's power:
  Know what I list, this all can not mee move,
But that (O me!) I both must write, and love.

*Idem*

## THE ELECTION

Some loves a woman for her Wit,
  Some Beauty does admire,
Some loves a handsome Leg or Foot,
  Some upwards does aspire;
Some loves a Mistress nice and coy,
  Some Freedom does approve;
Some like their Person to enjoy,
  Some for Platonick Love.
Some loves a widow, some a maid,
  Some loves the Old, some Young;
Some love until they be betray'd,
  Some till they be undone:
Some love for Money, some for Worth,
  Some love the Proud and High;
Some love for Fancy, some for Birth,
  Some love, and knows not why.
Some love the little, Plump and Fat,
  Some love the Long and Small:
Some loves for Kindness, and 'tis that
  Moves me beyond them all.

*The Marquess of Montrose* (?)

## THE GARDENER

The gardener stands in his bower door,
  With a primrose in his hand,
And by there cam a leal maiden,
  As jimp as a willow wand.

60

"O ladie can ye fancy me,
For to be my bride?
Ye'se get a' the flowers in my garden,
To be to you a weed.

The lily white shal be your smock,
It becomes your body best;
Your head shal be bask't wi' gilly-flower,
Wi' the primrose in your breast.

Your gown shal be the Sweet William;
Your coat the camovine;
Your apron o' the sallads neat,
That taste baith sweet and fine.

Your hose shal be the brade kail-blade
That is baith brade and lang;
Narrow, narrow at the cute,
And brade, brade at the brawn.

Your glaves shal be the marigold,
All glittering to your hand,
Weel spread owre with the blaewort
That grows amang corn-land."

"O fare ye weil, young man," she says,
"Fareweil, and I bid adieu;
Sin ye've provided a weed for me
Amang the simmer flowers,
I will provide anither for you,
Amang the winter-showers.

The new fall'n snaw to be your smock,
It becomes your bodie best;
Your head shal be wrapt wi' the eastern wind,
And the cauld rain on your breast."

*Anon.*

## THE GREENWOOD

The King's young dochter was sitting in her
     window,
  Sewing at her silken seam;
She lookt out o' a bow-window
  And she saw the leaves growing green,
     My luve,
And she saw the leaves growing green.

She stuck her needle into her sleeve,
  Her seam down by her tae,
And she is awa' to the merrie greenwood,
  To pu' the nit and the slae,
     My luve;
To pu' the nit and the slae.

             *Anon.*

## THE WHALE

God's might so peoples hath the sea
  With fish of divers sort,
That men therein may clearly see
  Great things for their comfort.

There is such great varietie,
  Of fishes of all kind,
That it were great impietie
  God's hand there not to find.

The Puffen, Torteuse, and Thorneback,
  The Scallop and the Goujeon,
The Shrimpe, the Spit-fish, and the Sprat,
  The Stock-fish, and the Sturgeon;

The Torteuse, Tench, and Tunnyfish,
  The Sparling and the Trout;
And Herring, for the poor man's dish,
  Is all the land about;

The Groundling, Gilt-head, and the Crab,
　　The Gurnard, Cockle, Oyster,
The Cramp-fish and als the Sea-Dog,
　　The Crefish and the Conger;


The Periwinkle and Twinfish—
　　It's hard to count them all;
Some are for oyle, some for the dish;
　　The greatest is the Whale!
　　　　　　　*Zachary Boyd* (1585–1653)


## THE BUSIE BRAIN

I find I'm haunted with a busie mind,
Swift as the Clouds, unstable as the Wind,
It sometimes gets it Wings, and soars aloft,
Anon it stoops into delights more soft,
It's sometimes serious, and it's sometimes vain,
Sometimes it's thoughts do please, and sometimes
　　pain;
　On while they're dark, and then they clear again;
Sometimes they'r cheerfull, sometimes they are sad;
They're sometimes good, and often they are bad;
Sometimes, myself, myself's their only Theam,
Sometimes, they grasp at more than Caesar's claim:
They bring forth Joy, they nourish Fear,
They towers into the Air do rear,
All things do seem within their Sphear:
O what a wandring thing's the Mind!
What contrares are there combin'd?
How shal't be held or where confin'd?
O what a Web's a busie Thought,
Where is it made? whence is it brought?
How is it warpt, how is it wrought?
　　　　*John Barclay, Minister of Cruden* (*fl.* 1670)

## HALLO! MY FANCY

In Conceit, like Phaeton,
I'll mount Phoebus' Chair!
Having ne'er a Hat on,
All my Hair's a-burning,
In my journeying,
Hurrying through the Air.
Fain would I hear his fiery Horses neighing!
And see how they on foamy Bitts are playing!
All the Stars and Planets I will be surveying!
Hallo! my fancy, whither wilt thou go?

O from what ground of Nature,
Doth the Pelican,
That self-devouring Creature
Prove so froward,
And untoward,
Her Vitals for to strain!
And why the subtile Fox, while in Death's wounds is
lying!
Doth not lament his Pangs by howling and by crying!
And why the milk-white Swan doth sing when she is
dying!
Hallo! my fancy, whither wilt thou go?

Fain would I conclude this,
At least make Essay,
What similitude is,
Why Fowls of a Feather,
Flock and fly together,
And lambs know Beasts of Prey!
How Nature's Alchymists, these small laborious
Creatures,
Acknowledge still a Prince in ordering their Matters
And suffer none to live, who slothing, lose their
Features!
Hallo! my fancy, whither wilt thou go?

64

Fain also would I prove this,
By considering,
What that which you call Love is:
Whether it be Folly,
Or a melancholy,
Or some Heroick thing!
Fain I'd have it prov'd, by one whom Love hath
wounded,
And fully upon one his Desire hath founded,
Whom nothing else could please, tho' the World
were rounded!
Hallo! my fancy, whither wilt thou go?

To know this World's Center,
Height, Depth, Breadth and Length,
Fain would I adventure,
To search the hid Attractions
Of Magnetick Actions
And Adamantick strength!
Fain would I know, if in some lofty Mountain,
Where the Moon sojourns, if there be Trees or
Fountain,
If there be Beasts of Prey, or yet be Fields to hunt in!
Hallo my Fancy.

Fain would I have it tried
By Experiment,
By none can be denied
If in this bulk of Nature
There be Voids less or greater
Or all remains compleat!
Fain would I know if Beasts have any Reason,
If Falcons killing Eagles do commit a Treason,
If Fear of Winter's want makes Swallows fly the
Season!

Hallo! my fancy, hallo!
Stay, stay at home with me,

65                                                      D

I can thee no longer follow;
For thou hast betrayed me,
And bewray'd me;
It is too much for thee.
Stay, stay at Home with me, leave off thy lofty
Soaring,
Stay thou at Home with me and on thy Books be
poring.
For he that goes abroad, lays little up in Storing.
Thou'rt welcome Home, my Fancy, welcome home
to me.

*William Cleland* (1661–1689)

## GOOD DOG

Calm tho' not mean, courageous without rage,
Serious not dull, and without thinking sage;
Pleased at the lot that nature has assign'd,
Snarl as I list, and freely bark my mind,
As churchman wrangle not with jarring spite,
Nor statesman-like caressing whom I bite;
View all the canine kind with equal eyes,
I dread no mastiff, and no cur despise.
True from the first, and faithful to the end,
I balk no mistress, and forsake no friend.
My days and nights one equal tenor keep,
Fast but to eat, and only wake to sleep.
Thus stealing along life I live incog,
A very plain and downright honest dog.

*William Hamilton of Bangour*

## ON THE ROBING OF THE KING AND
## QUEEN OF FAIRY

### 1. *The King*

Upon a time the fairy elves
Having first arrayed themselves,
They thought it meet to clothe their King,
In robes most fit for revelling.

66

He had a cobweb shirt more thin
Than ever spiders since could spin,
Bleached in the whiteness of the snow,
When that the northern winds do blow.

And in that vast and open air
No shirt is half so fine or fair;
A rich waistcoat they did him bring
Made of a trout-fly's golden wing.

Dyed Crimson in a maiden's blush
And lined with humming bees' soft plush.
At which his Elfship 'gan to fret,
And swore 'twould cast him in a sweat.

He for his coolness needs would wear
A waistcoat made of downy hair,
New taken from a eunuch's chin;
It pleased him well, 'twas wondrous thin.

His hat was all of ladies' love,
So passing light that it would move,
If any gnat or humming fly
But beat the air in passing by.

About it went a wreath of pearl
Dropt from the eyes of some poor girl,
Pinched because she had forgot
To leave clean water in the pot.

His breeches and his cassock were
Made of tinsel gossamer:
Down by its seam there went a lace
Drawn by an unctuous snail's slow pace.

### 2. *The Queen*

No sooner was their King attired
As never prince had been,

But as in duty was required
   They next array their Queen.

On shining thread shot from the sun
   And twisted into line
On the light Wheel of Fortune spun
   Was made her smock so fine.

Her gown was vari-coloured fair,
   The rainbow gave the dip,
Perfumed by an amber-air
   Breathed from a virgin's lip.

The stuff was of a morning dawn
   When Phoebus did but peep,
But by a poet's pencil drawn
   In Chloris' lap asleep.

Her shoes were all of maidenheads
   So passing thin and light
That all her care was how she treads—
   A thought had burst them quite.

The revels ended, she put off,
   Because her Grace was warm:
She fanned her with a lady's scoff,
   And so she took no harm.

*Archibald Pitcairn, M.D.*

## VIGNETTE

A green kail-yard, a little fount,
   Where water poplan springs;
There sits a wife with wrinkled front,
   And yet she spins and sings.

*Allan Ramsay*

## WOMAN IN LOVE

Patie to me is dearer than my breath:
But want of him I dread nae other skaith.
There's nane of a' the herds that tread the green
Has sic a smile, or sic twa glancing een.
And then he speaks with sic a taking art,
His words they thirle like musick thro' my heart.
How blythly can he sport, and gently rave,
And jest at feckless fears that fright the lave!
Ilk day that he's alane upon the hill,
He reads fell books that teach him meikle skill.
He is—but what need I say that or this?
I'd spend a month to tell you what he is!

*Idem*

## THE CORDIAL

O happy love! where love like this is found,
O heartfelt raptures! bliss beyond compare!
If Heaven a draught of heavenly pleasure spare,
　One cordial in this melancholy vale,
'Tis when a youthful, loving, modest pair,
　In other's arms breathe out the tender tale,
　Beneath the milk-white thorn that scents the
　　evening gale.

*Idem*

## LOVE SCENE

Last morning I was gay and early out,
Upon a dike I lean'd glowring about,
I saw my Meg come linkan o'er the lee;
I saw my Meg, but Meggy saw na me:
For yet the sun was wading thro' the mist,
And she was closs upon me ere she wist;
Her coats were kiltit, and did sweetly shaw
Her straight bare legs that whiter were than
　　snaw;

69

Her cockernony snooded up fou sleek,
Her haffet-locks hang waving on her cheek;
Her cheek sae ruddy, and her een sae clear;
And O! her mouth's like ony hinny pear.
Neat, neat, she was, in bustine waste-coat clean,
As she came skiffing o'er the dewy green.
Blythsome, I cry'd, My bonny Meg, come here,
I ferly wherefore ye're sae soon asteer;
But I can guess, ye'er gawn to gather dew:
She scour'd awa, and said, What's that to you?
Then fare ye well, Meg Dorts, and e'ens ye like,
I careless cry'd, and lap in o'er the dike.
I trow, when that she saw, within a crack,
She came with a right thievless errand back;
Misca'd me first—then bade me hound my dog
To wear up three waff ews stray'd on the bog.
I leugh, and sae did she; then with great haste
I clasp'd my arms about her neck and waste,
About her yielding waste, and took a fouth
Of sweetest kisses frae her glowing mouth.
While hard and fast I held her in my grips,
My very saul came lowping to my lips.

*Idem*


## MY PEGGY

My Peggy is a young thing,
   Just enter'd in her teens,
Fair as the day, and sweet as May,
Fair as the day, and always gay.
   My Peggy is a young thing,
      And I'm not very auld;
   Yet well I like to meet her, at
      The wawking of the fauld.


My Peggy speaks sae sweetly,
   Whene'er we meet alane,

I wish nae mair to lay my care,
I wish nae mair of a' that's rare.
  My Peggy speaks sae sweetly,
    To a' the lave I'm cauld;
    But she gars a' my spirits glow
      At wawking of the fauld.

My Peggy smiles sae kindly,
  Whene'er I whisper love,
That I look down on a' the town,
That I look down upon a crown.
  My Peggy smiles sae kindly,
    It makes me blyth and bauld;
    And naething gi'es me sic delight,
      As wawking of the fauld.

My Peggy sings sae saftly,
  When on my pipc I play,
By a' the rest it is confest,
By a' the rest that she sings best.
  My Peggy sings sae saftly,
    And in her sangs are tauld,
    In innocence, the wale of sense,
      At wawking of the fauld.
                *Idem*

## A SONG OF FOXES

Ho! Ho! Ho! the foxes!
Would there were more of them,
I'd give heavy gold
For a hundred score of them!

My blessing with the foxes dwell,
For that they hunt the sheep so well!

Ill fa' the sheep, a grey-faced nation,
That swept our hills with desolation!

71

Who made the bonnie green glens clear,
And acres scarce, and houses dear;

The grey-faced sheep, who worked our woe,
Where men no more may reap or sow,

And made us leave for their green pens
Our bonnie braes and grassy glens,

Where we were reared, and gladly grew
And lived to kin and country true;

Who bared the houses to the wind,
Where hearths were warm, and hearts were kind,

And spread the braes with wreck and ruin
The grey-faced sheep for our undoing!

And when they came were seen no more
Harrow or hoe on slope or shore,

And on the old and friendly places
New people sit with loveless faces;

And the good grey mare no more is seen
With its frisking foal on the open green,

And I seek in vain for the cow that lay
Licking its calf on the bonnie green brae!

And the bonnie milkmaids, ohon! ohon!
Are seen no more when the kine are gone!

And there's now no work for the lads to do
But to herd the sheep—some one or two!

And the goats, whose milk was good and cheap
They too must go, to make way for the sheep!

And the roe in the rocky glade that lies
Is waked no more by the fawn when it cries.

For stags will flee, and mothers will weep
When gentlemen live to make money by sheep!

And foresters now can earn no penny
When stags are few and sheep are many.

He earns from me no kindly will
Who harms the fox upon the hill;

May he die the death of a hog
Against a fox who drives a dog!

On the hill-side may he rot
Who fires on Reynard with cruel shot!

And may the young cubs prosper well
Where snug in rocky holes they dwell

And if my prayer with Heaven prevail
No trap shall grip their bushy tail!

And may they live on tasteful food
And die as wise old foxes should!
*Duncan Ban MacIntyre*

## MORNING ON BEN DORAIN

B' ionmhuinn leam ag éirigh
'San òg-mhaduinn,
Timchioll air na sléibhtean
'M bu chòir dhaibh bhith,
Cupal chunntas cheud,
Luchd nan ceann gun chéill
A' mosgladh gu neo-bheudar
Mòr-shòlasach;

D 2

Is osgarra o'm beul
Tormain socair, réidh,
'S glan an corp 's an cré
    Seinn an dreòcaim ud:
Broc-liath chorrach eild'
An lod g'a loireadh théid,
Cuid g'a farraid fhéin
    'N uair bu deònach leatha
'S annsa leam 'n uair théid
    Iad air chrònanaich,
Na na th'ann an Eirinn
    De cheòlmhoireachd;
'S binne na gach beus
Anail mhic an fhéidh
A' langanaich air eudan
    Beinn-Dòbhrain.

*Idem*

# ANN MORRISON

. . . . . .

Ach labhair i gu h-àilghiosach faiteagach, rium,
"Cha 'n fhair thu bhi làimh rium do chàradh mo
    chinn;
Tha siathnar 'g am iarruidh o bhliadhna de thìom,
'S cha b' àraidh le càch thu thoirt bàrr os an cinn."
Ha, ha, ha! an d' fhàs thu gu tinn,
Mas e 'n gaol a bheir bas ort gu 'm paigh thu d' a
    chinn!

Ach cionnus bheir mu fuath dhuit, ged dh'
    fhuaraich thu rium,
'N uair 's feargaich' mo sheanchas mu t' ainm air
    do chùl,
Thig t' ìomhaigh le h-annsachd, mar shamhladh 'n
    am ùigh,
Is saoilidh mi gur gaol sin, nach caochail a chaoidh.

74

Is théid air a ràth, gu'n dh-fhas e as ùr,
Is fàsaidh e 'n tràth sin cho àrda r tùr.

O 'n chualas gu'n gluaiseadh tu uam leis an t-Saoir,
Tha mo shuain air a buaireadh le bruadraichean
    gaoil;
Do 'n chàirdeas a bha sud, cha 'n fhàir mi bhith
    saor,
Gun bhàrnaigeadh làimh riut, tha 'n gràdh dhomh
    'n a mhaor.
Ach, ma tha mi'g a do dhith,
B' fheàirde mi pàg uait fàg thu an tìr.

*Rob Donn*

## PÒSADH MHIC LEOID

.    .    .    .

A Ruairidh Ruairidh
Ruairidh an Dùin ud,

Is tù mo mhire
Is mo cheòl sùgraidh:

Is tù mo phaidirean
Mo chìr-chùil thu:

Mo ghàradh mheas
Am bi na h-ùblan.

Càite a bheil
A h-aon riut coltach,

O nach maireann
Fionn no Oisean,

Diarmaid donn no
Goll no Osgar?

*Mary Macleod*

75

## MIDWINTER

Now mirk December's dowie face
Glowers o'er the rigs wi' sour grimace,
While, through his minimum of space
    The bleer-e'ed sun,
Wi' blinkin' light and stealing pace
    His race doth run.

Frae naked groves nae birdie sings
To shepherd's pipe nae hillock rings,
The breeze nae od'rous flavour brings
    Frae Borean cave,
And dwinin' Nature droops her wings
    Wi' visage grave.

*Robert Fergusson*

## SUB TEGMINE FAGI

Now when the dog-day heats begin
To birsle and to peel the skin,
May I lie streckit at my ease
Beneath the caller shady trees
(Far frae the din o' Borrowstown),
Where water plays the haughs bedown;
To jouk the summer's rigour there,
And breathe awhile the caller air,
'Mang herds, and honest cottar folk,
That till the farm and feed the flock;
Careless o' mair, wha never fash
To lade their kist wi' useless cash,
But thank the gods for what they've sent
O' health eneugh, and blythe content,
And futh that helps them to stravaig
Ower ilka cleugh and ilka craig;
Unkenned to a the weary granes
That aft arise frae gentler banes,

76

On easy chair that pampered lie,
Wi' baneful viands gustit high,
And turn and fauld their weary clay,
To rax and gaunt the live-lang day.

*Idem*


## BRAID CLAITH

Ye who are fain to hae your name
Wrote i' the bonnie book o' fame,
Let merit nae pretension claim
    To laurell'd wreath,
But hap ye weel, baith back and wame
    In gude braid claith.

Waesuch for him wha has nae feck o't!
For he's a gowk they're sure to geck at;
A chiel that ne'er will be respeckit
    While he draws breath,
Till his four quarters are bedeckit
    Wi' guid braid claith.

On Sabbath-days the barber spark
When he has done wi' scrapin' wark,
Wi' siller broachie in his sark,
    Gangs trigly, faith!
Or to the Meadows, or the Park
    In gude braid claith.

Braid claith lends fouk an unco heeze,
Maks mony kail-worms butterflees,
Gies mony a doctor his degrees
    For little skaith:
In short, you may be whay you please
    Wi' gude braid claith.

For tho' ye had as wise a snout on
As Shakespeare or Sir Isaac Newton,

Your judgment fouk would hae a doubt on,
    I'll tak' my aith,
Till they could see ye wi' a suit on
    O' gude braid claith.

*Idem*

## THE YELLOW-HAIR'D LADDIE

The yellow-hair'd laddie sat down on yon brae,
Cries, "Milk the ewes, lassie, let nane of them gae."
And ay she milked, and ay she sang:
"The yellow-hair'd laddie shall be my gudeman.

The weather is cauld, and my claithing is thin;
The ewes are new clipped, they winna bught in:
They winna bught in tho' I should die,
O yellow-hair'd laddie, be kind to me."

The goodwife cries butt the house, "Jenny, come ben,
The cheese is to mak', and the butter's to kirn".
"Tho' butter, and cheese, and a' should sour,
I'll crack and kiss wi' my love ae half-hour:
It's ae half-hour, and we's e'en mak' it three,
For the yellow-hair'd laddie my husband shall be."

*Anon.*

## THE INDUCEMENT

"Whistle, whistle, auld wife,
    An' ye'se get a hen."
"I wadna whistle", quo' the wife,
    "Though ye wad gie me ten."

"Whistle, whistle, auld wife,
    An' ye'se get a cock."
"I wadna whistle", quo' the wife,
    "Though ye'd gie me a flock."

"Whistle, whistle, auld wife,
    An' ye'll get a goun."
"I wadna whistle", quo' the wife,
    "For the best ane i' the toun."

"Whistle, whistle, auld wife,
    An' ye'se get a coo."
"I wadna whistle", quo' the wife,
    "Though ye wad gie me two."

"Whistle, whistle, auld wife,
    An' ye'se get a man."
"Wheeple-whauple", quo' the wife,
    "I'll whistle gin I can."

*Anon.*

## BLESSING OF THE KINDLING

Cogaidh mi mo theine an diugh,
An lathair ainghlean naomha neimh,
An lathair Airil is ailde cruth,
An lathair Uiril nan uile ageimh.
Gun ghnu, gun thu, gun fharmad.
Gun ghiomh, gun gheimh roimh neach fo'n ghrein,
Ach Naomh Mhac De da m'thearmad.

    Gun, ghnu, gun thu, gun fharmad,
    Gun ghiomh, gun gheimh, roimh neach fo'n
      ghrein,
    Ach Naomh Mhac De da m'thearmad.

Dhe fadaidh fein na m'chridhe steach,
Aingheal ghraidh do m'choimhearsnach,
Do 'n t-saoidh, do 'n daoidh, do 'n traille.
A Mhic na Moire min-ghile,
Bho'n ni is isde crannachaire,
Gu ruig an t-Ainm is airde.

    A Mhic na Moire min-ghile,
    Bho 'n ni is isde crannachaire,
    Gu ruig an t-Ainm is airde.

*Anglice*

I will kindle my fire this morning
in presence of the holy angels of heaven,
in presence of Ariel of the loveliest form,
in presence of Uriel of the myriad charms,
without malice, without jealousy, without envy,
without fear, without terror of any one under the sun,
but the Holy Son of God to shield me.
Without malice, without jealousy, without envy,
Without fear, without terror of any one under
the sun
but the Holy Son of God to shield me.

God, kindle Thou in my heart within
a flame of love to my neighbour,
to my foe, to my friend, to my kindred all,
to the brave, to the knave, to the thrall,
O Son of the loveliest Mary,
From the lowliest thing that liveth,
to the Name that is highest of all.
O Son of the loveliest Mary,
from the lowliest thing that liveth,
to the Name that is highest of all.

*Carmina Gadelica*

## THE MERRY WIDOWER

O fare ye weel, my auld wife!
Sing bum, biberry bum.
O fare ye weel, my auld wife!
Sing bum.
O fare ye weel, my auld wife!
Thou steerer up o' sturt and strife!
The maut's aboon the meal the nicht
Wi' some.

And fare ye weel, my pike-staff!
Sing bum, biberry bum.

And fare ye weel my pike-staff!
　Sing bum.
And fare ye weel my pike-staff—
Nae mair wi' thee my wife I'll baff!
The maut's aboon the meal the nicht
　Wi' some.

Fu' white white was her winding sheet!
　Sing bum, biberry bum.
Fu' white white was her winding sheet!
　Sing bum.
I was ower gladsome far to greet
I danced my lane, and sang to see't.
The maut's aboon the meal the nicht
　Wi' some.

　　　　　　　　　　　　　*Anon.*

## GLASGOW KISSES

Kiss'd yestreen, and kiss'd yestreen,
Up the Gallowgate, down the Green:
I've woo'd wi' lords, and woo'd wi' lairds,
I've mool'd wi' carles and mell'd wi' cairds,
I've kiss'd wi' priests—'twas done i' the dark,
Twice in my gown and thrice in my sark;
But priest, nor lord, nor loon can gie
Sic kindly kisses as he gave me.

　　　　　　　　　　　　　*Anon.*

## LASSIE, GIN YE LO'E ME

I hae laid a herring in saut,
　　*Lass, gin ye lo'e me, tell me now!*
I hae brewed a forpit o' maut,
　　*And I canna come ilka day to woo.*
I hae a calf will soon be a cow
　　*Lass, gin ye lo'e me tell me now!*
I hae a pig will soon be a sow,
　　*And I canna come ilka day to woo*

81

I've a house on yonder muir,
*Lass, gin ye lo'e me, tell me now!*
There sparrows may dance on the floor,
*And I canna come ilka day to woo.*
I hae a but and I hae a ben,
*Lass, gin ye lo'e me, tell me now!*
I hae three chickens and a fat hen,
*And I canna come ilka day to woo.*

I've a hen wi' a happity leg,
*Lass, gin ye lo'e me, tell me now!*
Which ilka day lays me an egg,
*And I canna come ilka day to woo.*
I hae a kebbuck upon my shelf,
*Lass, gin ye lo'e me, tak me now!*
I downa eat it all myself
*And I winna come ony mair to woo.*

*James Tytler*

## "MAIR SPIER NA, NOR FEAR NA"

It's hardly in a body's power,
To keep at times frae being sour,
  To see how things are shared,
How best o' chiels are whiles in want,
While coofs on countless thousands rant,
  And ken na how to wair 't,
But, Davie, lad, ne'er fash your head,
  Though we hae little gear,
We're fit to win our daily bread,
  As lang's we're hale and fier:
    "Mair spier na, nor fear na",
    Auld age ne'er mind a feg,
  The last o't, the warst o't,
    Is only but to beg.

*Burns*

82

## THE SUMMING-UP

I hae been blithe wi' comrades dear;
   I hae been merry drinkin'!
I hae been joyfu' gathr'in' gear;
   I hae been happy thinkin':
But a' the pleasures e'er I saw,
   Though three times doubled fairly,
That happy night was worth them a'
   Amang the rigs o' barley.

*Idem*

## SECRET LOVE

O May, thy morn was ne'er sae sweet
   As the mirk night o' December!
For sparkling was the rosy wine,
   And private was the chamber,
And dear was she I darena name,
   But I will ay remember.

And here's to them that, like oursel',
   Can push about the jorum!
And here's to them that wish us weel:
   May a' that's guid watch o'er 'em!
And here's to them we darena tell,
   The dearest o' the quorum!

*Idem*

## A MAUCHLINE WEDDING
### (FRAGMENT)

When Eighty-five was seven months auld
   And wearing through the aught,
When rolling rains and Boreas bauld
   Gied farmer folks a faught,
Ae morning quondam Mason W—
   Now Merchant Master Miller,

Gaed down to meet wi' Nansie B—
   And her Jamaica siller
      To wed that day.

The rising sun o'er Blacksideen
   Was just appearing fairly
When Nell and Bess got up to dress
   Seven lang half-hours o'er early!
Now presses clink and drawers jink,
   For linens and for laces
But modest Muses only *think*
   What ladies' underdress is
      On sic a day!

But we'll suppose the stays are lac'd
   And bonie bosoms steekit,
Tho' thro' the lawn—but guess the rest!
   An angel scarce durst keek it.
Then stockin's fine o' silken twine
   Wi' cannie care are drawn up,
An' gartered tight whare mortal wight

    .       .     .        .

[*As I never wrote it down, my recollection does
    not entirely serve me.*]

But now the gown wi' rustling sound
   Its silken pomp displays;
Sure there's nae sin in being vain
   O' siccan bonie claes!
Sae jimp the waist, the tail sae vast—
   Trouth, they were bonie birdies!
O Mither Eve, ye wad been grieve
   To see their ample hurdies
      Sae large that day!

Then Sandy, wi's red jacket braw,
   Comes whip-jee-woa! about,

And in he gets the bonie twa—
    Lord, send them safely out!
And auld John Trot wi' sober phiz,
    As braid and braw's a Bailie,
His shouthers and his Sunday's jiz
    Wi' powther and wi' ulzie
        Weel smear'd that day.

    .       .       .

*Idem*

## THE FRUGAL WISH

May I enjoy a state of health,
Free from both poverty and wealth;
And may I ever have a friend,
In whom I safely may depend;
To crack a joke, or tell a tale,
Or share a pint of nappy ale:
And also a good sneeshin mill;
And of the best rappee her fill;
With good tobacco, pipe and box,
And some to spare a friend who smokes.
And, in the morning when I rise,
A single glass to clear my eyes:
With some choice books to read at leisure,
To edify and some for pleasure.
Likewise a kind industrious wife,
Who nothing hates so much as strife;
A snug thack'd house, a canty fire;
A new-cal' cow to fill my byre.
A bonnie burnie trotting by,
Wherein to fish at hake and manger;
An orrow bed, to lodge a stranger.
Thus may I spin the thread of life,
Remote from bustle, din and strife:
And when at last death takes me aff,
May I deserve this epitaph—

"Interr'd below this silent sod,
Lies one who always feared God:
And, when he liv'd, by God's assistance,
Held cold and craving at a distance."
*Anon. (late 18th or early 19th cent.)*


## FARMER'S BOY

"Saw ye Johnnie comin'?" quo' she,
"Saw ye Johnnie comin';
Wi' his blue bonnet on his head
And his doggie runnin'?
Yestreen, about the gloamin' time
I chanced to see him comin',
Whistlin' merrily the tune
That I am a' day hummin'," quo' she;
"I am a' day hummin'."


"Fee him, faither, fee him", quo' she,
"Fee him, faither, fee him;
A' the wark about the house
Gaes wi' me when I see him;
A' the wark about the house,
I gang lightly through it:
And though ye pay some merks o' gear,
Hoot! ye winna rue it," quo' she;
"No, ye winna rue it."


"What wad I do wi' him, hizzy?
What wad I do wi' him?
He's ne'er a sark upon his back,
And I hae nane to gie him."
"I hae two sarks into my kist,
And ane o' them I'll gie him;
And for merk o' mair fee,
O dinna stand wi' him," quo' she.
"Dinna stand wi him."

86

"Weel do I lo'e him," quo' she,
  "Weel do I lo'e him;
The bravest lads about the place
  Are a' but hav'rels to him.
O fee him, faither; lang, I trow,
  We've dull and dowie been;
He'll haud the plough, thrash i' the barn,
And crack wi' me at e'en," quo' she,
  "Crack wi' me at e'en."

*Joanna Baillie*

## MORNING

But who the melodies of morn can tell?
The wild brook babbling down the mountain
    side;
The lowing herd; the sheepfold's simple bell;
The pipe of early shepherd dim descried
In the lone valley; echoing far and wide
The clamorous horn along the cliffs above;
The hollow murmur of the ocean-tide,
The hum of bees, the linnet's lay of love,
And the full choir that wakes the universal grove.

The cottage curs at early pilgrim bark;
Crown'd with her pail the tripping milkmaid
    sings;
The whistling ploughman stalks afield; and,
    hark!
Down the rough slope his ponderous waggon
    rings;
Through rustling corn the hare astonish'd
    springs;
Slow tolls the village clock the drowsy hour;
The partridge bursts away on whirring wings;
Deep mourns the turtle in sequester'd bower,
And shrill lark carols clear from her aërial tour.

*James Hay Beattie*

## WINTER DISCONTENT

Gane were but the winter cauld,
And gane were but the snaw,
I could sleep in the wild woods
Where the primroses blaw.

*Allan Cunningham*

## EXCERPTS FROM THE LIFE OF
## MARY QUEEN OF SCOTS

### 1. *Her Birth and Education*

Poor Mary Queen of Scots was born
With all the graces which adorn
Her birthday is so very late
That I do now forget the date
Her education was in France
There she did learn to sing and dance
There she was married to the dauphin
But soon he was laid in a coffin
Then she at once from France retired
Where she had been so much admired
Fare well dear France she cried at last
While a despairing look she cast.

### 2. *The Tragedy of Rizzio and its Sequel*

Mary was charmed with a player
Of whom she took a great great care
He fed upon the finest fair
He was her greatest favourite
Him she caressed with all her might
She gave him food and she gave him wine
When he was gone she would repine
The King heard this with anger sore
This is not all there is much more
For he did murder the poor player
Of whom she took so great a care

88

In agony she heaved a sigh
For on the King she did relie
Bad hatered at length found a way
It was a little more than play
An awful day at last arrived
Which was the last that he survived
For she went to a masquerade
But for that thing he dearly paid
For in her absence what was done
The thing would not I'm sure give fun
The house in which the King did lie
I cannot think without a sigh
Was blowen up at too next day
The King was killed I'm sorry to say.

3. *Mary and Elizabeth compared*

Elisbeth was a cross old maid
Now when her youth began to fade
Her temper was worse than before
And people did not her adore
But Mary was much loved by all
Both by the great and by the small
But hark her soul to heaven did rise
And I do think she gained a prise
For I do think she would not go
Into that awfull place below
There is a thing that I must tell
Elisbeth went to fire and hell
Him who will teach her to be cevel
It must be her great friend the divil.
                              *Marjory Fleming*

# FARM CAT

I had a Cat, o' cats the wale,
A bonnie brute frae snout to tail,
Soft as the silk his massy paw,
His skin as white as mountain snaw,

Save where the gowden spraings confest
Shone glancin' on his wally chest;
His smell like ony sluth-hund's keen,
An' quick his rowin hazel e'en;
Firm, portly on his legs he stood,
An' luik't a cat o' princely bluid.
Yet tho' he seem'd o' guid descent,
His pedigree I never kent.

I never sneckt an amrie door,
Tam never steal'd tho' he was poor;
My confidence he ne'er abus'd,
An' aft the proffer'd bite refus'd,
Wi modest face withdrew his e'en,
As if the gift he hadna seen;
Nor, tho' it savoury stood beside him,
Wad steal the bit I had denied him.

At e'en he prowl'd baith house an' barn,
Ilk ee red glancin' like a starn,
Wad every corner keen explore
Whar he could find a hole or bore;
Wi snout erect snuff up the ait,
As if he smelt his object there;
Down ilka paw sae saftly set,
As wadna scaith'd a spider's net;
Syne whan the mice began to stir,
Squat on the floor he ceas'd to purr,
An' caum as he had been asleep,
Saw them frae out their hidins peep;
Then neither age nor sex he spar'd,
But springing, like the furious pard,
Snap gaed his jaw, an' in a breath
Crush'd some poor hapless wretch to death.

Tho' a full tide o' noble bluid
Pour'd thro' his veins its crimson fluid:

Tho' he a tyger's fury knew
Whane'er his game he had in view,
Yet, quait, aside the fire himlane,
Was harmless as the soukin' wean;
Wi' all the bairns he was a pet,
An sad and sair they mourn him yet.
He ne'er wad wi' his neighbour squabble,
Nor herdit wi' the common rabble;
Till ance arriv'd at hoary age
He hirsl'd quaitly off the stage.

*Ebenezer Picken* (*fl.* 1813)

## ROVING LOVE

"A weary lot is thine, fair maid,
　A weary lot is thine!
To pull the thorn thy brow to braid,
　And press the rue for wine!
A lightsome eye, a soldier's mien,
　A feather of the blue,
A doublet of the Lincoln green,—
　No more of me you knew,
　　　　My love!
No more of me you knew.

This morn is merry June, I trow,
　The rose is budding fain;
But she shall bloom in winter snow,
　Ere we two meet again."
He turn'd his charger as he spake,
　Upon the river shore,
He gave his bridle-reins a shake,
　Said, "Adieu for evermore,
　　　　My love!
And adieu for evermore".

*Scott*

## THE LONELY HEART

Why should I sit and sigh
  When the greenwood blooms sae bonnie?
Laverocks sing, flow'rets spring,
  A' but me are cheery.
Ochon, O ri! There's something wanting,
  Ochon, O ri! I'm weary;
Nae young, blithe and bonnie lad,
  Comes o'er the knowe to cheer me.

When the day wears away
  Sair I look down the valley.
Ilka sound wi' a stound
  Sets my heart a-thrilling.
When I see the plover rising
  Or the curlew wheeling,
Then I trow some bonnie lad
  Is coming to my shieling.

Come away, come away,
  Herd or hind or boatman laddie;
I hae cow, kid and ewe,
  Gowd and gear to gain thee!
My wee cot is blessed and happy,
  Oh, 'tis neat and cleanly!
Sweet the briar that blooms beside it,
  Kind the heart that's lanely!
  Ochon, O ri! there's something wanting
    Ochon, O ri! I'm weary
  Nae young, blithe and bonnie lad
    Comes o'er the knowe to cheer me.
              *James Hogg*

## A BOY'S SONG

Where the pools are bright and deep
Where the grey trout lies asleep,

Up the river and o'er the lea,
That's the way for Billy and me.

Where the blackbird sings the latest,
Where the hawthorn blooms the sweetest,
Where the nestlings chirp and flee,
That's the way for Billy and me.

Where the mowers mow the cleanest,
Where the hay lies thick and greenest,
There to trace the homeward bee,
That's the way for Billy and me.

Where the hazel bank is steepest,
Where the shadow falls the deepest,
Where the clustering nuts fall free,
That's the way for Billy and me.

Why the boys should drive away
Little sweet maidens from the play,
Or love to banter and fight so well,
That's the thing I never could tell.

But this I know, I love to play,
Through the meadows, among the hay,
Up the water and o'er the lea,
That's the way for Billy and me.

*Idem*

## LAMENT FOR CAPTAIN PATON

Touch once more a sober measure,
　　And let punch and tears be shed,
For a prince of good old fellows,
　　That, alack-a-day! is dead;

For a prince of worthy fellows,
    And a pretty man also,
That has left the Saltmarket
    In sorrow, grief, and wo.
Oh! we ne'er shall see the like of Captain Paton no
    mo'.

His waistcoat, coat, and breeches,
    Were all cut off the same web,
Of a beautiful snuff-colour,
    Or a modest genty drab;
The blue stripe in his stocking
    Round his neat slim leg did go,
And his ruffles of the cambric fine
    They were whiter than the snow.
Oh! we ne'er shall see the like of Captain Paton no
    mo'.

His hair was curled in order,
    At the rising of the sun,
In comely rows and buckles smart
    That about his ears did run,
And before there was a toupee
    That some inches up did go,
And behind there was a long queue
    That did o'er his shoulders flow.
Oh! we ne'er shall see the like of Captain Paton no
    mo'.

And whenever we foregathered,
    He took off his wee three-cockit,
And he proffered you his snuff-box,
    Which he drew from his side-pocket;
And on Burdett or Bonaparte,
    He would make a remark or so,
And then along the plainstones
    Like a provost he would go.
Oh! we ne'er shall see the like of Captain Paton no
    mo'.

In dirty days he picked well
   His footsteps with his rattan;
Oh! you ne'er could see the least speck
   On the shoes of Captain Paton;
And on entering the coffee-room
   About two, all men did know,
They would see him with his *Courier*
   In the middle of the row.
Oh! we ne'er shall see the like of Captain Paton no
   mo'.

Now and then upon a Sunday
   He invited me to dine,
On a herring and a mutton chop
   Which his maid dressed very fine;
There was also a little Malmsey,
   And a bottle of Bordeaux,
Which between me and the Captain
   Passed nimbly to and fro.
Oh! I ne'er shall take pot-luck with Captain Paton
   no mo'.

Or if a bowl was mentioned,
   The Captain he would ring,
And bid Nelly to the West-port,
   And a stoup of water bring;
Then would he mix the genuine stuff,
   As they made it long ago,
With limes that on his property
   In Trinidad did grow.
Oh! we ne'er shall taste the like of Captain Paton's
   punch no mo'.[1]

And then all the time he would discourse,
   So sensible and courteous;

[1] See page 383 for the genuine stuff, as well as it can be composed in these degenerate days.

Perhaps talking of the last sermon
   He had heard from Dr. Porteous,
Or some little bit of scandal
   About Mrs So-and-So,
Which he scarce could credit, having heard
   The *con* but not the *pro*.
Oh! we ne'er shall hear the like of Captain Paton
  no mo'.

Or when the candles were brought forth,
   And the night was fairly setting in,
He would tell some fine old stories
   About Minden-field or Dettingen—
How he fought with a French major,
   And despatched him at a blow,
While his blood ran out like water
   On the soft grass below.
Oh! we ne'er shall hear the like of Captain Paton
  no mo'.

But at last the Captain sickened,
   And grew worse from day to day,
And all missed him in the coffee-room,
   From which now he stayed away;
On Sabbaths, too, the Wee Kirk
   Made a melancholy show,
All for wanting of the presence
   Of our venerable beau.
Oh! we ne'er shall see the like of Captain Paton
  no mo'.

And in spite of all that Cleghorn
   And Corkindale could do,
It was plain from twenty symptoms,
   That death was in his view;
So the Captain made his Test'ment,
   And submitted to his foe,

And we laid him by the Rams-horn Kirk—
'Tis the way we all must go.
Oh! we ne'er shall see the like of Captain Paton
  no mo'.

Join all in chorus, jolly boys,
  And let punch and tears be shed,
For this prince of good old fellows,
  That, alack-a-day! is dead;
For this prince of worthy fellows,
  And a pretty man also,
That has left the Saltmarket,
  In sorrow, grief, and wo!
For it ne'er shall see the like of Captain Paton
  no mo'.

*John Gibson Lockhart*

## DRINKIN' DRAMS

He ance was holy
An' melancholy,
Till he found the folly
  O' singin' psalms:
He's now as red's a rose,
And there's pimples on his nose,
And in size it daily grows
  By drinkin' drams.

He ance was weak,
An' couldnae eat a steak
Without gettin' sick
  An' takin' qualms;
But now he can eat
O' ony kind o' meat,
For he's got an appeteet
  By drinkin' drams.

He ance was thin,
Wi' a nose like a pen,

E

An' haunds like a hen,
　　An' nae hams;
But now he's round and tight,
An' a deevil o' a wight,
For he's got himsel' put right
　　By drinkin' drams.

He ance was saft as dirt,
An' as pale as ony shirt,
An' as useless as a cart
　　Without the trams;
But now he'd race the deil,
Or swallow Jonah's whale—
He's as gleg's a puddock's tail
　　Wi' drinkin' drams.

Oh! pale, pale, was his hue,
An' cauld, cauld was his broo,
An' he grumbled like a ewe
　　'Mang libbit rams;
But noo his broo is bricht,
An' his een are orbs o' licht,
An' his nose is just a sicht
　　Wi' drinkin' drams.

He studied mathematics,
Logic, ethics, hydrostatics,
Till he needed diuretics
　　To lowse his dams;
But now, without a lee,
He could make anither sea,
For he's left philosophy
　　An' taen to drams.

He found that learnin', fame,
Gas, philanthropy, an' steam,
Logic, loyalty, gude name,
　　Were a' mere shams;

That the source o' joy below,
An' the antidote to woe,
An' the only proper go,
Was drinkin' drams.
*George Outram*


## NO MAN LIVETH UNTO HIMSELF ALONE

Wherever men are gathered, all the air
  Is charged with human feeling, human thought;
Each shout and cry and laugh, each curse and prayer,
  Are into its vibrations surely wrought;
Unspoken passion, wordless meditation,
Are breathed into it with our respiration;
  It is with our life fraught and overfraught.

So that no man there breathes earth's simple breath,
  As if alone on mountains or wide seas,
But nourishes warm life or hastens death
  With joys and sorrows, health and foul disease,
Wisdom and folly, good and evil labours,
Incessant of his multitudinous neighbours;
  He in his turn affecting all of these.
*James Thomson* ("*B.V.*")


## THE DELUSION

How the moon triumphs through the endless nights!
  How the stars throb and glitter as they wheel
Their thick processions of supernal lights
  Around the blue vault obdurate as steel!
And men regard with passionate awe and yearning
The mighty marching and the golden burning,
  And think the heavens respond to what they feel.
*Idem*

99

## DIFFUGERE NIVES

Noo swallow-birds begin to big
   An' primrose-flowers to blaw;
An' Jockie whistles doun the rig
   A fareweel to the snaw;

An' glints o' sunshine glancin' gleg,
   Licht up the buddin' shaw
An' westlin' winds are playin' tig
   Round ae bewildered craw.

Auld Tammas to the garle-wa'
   Nails up a cherry-twig;
An' Mar'an waters, raw by raw,
   Her bleachin' wi' a pig;

An' yonder—he's been lang awa'—
   Comes Packie owre the brig,
An' country lads may noo gang braw,
   An' country lasses trig.
          *James Logie Robertson*

## THE LAMENTATION OF BALVA THE
## MONK

Balva the old monk I am called: when I was young,
   Balva Honeymouth.
That was before Colum the White came to Iona in
   the west.
She whom I loved was a woman whom I won out of
   the South.
And I had a good heaven with my lips on hers and
   with breast to breast.

Balva the old monk I am called: were it not for the
   fear
That the soul of Colum the White would meet my
   soul in the Narrows

100

That sever the living and dead, I would rise up from
 here,
And go back to where men pray with spears and
 arrows.

Balva the old monk I am called: ugh! ugh! the cold
 bell of the matins—'tis dawn!
Sure it's a dream I have had that I was in a warm
 wood with the sun ashine,
And that against me in the pleasant greenness was a
 soft fawn,
And a voice that whispered, "Balva Honeymouth, I
 am thy wine".

William Sharp

## ADVENTURE OF A POET

As I was walking down the street
  A week ago,
Near Henderson's I chanced to meet
  A man I know.

His name is Alexander Bell,
  His home Dundee;
I do not know him quite so well
  As he knows me.

He gave my hand a hearty shake,
  Discussed the weather,
And then proposed that we should take
  A stroll together.

Down College Street we took our way,
  And there we met
The beautiful Miss Mary Grey,
  That arch coquette,
Who stole last spring my heart away
  And has it yet.

That smile with which my bow she greets,
    Would it were fonder!
Or else less fond—since she its sweets
    On all must squander.
Thus, when I meet her in the streets,
    I sadly ponder,
And after her, as she retreats,
    My thoughts will wander.

And so I listened with an air
    Of inattention,
While Bell described a folding-chair
    Of his invention.

And when we reached the Swilcan Burn,
    "It looks like rain,"
Said I, "and we had better turn".
    'Twas all in vain.

For Bell was weather-wise, and knew
    The signs aerial,
He bade me note a strip of blue
    Above the Imperial,

Also another patch of sky
    South-west by south,
Which meant that we might journey dry
    To Eden's mouth.

He was a man of information
    On many topics:
He talked about the exploration
    Of Poles and Tropics.

The scene in Parliament last night,
    Sir William's letter;
"And do you like electric light
    Or gas-lamps better?"

The strike amongst the dust-heap pickers
    He said was over;
And had I read about the liquors
    Just seized at Dover?

Or the unhappy printer lad
    At Rothesay drowned?
Or the Italian ironclad
    That ran aground?

He told me stories (lately come)
    Of town society,
Some slightly tinged with truth, and some
    With impropriety.

He spoke of duelling in France,
    Then lightly glanced at
Mrs Mackenzie's monster dance,
    Which he had danced at.

So he ran on, till by and by
    A silence came,
For which I greatly fear that I
    Was much to blame.

Then neither of us spoke a word
    For quite a minute,
When presently a thought occurred
    With promise in it.

"How did you like the Shakespeare play
    The students read?"
By this the Eden like a bay
    Before us spread.

Near Eden many softer plots
    Of sand there be;
Our feet like Pharaoh's chariots,
    Drave heavily.

And ere an answer I could frame,
 He said that Irving
Of his extraordinary fame
 Was undeserving.

And for his part he thought more highly
 Of Ellen Terry;
Although he knew a girl called Riley
 At Broughty Ferry,

Who might be, if she only chose,
 As great a star.
She had a part in the tableaux
 At the bazaar.

If I had said but little yet
 I now said less,
And smoked a home-made cigarette
 In mute distress.

The smoke into his face was blown
 By the wind's action,
And this afforded me, I own,
 Some satisfaction.

But still his tongue received no check
 Till, coming home,
We stood beside an ancient wreck
 And watched the foam

Wash in among the timbers, now
 Sunk deep in sand,
Though I can well remember how
 I used to stand

On windy days and hold my hat
 And idly turn
To read "Lovise, Frederikstad"
 Upon her stern.

Her stern long since was buried quite,
 And soon no trace
The absorbing sand will leave in sight
 To mark her place.

This reverie was not permitted
 To last too long.
Bell's mind had left the stage, and flitted
 To fields of song.

And now he spoke of *Marmion*
 And Lewis Morris;
The former he at school had done
 Along with Horace.

His maiden aunts no longer young,
 But learned ladies,
Had lately sent him *Songs Unsung*,
 *Epic of Hades*,

*Gycia* and *Gwen*. He thought them fine;
 Not like that Browning,
Of whom he could not read a line,
 He told me frowning.

Talking of Horace—very clever
 Beyond a doubt,
But what the Satires meant he never
 Yet could make out.

I said I relished Satire Nine
 Of the First Book;
But he had skipped to the divine
 Eliza Cook.

He took occasion to declare
 In tones devoted,
How he admired her *Old Arm-chair*,
 Which now he quoted.

And other poets he reviewed
    Some two or three,
Till, having touched on Thomas Hood,
    He turned to me.

"Have *you* been stringing any rhymes
    Of late?" he said.
I could not lie, but several times
    I shook my head.

The last straw to the earth will bow
    Th' o'erloaded camel,
And surely I resembled now
    That ill-used mammal.

This is the recompense we meet
    In our vocation.
We bear the burden and the heat
    Of inspiration;

The beauties of the earth we sing
    In glowing numbers,
And to the "reading public" bring
    Post-prandial slumbers;

We save from Mammon's gross dominion
    These sordid times. . . .
And all this in the world's opinion
    Is "stringing rhymes".

It is as if a man should say
    In accents mild,
"Have you been stringing beads to-day,
    My gentle child?"

(Yet even children fond of singing
    Will pay off scores,
And I to-day at least am stringing
    Not beads but bores.)

And now the sands were left behind,
    The Club-house past,
I wonder, Can I hope to find
    Escape at last,

Or must I take him home to tea,
    And bear his chatter
Until the last train to Dundee
    Shall solve the matter?

But while I shuddered at the thought
    And planned resistance,
My conquering Alexander caught
    Sight in the distance

Of two young ladies, one of whom
    Is his ambition;
And so, with somewhat heightened bloom,
    Bell asked permission

To say good-bye to me and follow.
    I freely gave it,
And wished him all success. *Apollo*
    *Sic me servavit.*

                    *R. F. Murray*

## THE WHITE FLAG [1]

As notions wail thy jeer an' grin a vows an' isify,
A soothing theme an ziral dreams letters peterfy.
An o'er some howl as warrior's guess, an quivers
    ever so,
Entations oil forbid an' princes ly below.

[1] Let there be no mistake. These two specimens of Thomson's work belong here, and anyone who thinks they would find a more proper place in the next section proclaims himself a Philistine; for how, if he cannot appreciate Thomas Thomson, can he be expected to appreciate some of the most admired literary experiments of the present day? It is only just that this ingenious precursor of Joyce and MacDiarmid should have some belated recognition. Thomson was for many years a well-known "character" in Dalbeattie, where he died in 1924, aged 87.—Edd.

Awake! awake! an' sanctify, as years restore in love,
Rivers overflow, an' locust high above.
As lions growl an' whelps aft oul, as domotars
    pursue,
Chaff an' kinsmen kiss, an' querila bans o' you

  .     .     .     .     .

Noo, what o' gourr an' wither'd stock o' wax an'
    prophesi,
Doleful prayers are heard an' strains o' equity.
As some sellor pang prevail an' lips averse from war,
Prunning hooks are taen, an' Methuesla ajar,
Now lying wait me soul. O Lord, as numbert id
    declare,
Restore me foes me voice o cry an' bear,
An o'er thy path in reverence rocks an' miry clay,
As quiet waters be an' querilla sums o' lay.

                                  *Thomas Thomson*

## HYFONS, HYFONS

Noo slings aboot an' stars a' oot, an' auld moon
    chowin' sin,
  Here ye wonner really at the din,
As fit aboot of ebbs salute, and fetters all the score,
  Hyfon pland often really soar.
Of slang aboot and Sunday loot and ithers coortin'
    fame,
  Claim gaits and prayers of mony weans,
Noo fit aboot and faulds divine, and whirling ever
    soar,
  Quira sauce and bogles of the score.
As I houk my heid in anger, dote on hinges prest
    of long,
  Vaunting leers some may rule the throng,
An' marl't slings forgi'ein jars, stare an' rainbows
    flat,
  Of shoals and prayers blinding wonder at.

                                          *Idem*

## TO A SKYLARK SINGING ABOVE A POORHOUSE

What blast of Fate, melodious Mocker, say,
   Has blown thee *here*: in airy, spendthrift glee,
   Wasting thy wealth of liquid ecstasy
On hearts too cold to kindle at thy lay?
Thou sing'st of Hope above Hope's grave. . . .
     Away!
   Flee this dark Hall of Eblis, thro' whose aisles
   Frail phantoms totter, or with senile smiles
Rake the spent ashes of dead yesterday!

Flung from Life's boiling tumult, bruised and sore;
   Sick with the shame of what I have become,
   My wistful gaze follows thy flight afar;—
As some late Reveller, when the Rout is o'er,
   Pauses in his uncertain steps for home,
    With blear'd eyes blinking at the Morning Star.
          *Roger Quin (the younger)*

## MY NATIVE LAND [1]

My native land! which oft with heart afire,
   In Patriotic zeal *mine own* I call,
It damps my ardour that I must admire
   From this side of a somewhat lofty wall.

Yon lordly height I might ascend, and there
   Survey the scene as from God's hand it came—
'Tis rented by a Yankee millionaire,
   I must not trespass or disturb the game.

Beside this gentle stream then let me stray,
   And from the city's din find welcome peace—
A careful landlord, though, has blocked the way,
   Untrodden lies the walk, for he's at Nice.

[1] These prophetic verses were written some years before the
Great War.—Edd.

Our fathers fought, so runs the glorious tale,
　To save you, country mine, from tyrants rash,
And now their bones and you are up for sale,
　The smartest bidder buys for ready cash.

What comforts to be privileged to give
　My body's labour, so I may command
The wondrous right to be allowed to live
　On you my own (*i.e.* Lord Blythswood's) land!

And when a naughty foe insults our King,
　And foreign landlords want Lord Blythswood's
　　earth,
My good Lee-Enfield manfully I'll sling,
　And forth to battle for *his* home and hearth.

And having fought and bled, when I return,
　And bread is scarce and rent is overdue,
From Sheriff-officers I quickly learn,
　Dear native land, the share I have in you.

But, discontented soul, why fume and fret?
　Keep but thy life insurance well in hand,
And (Land-) Lord willing, you at last shall get
　Six feet by two—your own *dear* native land.
　　　　　　　　　　　　　　　*J. R. Christie*


# A LIVING DOG

King Arthur ruled the land, he did;
　His lance was keen, his right arm strong,
His aim (ostensibly) to rid
　The world or thereabouts of wrong.
He was a wight of high degree,
　And knew how many beans make five,
But now he's not a patch on me,
　For he is dead and I'm alive.

For Milo and his morning walk
  I own to admiration; it
Would doubtless cause no end of talk
  If he were matched with Hackenschmidt;
But though some records once he made,
  At which I never can arrive,
To-day I flout him unafraid,
  For he is dead and I'm alive.


The brain that lodged in Homer's head
  May have outweighed by half a stone
The one which kindly friends have said
  Has made its dwelling in my own;
And through his burning heart divine
  What fiery dreams were wont to drive!
Cold are they now compared with mine,
  For he is dead and I'm alive.


And all the gay deceased of old—
  The wise, the generous, the good,
The poet sage, the warrior bold,
  The man of brain, the man of blood—
Their songs I grant, were wild and free,
  To match their deeds I would not strive,
But put your money, boys, on me,
  For they are dead and I'm alive.
                        *The Rev. T. L. Douglas*


## FOR CHOICE

Sages sacred and profane
  Nail this dogma to the mast:
Pleasures have for relish pain,
  Feasts an antecedent fast;
All of which, with judgment ripe,
I consider utter tripe.

Give me skies for ever blue,
    Breakfasts uniformly warm,
Ties that never go askew,
    Friends consistently in form,
Every good by me enjoyed
Absolutely unalloyed.

*Idem*

## THE BEST-DRESSED HIGHLANDER

["A Prize of £5 to be awarded to the best-dressed
Highlander at his own expense."—*Programme of
any Highland Gathering*.]

My name is John Macleod—from Chiefs descended
    Distinguished for their courage and their size.
A Highland gathering lately I attended,
    Because I saw there was to be a prize
        For the best-dressed Highlander,
        The best-dressed Highlander,
The best-dressed Highlander at his own expense.

*Chorus*

    At his own expense,
    At his own expense,
The best-dressed Highlander at his own expense.

My kilt and tartan stockings I was wearing,
    My claymore and my dirk and skian-dhu,
And when I sallied forth with manly bearing
    I heard admiring whispers not a few—
        "He's the best-dressed Highlander,
        The best-dressed Highlander,
The best-dressed Highlander at his own expense."
    *Chorus*.—At his own expense, etc.

The ladies, bless them! came and gathered round
        me,
    And gazed upon my form so strong and proud.

With ties of gratitude and love they bound me,
   When they declared 'twas clear that John Macleod
      Was the best-dressed Highlander,
      The best-dressed Highlander,
The best-dressed Highlander at his own expense.
     *Chorus.*—At his own expense, etc.

The judge—a man of sense and penetration—
   Would go no further when he came to me.
"This is", he said, with hearty approbation,
   "As every one with half an eye can see,
      Just the best-dressed Highlander,
      The best-dressed Highlander,
The best-dressed Highlander at his own expense".
     *Chorus.*—At his own expense, etc.

The world has many shining paths of glory,
   And I have chosen out this path for me—
That John Macleod, until he's old and hoary,
   Will always and incomparably be
      Quite the best-dressed Highlander,
      The best-dressed Highlander,
The best-dressed Highlander at his own expense.

     *Grand Chorus* (*Crescendo*)
     At his *own* expense,
     At his own expense,
THE BEST-DRESSED HIGHLANDER AT HIS OWN
EXPENSE

                  *D. M. McKay*

## WOOD MAGIC

I will walk warily in the wise woods on the fringes
   of eventide,
   For the covert is full of noises and the stir of
     nameless things,
I have seen in the dusk of the beeches the shapes of
   the lords that ride,

And down in the marish hollow I have heard the
    lady who sings,
And once in an April gloaming I met a maid on the
    sward,
    All marble-white and gleaming and tender and
        wild of eye;
I, Jehan the hunter, who speak am a grown man,
    middling hard,
    But I dreamt a month of the maid, and wept I
        knew not why.


Down by the edge of the firs, in a coppice of heath
    and vine,
    Is an old moss-grown altar, shaded by briar and
        bloom,
Denys, the priest, hath told me 'twas the lord
    Apollo's shrine
In the days ere Christ came down from God to the
    Virgin's womb.
I never go past but I doff my cap and avert my
    eyes—
    (Were Denys to catch me I trow I'd do penance
        for half a year.)—
For once I saw a flame there and the smoke of a
    sacrifice
    And a voice spake out of the thicket that froze my
        soul with fear.


Wherefore to God the Father, the Son, and the Holy
    Ghost,
    Mary the Blessed Mother, and the kindly Saints
        as well,
I will give glory and praise, and them I cherish the
    most,
    For they have the keys of Heaven, and save the
        soul from Hell.

But likewise I will spare for the Lord Apollo a grace,
   And a bow for the lady Venus—as a friend but
     not as a thrall,
'Tis true they are out of Heaven, but some day they
     may win the place;
For gods are kittle cattle, and a wise man honours
     them all.

*John Buchan*


## THE SHORTER CATECHISM

When I was young and herdit sheep,
   I read auld tales o' Wallace wight;
My heid was fou o' sangs and threep
   O' folk that feared nae mortal might.
But now I'm auld and weel I ken
   We're made alike o' gowd and mire;
There's saft bits in the stievest men,
   The bairnliest's got a spunk o' fire.
     Sae hearken to me, lads,
       It's truith that I tell;—
     There's nae man a' courage—
       I ken by mysel'.


I've been an elder forty year,
   I've tried to keep the narrow way,
I've walked afore the Lord in fear,
   I've never missed the kirk a day,
I've read the Bible in an' oot,
   I ken the feck o't clean by he'rt;—
But still and on I sair misdoot
   I'm better noo than at the stert,
     Sae hearken to me, lads,
       It's truith I maintain!—
     Man's works are but rags, for
       I ken by my ain.

115

I hae a name for dacent trade;
 I'll wager a' the countryside
Wad swear nae trustier man was made
 The ford to soom, the bent to bide.
But when it comes to coupin' horse
 I'm juist like a' that e'er were born,
I fling my heels and tak my course—
 I'd sell the minister the morn.
  Sae hearken to me, lads,
   It's truith that I tell:—
  There's nae man deid honest—
   *I ken by mysel'*.

*Idem*

## JUVENIS AND PISCATOR

*Juv.* Canny Fisher Jamie, comin' hame at e'en,
 Canny Fisher Jamie, whaur have ye been?
*Pisc.* Mony lang miles, laddie, o'er the Kips sae green.
*Juv.* Fishin' Leithen Water?
*Pisc.*                          Nay, laddie, nay.
 Just a wee burnie rinnin' doun a brae,
 Fishin' a wee burnie nae bigger than a sheugh.
*Juv.* Gat ye mony troots, Jamie?
*Pisc.*                          I gat eneugh—
 Eneugh to buy my baccy, snuff, and pickle tea,
 And lea me tippence for a gill, and that's eneugh
  for me.
   *—Noted from oral tradition by John Buchan*

## AY, FEGS

Ay, fegs, an' fat dae ye think o' my legs?
 Ye hanna seen me i' my sodger's kilt for weeks,
For aye as I'm mairchin' by, some limmer is sure to
  cry,
 "Wi' shanks like that ye'd better hae stuck to
  breeks".

Na, fegs, they needna laugh at my legs,
  For mony a weary fecht they've brocht me
    through.
Ay, fegs, gin't hadna been for my legs
  O I would be a cauld corp noo.


Ay, fegs, when the sergeant saw my legs
  He was handin' ower the shillin' afore he spoke,
He kent brawly fat ye need to wyde amo' fire an'
    bleed,
  Sae he clappit me on the shou'der an' ca'ed me
    "Jock".
      Na, fegs, he didna laugh at my legs,
        He kent the weary fechts they'd bring me
          through.
      Ay, fegs, gin't hadna been for my legs.
      O I wad be a cauld corp noo.


Eh, mon, sic a terrible day was thon,
  The bullets and ba's were fleein' about like
    snaw;
"Strike oot" they cried for hame, but the feck o'
    lave was lame,
  An' I got there twa days afore them a'.
      Ay, fegs, sic a handy thing is your legs,
        An' mony a weary fecht they bring you
          through.
      Na, fegs, gin't hadna been for my legs
      O I wad be a cauld corp noo.


Ay, fegs, when a cannon ba' grazed my legs
  It mindet me upon something I'd forgot,
My auld mither ower the sea, sittin' wearyin' sair
    for me,
  For wha would dibble her kail gin I was shot?

Ay, fegs, she aye admired my legs,
　　An' here I'm back i' the Cabrach wi' the coo.
Na, fegs, gin't hadna been for my legs
　　O I wad be a cauld corp noo.

Charles Murray

## THE SONG OF THE SWORD OF THE ETERNAL

A sword, a sword,
whetted and polished,
whetted to slay,
polished to flash like lightning . . .
handed to slayers
to wield,
whetted and polished
for slayers to handle!
Shriek, son of man, and howl;
it is drawn against my people,
against all Israel's leaders—
they and my people
surrendered to the sword!
Smite your breast despairingly,
for I spurn them in my wrath,
says the Lord the Eternal.

Prophesy, then, son of man,
call the doom down,
swing the sword twice, thrice,
the sword of mortal wounds,
the huge sword of mortal wounds,
that hems them in.

Scare them till their hearts are trembling,
and dead lie heaped at every gate.
They are abandoned to the slaughtering sword,
flashing like lightning,
whetted for slaughter.

Whirl to the rear, sword,
right, front, left—
wherever your edge must whirl;
and I will clap you on,
I will glut my fury—
I, the Eternal, have said it!
            *Ezekiel (Dr. Moffatt's Version)*


## THE CROCODILE

Can you pull out the crocodile with a hook,
Or tie his tongue down with a string,
Or run a cord through his gills,
Or carry him with a gaff between his jaws?
Will he make many a prayer to you?
Will he speak softly to you?
Will he come to terms with you,
        Always be at your service?
Will you play with him like a pet bird,
Or cage him to amuse your maidens?
Will fishermen make a meal of him?
        Will traders cut him up?
Can you plant harpoons in his skin,
Or pierce the head of him with spears?
Just lay a hand on him!—just once!—
        You will not forget the fray!
Who can strip off his hide?
Who can pierce his armoured scales?
Who can force open his jaws?
        His teeth are a terror!
His back is row on row of shields,
        sealed close and tight,
One scale so near another
        that no air can pass between,
Welded each to each,
        clasped till they cannot be parted.

The light plays on his snorting snout;
His eyes flash like the morning rays,
Flames issue from his mouth,
      and sparks fly out,
Steam pours out of his nostrils,
As from a seething, boiling pot
His breath would kindle coals,
      with the fire from his mouth.


Strength is seated in his neck—
      all creatures twitch in terror at him.
Firm are the flakes of his flesh;
      his heart is stout as a millstone.
When he comes up, strong men are terrified,
      scared by the swirl in the water;
No sword avails against him,
      no spear, no dart, no arrow;
He treats a harpoon like a straw,
A bronze lance is like rotten wood;
No arrow makes him fly,
Stones from a sling to him are merely stubble,
Bludgeons are mere bulrushes,
      and whizzing javelins he derides.


His lair is the sharp rocks;
      he rests his loins upon the mud.
He makes the water boil and foam,
Churning the deep like unguents in a pot;
He leaves a shining furrow in his wake—
One would think the deep was hoary.
Nowhere on earth is there the like of him,
      a creature born to know no fear;
Wild animals are all in fear of him,
      the monarch of proud creatures.

                *Job (Dr. Moffatt's Version)*

# FAITH

Though the fig-tree may not blossom,
Though no fruit is on the vine,
Though the olive crop has failed,
Though the fields give us no food,
Though the folds have lost their flocks,
And in the stalls no cattle lie,
Yet in the Eternal we will find our joy,
We will rejoice in the God who saves us.
The Lord, the Eternal, is our strength,
He makes our feet sure as the feet of hinds,
Helps us to keep our footing on the heights.
*Habakkuk (Dr. Moffatt's Version)*

## ON A CAT AGEING

He blinks upon the hearth-rug
And yawns in deep content,
Accepting all the comforts
That Providence has sent.

Louder he purrs, and louder,
In one glad hymn of praise
For all the night's adventures,
For quiet, restful days.

Life will go on for ever,
With all that cat can wish:
Warmth and the glad procession
Of fish and milk and fish.

Only—the thought disturbs him—
He's noticed once or twice,
That times are somehow breeding
A nimbler race of mice.
*Alexander Gray*

## SHOOTING GUEST, NONCONFORMIST

You promised I should see the golden eagle;
Speckled brown adders basking in the sun;
Proud antlered stags and herds of red hinds leaping
Across great rocky corries, rainbow-spanned;
Peat mosses where three thousand feet on high
The luscious scarlet averens [1] are glowing;
Pools where the otter stalks for salmon flesh;
Heron, grey on a green sky, solemn floating.

But these I saw while you to butts were striding
Guided by servile gillies to your sport.
*Fast-rooted bracken where the corn once ripened;*
*Roofless and ruined homesteads by the score;*
*Once-fertile gardens, mildewed, choked with weed,*
*Hemlock and nettle where the children played.*
                              *Helen B. Cruickshank*

[1] Cloudberries.

## A MOMENT IN ETERNITY

The great song ceased
—Aye, like a wind was gone,
And our hearts came to rest,
Singly as leaves do,
And every leaf a flame.

My shining passions stilled
Shone in the sudden peace
Like countless leaves
Tingling with the quick sap
Of immortality.

I was a multitude of leaves
Receiving and reflecting light,
A burning bush
Blazing for ever unconsumed,
Nay, ceaselessly,

Multiplying in leaves and light
And instantly,
Burgeoning in buds of brightness,
—Freeing like golden breaths
Upon the cordial air
A thousand new delights,
—Translucent leaves
Green with the goodness of Eternity,
Golden in the Heavenly light
—The golden breaths
Of my eternal life,
Like happy memories multiplied,
Shining out instantly from me
And shining back for ever into me,
—Breaths given out
But still unlost,
For ever mine,
In the infinite air,
The everlasting foliage of my soul
Visible awhile
Like steady and innumerable flames,
Blending into one blaze
Yet each distinct
With shining shadows of difference.

A sudden thought of God's
Came like a wind
Ever and again
Rippling them as waters over stars,
And swiftlier fanning them
And setting them a-dance,
Upflying, fluttering down,
Moving in orderly intricacies
Of colour and of light,
Delaying, hastening,
Blazing and serene,
Shaken and shining in the turning wind,
Lassoing cataracts of light

With rosy boughs,
Or clamouring in echoing unequalled heights,
Rhythmical sprays of many-coloured fire
And spires chimerical
Gleaming in fabulous airs,
And suddenly
Lapsing again
To incandescence and increase.
And again the wind came
Blowing me afar
In fair fantastic fires,
—Ivies and irises invading
The upland garths of ivory;
Queen daisies growing
In the tall red grass
By pools of perfect peace,
And bluebells tossing
In transparent fields;
And silver airs
Lifting the crystal sources in dim hills
And swinging them far out like bells of glass
Pealing pellucidly
And quivering in faery flights of chimes;
Shivers of wings bewildered
In alleys of virgin dream;
Floral dances and revels of radiance
Whirling in stainless sanctuaries;
And eyes of Seraphim,
Shining like sunbeams on eternal ice,
Lifted towards the unexplored
Summits of Paradise.

*Hugh MacDiarmid*

## THE POET'S PASSING

I have known all the storms that roll.
I have been a singer after the fashion
Of my people—a poet of passion.

All that is past.
Quiet has come into my soul.
Life's tempest is done.
I lie at last
A bird cliff under the midnight sun.

*Idem*

## WHEESHT, WHEESHT

Wheesht, wheesht, my foolish hert,
For weel ye ken
I widna hae ye stert
Auld ploys again.

It's guid to see her lie
Sae snod and cool,
A' lust o' lovin' by—
*Wheesht, wheesht, ye fule!*

*Idem*

## THE FIRE-WHEEL

Time's a fire-wheel whose spokes the seasons turn,
And fastened there we, Time's slow martyrs, burn.
To some that rage is but a pleasant heat,
And the red fiery bower as summer sweet.
Others there are who lord it in the flame,
And, while they're burning, dice for power and
    fame.
A choicer company ignore the pyre,
And dream and prophesy amid the fire.
And a few with eyes uplifted through the blaze
Let their flesh crumble till they're all agaze
Glassing that fireless kingdom in the sky
Which is our dream as through Time's wood we fly
Burning in silence or crying the ancient rhyme:
"Who shall outsoar the mountainous flame of Time?"

*Edwin Muir*

## THE INDWELLER

Packed in my skin from head to toe
Is one I know and do not know.
He never speaks to me, yet is at home
More snug than embryo in the womb.
His lodgings are but poor; they neither please
Nor irk him greatly, though he sees
Their cracks, rents, flaws, impossibilities,
He sits secure and will not out.

His name's Indifference.
Nothing offending he is all offence;
Can stare at beauty's bosom coldly
And at Christ's crucifixion boldly;
Can note with a lack-lustre eye
Victim and murderer go by;
Can pore upon the maze of lust
And watch the lecher fall to dust
With the same glance; content can wait
By a green bank near Eden's gate
To see the first blood flow and see naught then
Except a bright and glittering rain.
If I could drive this demon out
I'd put all Time's display to rout.
Its wounds would turn to flowers and nothing be
But the first Garden. The one Tree
Would stand for ever safe and fair
And Adam's hand stop in the air.
Or so I dream when at my door
I hear my Soul, my Visitor.

He comes but seldom and I cannot tell
If he's myself to one that loves me well
And comes in pity, for he pities all:
Weeps for the hero's and the beggar's fall;
The conqueror before his fallen foe
(Fingering his useless sword he cannot go,

But stands in doltish silence, unappeased);
Bereavement that, by deathless memory teased,
Pores on the same for-ever-altered track,
Turns, always on the old blind way turns back;
Lost Love that flies aghast it knows not where
And finds no foothold but the dreadful air;
The unending open wound in Jesus' side;
And all that has to die and that has died.

Pity would cancel what it feeds upon,
And gladly cease, its office done.
Yet could it end all passion, flaw, offence,
Would come my homespun fiend Indifference
And have me wholly. On these double horns
I take my comfort, they're my truckle-bed;
Could Pity change the crown of thorns
To roses peace would soon be fled,
And I would have no place to rest my head.

Then must dead Pity, quickened by my plight,
Start up again and make for my delight
A mimic stage where all the day
A phantom hound pursues a phantom prey,
Where the slain rise and smile upon the slayer,
And the crowned victor is a harmless player,
And cunning is a fond deceit,
Treachery feigned and loss imaginary,
And friends consent to meet
To stage a slaughter and make up a story.

Oh, then, at such deceitful art,
Tears, real and burning, from my lids would start,
And peace would burst into my heart.

*Idem*

127

## GUID ENOUGH FOR ME

I've pandit my engagement ring,
  My marriage ring as weel,
I've ha'en a row wi' my guidman
  An' sent him to the Deil.

Ye see that wee ring wi' the stane,
  It's mair than worth his twa,
I got if frae my puir mither
  That's deid an' buried an' a'.

She's deid an' buried in her grave,
  The guid Lord rest her noo,
She thought I'd got a man to wed
  And no a muckle soo.

Last night I pand the chest o' drawers,
  I got ten bob for that,
I pandit Mickie's Sunday coat,
  I pand his Sunday hat.

Cheer up, my hen, and no be dull,
  I've got a lad in Fife,
A chiel frae Inverkeithen toon
  Wha wants me for his wife.

Ye haena got divorce, guidwife,
  They'll pit ye in the nick;
Ye canna hae another man
  Till ye get rid o' Mick.

Divorce be damned, divorce be damned,
  The gile be damned—ye see!
I've ta'en and burned my marriage lines,
  That's guid enough for me.
*William Ogilvy*

## THE FIRST SUPPER

At the First Supper
   The guests were but one:
A maiden was the hostess,
   The guest her son.

At the First Supper
   No candles were lit:
In darkness hay-scented
   They both did sit.

At the First Supper
   No table was spread:
In the curve of her elbow
   She laid his head.

At the First Supper
   They poured no wine:
On milk of the rarest
   The guest did dine.

She held him very closely
   Against her breast,
Her fair one, her dear one,
   Her darling guest;

She held him very closely,
   Guessing that this
Is the last that any mother
   May know of bliss.

*Jan Struther*

## AT A DULL PARTY

In fifty years, at most, I shall be dead.
   These jaws, which now grind hard to scotch a yawn,
Will gape unchecked; and in a clay-cold bed
   Clamped fast, I'll wait a problematical dawn.
I have less than twenty thousand days to live,
   Six hundred months, a bare half-million hours;
And each new breath, heedless and fugitive,
   Another mouthful of my life devours:
Then Christ! What spendthrift folly brought me here
To breathe stale smoke, and drink, talk, think small
      beer?

*Eadem*

## "OCTOBER 6: SUMMER TIME ENDS"

"Summer Time Ends."
You need but turn a leaf
In this small book, whose brief
Laconic notes make up
A skeleton map
Of the year's delight and grief,
To see in black and white
What bone has felt, heart known:
Summer Time ends.

Leaves, which in spring were made
Marvellously of jade
And under summer's heat
Deepened to malachite,
Hang brittle now and brown:
One gale will bring all down.
Summer Time Ends.

Move back those cheating hands:
Time is not checked by lies.
Reclaim the hostage hour you gave in spring
To gain fool's paradise.

Come down again to earth.
Let clocks and hearts tell truth,
That brave, that bitter thing:
Summer Time Ends.

*Eadem*


## THE LOCOMOTIVE

The caked surface of black fuel
Which was to feed the slowness of my life
Evenly and without disturbance
Is broken, and falls into the living fire.
The breath of clean air rushes up through me
And I am white hot and seething within.
Trembling and roaring softly
I am ready for a long journey,
My eyes glitter like new lamps,
My ears hum, my heart races.

I am part of the order of things,
Made to run on steel flanged wheels
Held to an iron way.
My direction is set out in front of me,
My speed controlled by signals.
I can never leave the rails,
I can never fly.
I am made cunningly for the order of things
However great the pressure within me,
It cannot burst me into pieces.
I am made strong to bear without distortion
The power that strains every part of me;
I am made sensitive and scream in my agony,
Then people stand away from me
The shriek of my safety valve frightens them.
The signal drops, I take the strain,
I disturb the whole world near me,

I belch a fanfare of rushing clouds,
But I do no harm.
I go straight pulling the load I cannot see.
I go quicker and quicker,
I toil up the long hills,
I go slower and slower.
Am I the driver?
Am I the driven?
I am inside a mass of machinery,
I am outside anxiously watching,
I am power imprisoned,
I am letting power free.
Some day I shall jump the line
I shall crash at a crossing,
There will be some trouble and the track
    ripped up.
There will be a little delay
A scrapping of the old machine.
The order of things will make good again
The eternally permanent way.

*Patrick Miller*

# UNLUCKY NUMBERS
## *OR*
## *THE BAD BALLADS*

*Wink hard, and say the folks hae done their best.*
BURNS

# THE CASE AGAINST NOAH'S ARK

OLD doted foole! thy folly all may see,
Ingraven deepe, in thy great towre of tree,
If thou wilt have to be a mighty fort,
A towre of steel to save and to support
Thyself, thy sonnes, from peril and mishaps,
Which will the world swell with tempestuous claps.
How long's your ark, how high, how broad us tell,
Teach us, for yee in wisdom doe excell?
We heare the length three hundred cubits bee,
And that the breadth but fiftie which wee see,
And that the hight should thirtie cubits have,
Men, fowles, and beastes, from drowning for to
    save.
With all those, as it must be understood,
Yee must for all have ev'n sufficient food.
What if you with your sonnes and household dear,
And beastes and fowles remain there but a yeare?
Yea, if but half that space you there remaine,
Will the Ark you all, and food for you containe?
Bread for yourselves, and fodder for your Horses,
For Elephants, for Camells, and for Asses;
For Cowes and Sheepe, for Dogs and filthy Swine,
The Hart and Hind, for Goats and Porcupine;
For Weezles which haunt in the clefts of rocks,
For wittie Monkeys, and the wily Fox;
And thousands more of beasts and fowls also,
Which to the Ark, you must als make to goe?
There must be Peacocks, which with golden eyes,
Upon their feathers the beholders please;
There must be Lapwings, with their hooded tops,
And Eagles which still haunt among the rocks;
There must the Ostrich also have a place,
The Cran and Owle, with its ill-favor'd face;

The Swallow swift, and als the Cormorant,
The Brigander, Quaile, Barnacle, Feasant,
The Shovler, Brambline, Bitter and Hickway,
The Paret, Partridge, Dove, and the Ospray,
The Heron, Harefoot, Rooke, and the Woodpecker,
The Daker Hen, the Ganet, and the Plover,
The Kestrell, Cough, the Crow, Raven, Gull, the
    Jay,
The Jackdaw, and the Griphon strong for prey,
The Pelican, the Phenix, and the Thrush,
The Falcon fierce, which downe with force doth rush,
The Gosehawk, Tercell, Gerfalcon, and Seker,
The Merlin, Musket, Hobb, that's still a taker,
The Wagtail, Snipe, the Starling, and the Stork
The Cuckoo, Titling, Titmouse, and the Bat,
The Teele, and Mavis, and the chattering Py,
The Yelamber, and pratling Papingay,
The Goldfinch, Fieldfare, with Cock, Hen, and Kit,
And many moe, where will these fowles all sit?
What shall they eat if they continue long,
Within that house with beastes and fowles so strong?
Some eat but wormes, some grasse, and some but
    graine,
Some must have flesh their life for to maintaine;
For Horse, Kine, Sheep, and other beasts the fodder
Would fill an Ark that's longer, deeper, broader.
Count well your cubits, and consider all,
If that your Ark can beasts both great and small,
With fowles and foode within its bounds containe,
See if ye can by reason this maintaine.
Yet more of beastes and fowles all that be cleane,
Of every sort preserved must be sev'n;
Th' odde one for God a sacrifice must bee,
The other six must serve to multiplie;
The fodder, fowles, the beasts with biggest bulks,
Would surely fill a score of greater Hulks.

*Zachary Boyd*

## JONAH'S SOLILOQUY

Here apprehended I in prison ly,
What goods will ransom my captivity?
What house is this, where's neither fire nor candle,
Where I nothing but guts of fishes handle?
I and my table are both heere within,
Where day ne'er dawn'd, where sun did never shine.
The like of this on earth man never saw,
A living man within a monster's maw;
Buried under mountains which are high and steep
Plung'd under waters hundreth fathoms deep.
Not so was Noah in his house of tree,
For through a window hee the light did see;
He sailed above the highest waves a wonder,
I and my boat are all the waters under,
He in his ark might go and also come,
But I sit still in such a strait'ned roome
As is most uncouth, head and feet together
Among such grease, as would a thousand smother.
I find no way now from my shrinking hence,
But heere to lie and die for mine offence;
Eight prisoners were in Noah's hulk together,
Comfortable they were each one to other.
In all the earth like unto me is none,
Farre from all living I heere lye alone;
Where I entombed in melancholy sink,
Choak't suffocat with excremental stink.

*Idem*

## TO THE MEMORY OF SIR ALEXANDER FRASER OF DOORES, BT.

Let other Nations boast of Golden Mines,
Fragrant Spices, and of Noble Vines,
Of Flowry Meadows, and of Silver Springs,

Of Fields, and Folds, and all delightful things,
We look not on them with envious eyes,
Since Caledon, in Men, them all outvies.

We do not value all the Indian fruits,
Nor care to ruffle in the Asian suites,
Nor sport with African baboons and apes,
Nor yet to press French and Canary grapes:
Our Countrey in its Heroes doth delight,
Who are its fame abroad, at home its light.

Is that a barren Country, which affords
Men glorious by their pen, and by their swords,
Where Cicero's matched in his golden tongue,
And Poets sing, as sweet as Virgil sung
And such brave souls have therein had abodes,
As duller Ancients would have called gods?

Lo one of them to us doth here return,
But ah! he's wafted hither in his Urne,
Yet even his dust doth kind acceptance claim,
Our hearts are elevated by his name,
Two Princes' darling (yea, and Heaven's that's more)
Aboard this Vessel comes unto our Shore.

I know it's not great matter, of what kind
A man is come, if of a generous mind;
Yet since the world makes some reck'ning here,
They cannot for a mean birth at him jeer;
An Herauld may, unblushing, say aloud,
He's come of ancient honourable blood.

These lands which he by industry hath won,
And which he hath bequeathed to his Son,
His Ancestors (once rank'd among the best)
Hundreds of years, (entitl'd Thanes) possest:
Though they were as struck trees, yet from their race
Heaven watered this branch to fill their place.

When others, at the highest price might be,
Did rate their sufferings and their loyalty,
Claim'd great rewards, thought, all they could
    desire
Was for their service but too mean a hire:
He who both did and suffer'd more than many,
Was yet as modest in his suits as any.

To him it was enough, when he did see
His King and Country happy both to be,
It pleased him much more than any wealth
To see his Prince's face, and tend his health,
This comfort he enjoyed, and providence
Did unsought riches unto him dispense.

Descend ye famous hills and levelled be,
And borrow tears from your neighbouring Dee,
Or heave you upward, and draw from the clouds,
And then his grave bedew with brinish flouds;
This is but just, for now his dust is here,
Who was to Heaven, his Prince, and Country dear.

          *John Barclay, Minister of Cruden*

# THE VOICE OF GOD

Men may esteem the Trespass small, but I
Will after such Offender strictly try:
My hand shall find them out, I will not spare
That vile presumptuous Wratch who's bold to dare,
In his vile mouth to take my Hallowed Name
Without due Reverence, and a Praying Frame.
I'll smite him through with darts of fiercest Wrath
And Sharpest Vengeance; yea Eternall Death,
And hightned Fury on his Soul shall seize,
Without the least hours Respite, Sist, or Ease
His tongue shall Fry in hotest Pot of Hell,
That thus offends; yea and his Soul shall Dwell

In most exquisit Torments in that cave,
Which for the Devils I Prepared have.
    First to the Eye is represented there
Most dreadfull Spectres round them everywhere.
Hobgoblings dancing in prodigious Shapes,
Like Lyons, Tigers, Dragons, Bears, and Apes,
With Horns of Steel, and Iron—Teeth like Darts,
And forked Claws for tearing Sinners Hearts.
    Thou no glad Musick in that place shall hear,
Nor other Noise shall touch thy Cursed Ear,
But Ruefull Strikes, and Knocks of Ratling Chains,
And mutual Curses of Dire Ghosts in Pains,
Who One Another tempted have to Sin,
Plagueing the Day their 'quaintance did begin.
    No sweet Refreshing Smell shall there be found,
But noxious Savour Every Where abound,
Of all vile Filth, and stinking Sulphorous Smoak,
Least Smell of which all Mortal Flesh would Choak,
Were it not now so strongly Verg'd about
With thickest Earth that none thereof gets out.
    No softer Touch is there than Scorpions Stings,
And Byting Asps; yea all Tormenting Things,
Do there combine, and all their Force Unite
To Plague the Body, and Torment the Sp'rit:
The Worm of Conscience Gnawing Within,
When thou Reflects upon thy By-Past-Sin,
Its gentlest Byts much sharper are by Far
Than Dragons Claws or red-hot Pincers were,
Thy Heart and Bowels plucking out At Once;
Or Rav'nous Birds thy Flesh tear from thy Bones.
Hot Burning Coals of Juniper shall be
Thy Bed of Down, and then to Cover thee
A Quilt of Boyling Brimstone thou must take,
And Wrap thee in till thou full Payment make,
To Divine Justice for thy Great Offence,
In that thou hast without due Reverence,
My Hallowed Name Prophan'd, and tane in Vain.
Thou surely shall endure Eternal Pain,

Because thy Sufferings no Proportion have,
To that Infinite Offence which thou gave.
The Head, the Hand, the Nose, the Ear, the Eye,
Yea, every Member shall tormented be
Apart, and such exquisite Tortures fill
Each Joint as would great Leviathan kill.
Yet thy frail Body I'll make to subsist
Under such Torments, while I do exist.
  No Wine or Beer is there to quench thy Drowth
Nor liquid Drop at all to cool thy Mouth.
But bitter Dreggs of that great Cup of Wine
Of Indignation in my hand Divine;
Which without Mixture every Soul shall Take,
And Drink and Vomit in that Burning Lake.

*James Donaldson (fl. 1695)*

## UMPHREY MILNE, WATCHMAKER,
## BURGESS OF EDINBURGH

O! Monstruous death, and bloody foe, thou enemy of
    man!
Thou's barbled all thy arrows great, from earth now
    has him tane,
That was a credit to the land, known by all of great
    note,
Though he was born an English man, he was a real
    Scot,
He coost a copy to all men, who ever shall succeed,
He teacht brave men his noble art, did not eat iddle
    bread:
Many may lament full sore, that he is dead and
    gone,
Beside his wife, and dearest friends, the poor will
    him bemoan,
Death with his fearful bloody syth, has cutt this
    Sedar down,

But he has left his art behind, even to his great
    renown;
His name will blosome in the dust, his actions were
    so good,
He was so kind to poor and rich, and still he feared
    God,
He was belov'd of every one, and namely by the
    common,
Though he was call'd Episcopal, be sure he was no
    Roman:
He wore a badge of secresie, and well did know its
    worth;
There was a motto upon it, and that was called
    Truth;
None dare but venerat his name, pious, good, and
    kind;
He's gone from earth to heavens glore, left not his
    match behind.
My quill cannot descrive him right, the truth of this
    I know:
For any thing that I can guess, there's few like him
    below.
I will not name his parentage: his breeding, nor his
    birth;
But he that runs may read his life, he was a man of
    worth;
He valued not this earth below, although he had it
    *satis*,
He lov'd to lay his stock above, and now he is
    *beatis*.

*Idem*

## ON THE DEATH OF JAMES,
## SECOND MARQUESS OF MONTROSE

Chief of Grames Name, who always have been
    great,
Has seventy-one Kings Serv'd in War and State;

Has Thirteen hundred twenty-seven years stood:
With whom King Fergus-Second, Match'd in Blood:
To Royaltie may say, Truth to discover,
To King Eugenius-Second Bred Queen-Mother.
Thy jovial House, turns now the House of Woe,
No heart of Stone unbroke, can therein go:
Alace to see thy Lady Marquess state,
Heartless become, by this sad Stroke of Fate,
With her young Marquess sits whose doleful crys,
With Her to Joyn, moves all our Sphears and Skies;
Bereav'd of Her dear Lord, 'twixt whom was Love,
That Imitate Heavens Hierarchie above.
Ah! ah! young Marquess in Thy Bud, to see
Of Thy Paternal-root, Robed to be;
By which Thy Name and House Enervat are,
Of Chief and Master, of both who had Care.
  Chronologizers Theam t'inlarge long Story,
The Soul of Virtue now is gone to Glory.

*Mungo Murray*


## ON THE LAMENTED DEATH OF
## LORD BASIL HAMILTON

To this thrice worthy mate, an ample field
Is patent to her grief, she's big with child:
She weeps, the child shall ne'er his father see,
While the three born lisp out an elegie,
So great's her grief: sure she had lost her life,
Had not the Christian overcome the wife.
So great's his mother's sorrow, that her soul,
Were she not saint, would with his mount the pole.
Only well grounded hopes of his blest state,
Can their excessive agonies abate.

*Anon.* (1701)

143

## ON BILIOUSNESS

Not all the culinary arts can tame
To wholesome food the abominable growth
Of rest and gluttony; the prudent taste
Rejects like bane such loathsome lusciousness;
The languid stomach curses ev'n the pure
Delicious fat and all the race of oil,
For more the oily aliments relax
Its feeble tone, and with the eager lymph
(Fond to incorporate with all it meets)
Coyly they mix, and shun with slippery wiles
The woo'd embrace. Th' irresoluble oil,
So gentle late and blandishing, in floods
Of rancid bile o'erflows: what tumults hence
What horrours rise were nauseous to relate.
Chuse leaner viands, ye whose jovial make
Too fast the gummy nutriment imbibes,
Chuse sober meals, and rouse to active life
Your cumbrous clay, nor on th' enfeebling down
Irresolute protract the morning hours:
But let the man whose bones are thinly clad
With cheerful ease and succulent repast
Improve his habit if he can; for each
Extreme departs from perfect sanity.

*John Armstrong, M.D.*

## METABOLISM

For this the watchful appetite was giv'n,
Daily with fresh materials to repair
This unavoidable expense of life,
This necessary waste of flesh and blood:
Hence the concoctive pow'rs with various art
Subdue the cruder elements to chyle,
The chyle to blood, the foamy purple tide
To liquors, which through finer arteries

To diff'rent parts their winding course pursue,
To try new changes and new forms put on
Or for the publick or some private use.

*Idem*

## MELANCHOLY OCCURRENCE

Rang'd on the brink the weeping matrons stand,
  The lovely wreck of fortune to survey;
While o'er the flood he wav'd his beauteous hand,
  Or in convulsive anguish struggling lay,
  By slow degrees they view'd his force decay,
In fruitless efforts to regain the shore;
They view'd and mourn'd his fate—O Heaven, they
  cou'd no more!

*Thomas Blacklock, D.D.*

## PASTORAL

Her robe, around her loosely thrown,
  Gave to the shepherd's een
What could in innocence be shown;
  The rest was all unseen.

*Idem*

## LAMENTATION

Love too did oft our speech employ,
Love the pure source of social joy:
Love—but what visions, strike mine eyes!
What forms, what heav'nly forms arise?
Ammonia here!—ah me excuse
The sallies of a wanton muse,
That flies on fancy's wing away,
I cease—I cease the empty lay.

*James Boswell*

145

## MORE LAMENTATION

There was a time when this dull breast
   Throbb'd wild to all that flitted by;
An angel spirit was its guest,
   And nature charmed my laughing eye.

Has nature charms? or does the soul
   Give all the colour that we know?
Are those the orbs that wont to roll?
   Are these the streams that wont to flow?

Talk to the blind of joys of sight,
   And tell the deaf of music's art,
And spread the tinsel of delight
   Before a wounded broken heart.

She was—but let my accents fall——
   She is—but soars yon stars above!
I saw her in her father's hall
   We met, we gazed, and all was love.

Yes, Seraph! 'twas his mandate proud,
   That seas should part my love and me!
It was a father's wish. I bow'd,
   And bade adieu to hope and thee.

I wandered, but in every land,
   Thy lovely image wandered too;
Thy name I traced on every sand,
   And mingled drops with every dew.

Yes, I returned, and she, my love,
   No longer dwelt on Earth's bright scene;
Her angel spirit fled above,
   And all—as she had never been!

              *Sir Alexander Boswell*

## ODE TO DILIGENCE

Hail! mighty Pow'r, to whom we owe,
Beyond what words can fully show,
    Or any art express!
To thee, O Diligence! we bend
To thee! on whom we all depend,
      For bounties more or less!
        Before thee all
        May prostrate fall
When flushed with new success!

Should any object more inspire!
Should aught so far the grateful fire,
    Or such affection claim!
How highly ought we all to prize,
The means by which we justly rise,
      To wealth and endless fame!
        And may explore
        Immensely more
Than time permits to name!

When mountains heap'd on mountains high,
Approaching near the azure sky,
    Our progress seem to stop,
By thy kind hand we're gently led,
And taught with care their brow to tread
      Or mount their lofty top:
        The highest tree
        We climb by thee,
And all its branches lop!

When hard and intricate the course,
We find thee still the chief resource;
    Thou all prevailing spring!
May then each tongue in tuneful lays,
A grateful revenue of praise,

And honours to thee bring!
And may the Nine
Inspire each line,
While thus of thee we sing!

*George Hay* (*fl.* 1785)

## THE NAME OF STUART

Revered defender of beauteous Stuart,
Of Stuart, a name once respected—
A name which to love was the mark of a true heart,
But now 'tis despised and neglected.

Though something like moisture conglobes in my
eye
Let no one misdeem me disloyal;
A poor friendless wanderer may well claim a sigh,
Still more if that wanderer were royal.

*Burns*

## DAIRY PRODUCE

Besides the sweets of Ceres' reign,
The farmer boasts of lowing kine,
Whose lusty udders never fail
To fill the gold-begetting pail,
With many a white refulgent stream;
Whence the nectareous, mantling cream,
From which, express'd by homely toil,
The richly butyraceous oil:
The serous parts with equal ease,
Are formed into the lusty cheese,
Which is, in spite of all that's rare,
The chiefest still of Scotia's fare.

*John Bell* (*fl.* 1816)

148

## LOCHNAGAR

Away, ye gay landscapes, ye gardens of roses!
    In you let the minions of luxury rove,
Restore me the rocks, where the snow-flake reposes,
    Though still they are sacred to freedom and love:
Yet, Caledonia, beloved are thy mountains,
    Round their white summits though elements war;
Though cataracts foam 'stead of smooth-flowing
        fountains
    I sigh for the valley of dark Loch na Garr.

Ah! there my young footsteps in infancy wander'd,
    My cap was the bonnet, my cloak was the plaid;
On chieftains long perish'd my memory ponder'd,
    As daily I strode through the pine-cover'd glade,
I sought not my home till the day's dying glory
    Gave place to the rays of the bright polar star,
For fancy was cheer'd by traditional story,
    Disclosed by the natives of dark Loch na Garr.

Years have roll'd on, Loch na Garr, since I left you,
    Years must elapse ere I tread you again:
Nature of verdure and flow'rs has bereft you,
    Yet still are you dearer than Albion's plain.
England! thy beauties are tame and domestic
    To one who has roved o'er the mountains afar:
Oh for the crags that are wild and majestic!
    The steep frowning glories of dark Loch na
        Garr.

*Byron*

## O THOU OCEAN!

O thou Ocean! as a sea boy, I have lain upon thy
    breast,
Ere a dream of evil after-days could steal upon my
    sleep;

I have gazed upon thy beauty when thy spirit was
    at rest,
Till my heart's full founts o'erflowing made me turn
    away and weep.
I have plough'd thee in the tempest, I have plough'd
    thee in the calm,
I have plough'd thee when the cannon roar and
    battle din was loud,
At midnight, and at morn, when an Ether fraught
    with balm,
Was hanging o'er thy bosom in a rosy-colour'd
    cloud.

I have thought upon thy nature, but have found all
    efforts vain,
To make myself acquainted with the changes thou
    hast seen;
I have heard of mighty cities, but could find no
    stone remain,
To point me with a certainty where such a one has
    been.
But I loved thee in my boyhood, and will love thee
    in my age,
Thou vast unconquer'd element, which man would
    vainly brave!
And when my weary spirit has obtain'd her skyward
    gage,
Oh! in some of thy recesses, let my body find a
    grave.

*J. L. Denovan* (1798–1827)


## REUNITED

The priest undid two doors that hid
    The inn's adjacent room,
And there a lovely woman stood,
    Tears bathed her beauty's bloom.

One moment may with bliss repay
  Unnumbered hours of pain;
Such was the throb and mutual sob
  Of the Knight embracing Jane.
                              *Thomas Campbell*

## FALSE FERDINAND

Light rued false Ferdinand to leave a lovely maid
    forlorn,
Who broke her heart and died to hide her blushing
    cheek from scorn.
One night he dreamt he woo'd her in their wonted
    bower of love,
Where the flowers sprang thick around them, and
    the birds sang sweet above.


But the scene was swiftly changed into a church-
    yard's dismal view,
And her lips grew black beneath his kiss, from
    love's delicious hue.
What more he dreamt he told to none; but
    shuddering, pale, and dumb,
Look'd out upon the waves, like one who knew his
    hour was come.


'Twas now the deadwatch of the night—the helm
    was lashed a-lee,
And the ship rode where Mount Aetna lights the
    deep Levantine sea;
When beneath its glare a boat came, row'd by a
    woman in her shroud,
Who, with eyes that made our blood run cold, stood
    up and spoke aloud.

"Come, Traitor, down, for whom my ghost still
    wanders unforgiven!
Come down, false Ferdinand, for whom I broke my
    peace with Heaven!"
It was in vain to hold the victim, for he plunged to
    meet her call,
Like the bird that shrieks and flutters in the gazing
    serpent's thrall.


You may guess the boldest mariner shrunk daunted
    from the sight,
For the Spectre and her winding-sheet shone blue
    with hideous light;
Like a fiery wheel the boat spun with the waving of
    her hand,
And round they went, and down they went, as the
    cock crew from the land.

*Idem*


## DISILLUSION

And are all the gay pictures I've painted of life,
    Youth's dreams of romance, ever gone?
From scenes which with bliss, love, and beauty were
    rife,
    Must I now awaken to nothing but strife,
      But self and discordance alone?


To find we have got appellations for much
    Here rarely or ne'er to be found,
Ah! how much are we forc'd to acknowledge as
    such
Things shunning alike both the sight and the touch,
    And charming alone by the sound.

*Edward Allan* (1837)

## GLASGOW PATRIOTS

Loyal-hearted citizens!
Great news there's come to town;
I have not got the particulars yet,
But they'll be in the afternoon.

Loyal-hearted citizens!
Great news I've got to tell,
Of the wars in Spain and Portingall,
And how the town of Badajos fell.

There was one Aleck Pattison,
A man of great renown;
He was the first that did mount Badajos walls,
And the first that did tumble down.

He was a handsome tall young gentleman,
As ever my eyes did see;
A captain, colonel, or major,
He very soon would be.

I am the author of every word I sing,
Which you may very well see,
The music alone excepted,
But just of the poetree.

I've travelled the world all over,
And many a place beside:
But I never did see a more beautifuller city,
Than that on the banks of the navigatable
    river, the Clyde.

I left Inverness without e'er a guide,
And arrived in Glasgow city,
Where I've been informed that bold John Bull,
Again beat the French so pretty.

I came into the Star Inn and Hotel
First, they gave me brandy, and then they
    gave me gin;
Here's success, to all the waiters
Of the Star Hotel and Inn!

    *Alexander MacDonald* ("*Blind Alick*")


## THE ROYAL LANARKSHIRE VOLUNTEERS

For they're the men I do declare,
I mean the Royal Lanarkshire Volunteers.


The first comes Colonel Hunter,
    In a kilt see he goes,
Every inch is a man
    From the top to the toes.—


He is the loyal Editor,
    Of the *Herald* news-pa-per—
And no man at the punch-bowl,
    The punch can better stir.


Like the fiery god of war,
    Colonel Geddes does advance,
On a black horse, that belonged
    To the murdered King of France.


And then comes Major Paterson,
    You'll say he's rather slim;
But 'twill take a clever ball,
    For to hit the like of him.

    *Idem*

# QUEEN VICTORIA'S WELCOME
## TO DEESIDE

Ye hills and ye mountains surrounding Balmoral,
　　Ye groves and ye valleys, ye surely can tell,
Frae the mouth of the Dee to the fam'd Ballochbui,
　　Where cannons and pibrochs made a' the woods
　　　　yell?

The eighth of September will ne'er be forgotten,
　　A merrier day we never hae seen,
We ran and we jumpit ower moorlands and mosses
　　To bonnie Aboyne to welcome the Queen.

The Queen and her Consort and three bonnie
　　　　bairnies
　　Arrived at twelve on Charleston's Green;
The blackbirds were singin', the church bells were
　　　　ringin',
　　The minstrels o' Tarland played "God save the
　　　　Queen".

All in a sudden the royal coach started,
　　Wi' four bonnie steeds 'maist the colour o' cream;
Though the Queen was a stranger, she was in nae
　　　　danger,
　　They a' wished her weel to her ain Hieland hame.

Lang! lang may she reign as the Queen o' our
　　　　nation,
　　Wi' health and contentment and wealth at her
　　　　call,
Lang may she be spared to comfort her children,
　　And spouse to Prince Albert, the Laird o' Birkhall.

*Bothy song*

155

# WELCOME TO
# HARRIET BEECHER STOWE

[As sung at the Banquet given her in Edinburgh,
on Wednesday, 20th April 1853.]

Come, Scotland, tune your stock and horn,
And hail with song this joyous morn,
When on Love's eagle pinions borne,
    Harriet Beecher Stowe's come.

*Chorus*: Freedom's angel now's come,
        Mercy's sister now's come,
        Grim Oppression drees his doom:
        Harriet Beecher Stowe's come.

Through hostile ranks our sires of yore,
Fair Freedom's flag unsullied bore,
And still she fills our bosom's core:
    Harriet Beecher Stowe's come.

A woman's arm Truth's falchion bears,
A sweet low voice stern Conscience fears,
And stony hearts dissolve in tears:
    Harriet Beecher Stowe's come.

And far as rolls the ocean wave,
Is heard that voice now raised to save,
Alike the slaver and the slave:
    Harriet Beecher Stowe's come.

And tyrants scared the writing scan,
O'er-arching heaven with rainbow span,
MAN HATH NO PROPERTY IN MAN:
    Harriet Beecher Stowe's come.

Then welcome be that honoured name,
So dear to freedom and to fame;
Come, rend the welkin with acclaim:
    Harriet Beecher Stowe's come.
                    *James Ballantine*

# THE LIONS' DEN

There were two brothers, both noted warriors,
   Who fell in love with a lady gay;
And for to win her was their endeavour—
   They tried to gain her both night and day.
The one of them he was a captain,
   Commanded by brave Colonel Carr;
While the other he was a brisk lieutenant
   On board the *Tiger*, a man-of-war.

The lady made a bold resolution
   That she would wed no man but he
Who would prove himself to be a man of valour,
   Either on the land or on the sea.
She called her coach to be made ready
   In early morning by the break of day,
And with her two gallants rode o'er the mountains
   Until they came where the lions lay.

And when they came into the tower
   She threw her fan in the lions' den,
Saying—"Either of you that would gain a lady
   Must bring me back my fan again".
Then out did speak the faint-hearted captain,
   For he was sore distressed in mind—
"In battle I was ne'er called a coward,
   And to fight my foes I am well inclined;

"But among these lions, bears, and tigers,
   I think my life would no ransom prove;
I will not venture my life in danger,
   Though I should never gain your love".
Then out did speak the bold lieutenant,
   With a voice like thunder, both loud and shrill,
"Oh, I will venture my life in danger,
   All for to gain my love's goodwill".

157

So while they went into the tower
  The lions all looked fierce and grim,
But well behav'd the bold lieutenant,
  His looks were ten times as fierce as them.
Then from his side he drew a rapier,
  Two of the lions then he did kill;
When the others saw his manly courage
  Down at their conqueror's feet they fell.

He stooped down the fan to lift up,
  This courteous warrior made no delay;
While the lady in her coach sat trembling,
  Lest he'd become the lions' prey.
But when she saw the bold hero coming,
  And that to him no harm was done,
With open arms she did embrace him,
  Says—"Take the prize, love, ye now have won".

It was not long till the King got notice
  That two of his lions had been slain;
Yet he was not at all displeased,
  But gave him honour for the same.
He advanced him from being a first lieutenant,
  And made him Admiral of the Blue,
And soon the lady and he were married;
  This lets us see what love can do.

*Bothy song*

## ELLEN OF ABERDEEN

My earthly pleasures now are fled,
  My joyful days are done,
Since Ellen in her grave was laid
  And her sands of life are run.

No friends on earth young Ellen had
  To shed a silent tear,
Of parents both she was bereft
  In her eleventh year.

The trouble that my Ellen had
    Defied the doctor's skill;
She closed her eyes, and bade farewell
    At her Redeemer's will.

Her days were numbered on this earth,
    Her age scarce seventeen;
She was an honour to the female sex,
    And the pride of Aberdeen.

                  *Bothy song*

## HYMN FOR THE YOUNG

Would'st thou reap life's golden treasure?
    Young man, be wise!
Cease to follow where light pleasure
    Cheats blinking eyes,
Let no flattering voices win thee,
Let no vauntful echoes din thee,
But the peace of God within thee
    Seek, and be wise!

Where the fervid cup doth sparkle,
    Young man, be wise!
Where quick glances gleam and darkle,
    Danger surmise!
Where the rattling car is dashing,
Where the shallow wave is plashing,
Where the coloured foam is flashing,
    Feast not thine eyes!

Rocking on a lazy billow
    With roaming eyes,
Cushioned on a dreamy pillow,
    Thou art not wise;
Wake the power within thee sleeping,
Trim the plot that's in thy keeping;
Thou wilt bless the task when reaping
    Sweet labour's prize.

Since the green earth had beginning,
  Land, sea, and skies,
Toil their rounds with sleepless spinning,
  Suns sink and rise,
God, who with His image crowned us,
Works within, above, around us,
Let us, where His Will hath bound us,
  Work and be wise!

All the great, that won before thee
  Stout labour's prize,
Wave their conquering banners o'er thee;
  Up, and be wise!
Wilt thou from their sweat inherit,
Fruits of peace, and stars of merit,
While their sword, when thou should'st wear it,
  Rust-eaten lies?

Work, and wait, a sturdy liver
  (Life fleetly flies!);
Work, and pray, and sing, and ever
  Lift hopeful eyes;
Let no blaring folly din thee!
Wisdom, when her charm may win thee,
Flows a well of life within thee;
  Young man, be wise!

                  *John Stuart Blackie*

## THE NEW TAY BRIDGE

Beautiful new railway bridge of the silvery Tay,
With your strong brick piers and buttresses in so
    grand array;
And your thirteen central girders, which seems to
    my eye,
Strong enough all windy storms to defy.

And as I gaze upon thee my heart feels gay,
Because thou art the greatest railway bridge of the
    present day;
And can be seen for miles away,
From north, south, east, or west, of the Tay,
On a beautiful and clear sunshiny day,
And ought to make the hearts of the *Mars* boys feel
    gay;
Because thine equal nowhere can be seen,
Only near by Dundee and the bonnie Magdalen
    Green.

Beautiful new railway bridge of the silvery Tay,
With your beautiful side screens along your railway;
Which will be a great protection on a windy day,
So as the railway carriages won't be blown away;
And ought to cheer the hearts of the passengers
    night and day,
As they are conveyed along thy beautiful railway.
And towering above the silvery Tay,
Spanning the beautiful river from shore to shore;
Upwards of two miles and more,
Which is most wonderful to be seen—
Near by Dundee and the bonnie Magdalen Green.

Thy structure, to my eye, seems strong and grand,
And the workmanship most skilfully planned;
And I hope the designers, Messrs. Barlow & Arrol,
    will prosper for many a day,
For erecting thee across the beautiful Tay.
And I think nobody need have the least dismay,
To cross o'er thee by night or day;
Because thy strength is visible to be seen—
Near by Dundee and the bonnie Magdalen Green.

Beautiful new railway bridge of the silvery Tay,
I wish you success for many a year and day,

And I hope thousands of people will come from far
    away,
Both high and low, without delay,
From the north, south, east and the west,
Because as a railway bridge thou art the best;
Thou standest unequalled to be seen—
Near by Dundee and the bonnie Magdalen Green.

And for beauty thou art most lovely to be seen,
As the train crosses o'er thee with her cloud of steam;
And you look well painted with the colour of
    marone,
And to find thy equal there is none;
Which, without fear of contradiction, I venture to
    say,
Because you are the longest railway bridge of the
    present day;
That now crosses o'er a tidal river stream,
And the most handsome to be seen—
Near by Dundee and the bonnie Magdalen Green.

The New Yorkers boast about their Brooklyn Bridge,
But in comparison to thee it seems like a midge,
Because thou spannest the silvery Tay,
A mile and more longer I venture to say;
Besides the railway carriages are pulled across by a
    rope,
Therefore Brooklyn Bridge cannot with thee cope;
And as you have been opened on the 20th day of
    June,
I hope Her Majesty Queen Victoria will visit thee
    very soon;
Because thou art worthy of a visit from Duke, Lord,
    or Queen,
And strong and securely built, which is most worthy
    to be seen—
Near by Dundee and the bonnie Magdalen Green.

*William McGonagall*

162

## MR SPURGEON

Oh! mighty city of London, you are wonderful to
 see,
And thy beauties no doubt fills the tourist's heart
 with glee,
But during my short stay and while wandering there,
Mr Spurgeon was the only man I heard speaking
 proper English I do declare.

*Idem*


## THE HORRORS OF MAJUBA

'Twas after the great Majuba fight:
And the next morning, at daylight,
Captain Macbean's men were ordered to
 headquarters camp
So immediately Captain Macbean and his men set
 out on tramp.


And there they were joined by the Blue Jackets and
 58th men,
Who, for unflinching courage, no man can them
 condemn,
And that brave little band was commissioned to bury
 their dead,
And the little band numbered in all about one
 hundred.


And they were supplied with a white flag, fit emblem
 of death,
Then they started off to O'Neill's farm, with bated
 breath,
Where their comrades had been left the previous
 night,
And were lying weltering in their gore, oh! what a
 horrible sight.

163

And when they arrived at the foot of Majuba Hill
They were stopped by a Boer party, but they meant
    no ill,
Who asked them what they wanted without dismay,
And when they said their dead, there was no further
    delay.

Then the brave heroes marched on, without any
    dread,
To the Hill of Majuba to collect and bury their dead;
And to see them climbing Majuba it was a fearful
    sight,
And much more so on a dark pitch night.

And on Majuba there was a row of dead men,
Numbering about forty or fifty of them;
There were also numbers of wounded men lying on
    the ground,
And when Captain Macbean's party gazed on them
    their sorrow was profound.

Oh, heaven! what a sight of blood and brains!
While the grass was red all o'er with blood-stains;
Especially at the edge of the Hill, where the 92nd
    men were killed,
'Twas there that the eyes of Macbean's party with
    tears filled,

When they saw their dead and dying comrades-in-
    arms,
Who were always foremost in the fight during war's
    alarms;
But who were now lying dead on Majuba Hill,
And, alas! beyond the aid of all human skill.

They then went about two hundred yards down the
    Hill,
And collected fourteen more bodies, which made
    their blood run chill;

And, into one grave, seventy-five bodies they buried
    there,
All mostly 92nd men, who, I hope, are free from all
    care.


Oh! think of that little gallant British band,
Who, at Majuba, made such a heroic stand,
And, take them altogether, they behaved like brave
    men,
But, alas! they were slaughtered like sheep in a pen.


Poor fellows! there were a few of them left to retire,
Because undauntedly they faced that murderous fire,
That the mighty host poured in upon them, left and
    right,
From their numerous rifles, day and night.


The conduct of the 92nd was most brave through-
    out,
Which has always been the case, without any doubt;
At least, it has been the case in general with the
    Highland Brigade,
Because in the field they are the foremost, and
    seldom afraid.


And to do the British justice, at Majuba they behaved
    right well,
But by overwhelming numbers the most of them fell,
Which I'm very sorry to relate,
That such a brave little band met with such a fate.


The commanders and officers deserve great praise,
Because they told their men to hold Majuba for three
    days;
And so they did, until the most of them fell,
Fighting nobly for their Queen and country they
    loved right well.

But who's to blame for their fate I'm at a loss to
    know,
But I think 'twas by fighting too numerous a foe;
But there's one thing I know, and, in conclusion will
    say,
That their fame will be handed down to posterity,
    for many a day!

*Idem*

# EPIGRAMS, EPITAPHS AND
## OTHER TRIFLES

*Gude witt jumps.*

## LIBERA NOS DOMINE

DELIVER me, O Lord, from the errors of wise men, yea,
and of good men.—*Archbishop Leighton.*

## SIX MORAL EPIGRAMS

### On the True Test of Poverty

He that agreeth with his povertie
Is truly rich, while on the other part,
He's poore, who 'midst the superfluitie
Of wealth, in new desires consumes his heart:
    For 'tis an empty mind inflicts the curse
    Of poverty, and not an empty purse.

### On Self-conceit

Fond selfe-conceit likes never to permit
One's mind to see itselfe with upright eyes;
Whence many men might have attain'd to wit,
Had they not thought themselves already wise:
    To boast of wisedome then is foolishnesse,
    For while we thinke we're wise, we're nothing lesse.

### On Candour

Though all some errors doe commit, yet few
Having committed them would have them told:
That talke then being displeasing which is true,
Who cannot flatter, he his peace must hold;
    So hard a thing it is to say or pen,
    Without offence, the truth of living men.

### On mere Longevity

That aged man, we should, without all doubt
Of all men else the most disgraceful hold,

Who can produce no testimonie but
The number of his yeares that he is old;
  For of such men what can be testifyed
  But that being borne, they lived long, then dyed?

### On Sinning and Repenting

We sinne with joy: and having sin'd, we mourn;
Then kindle, after teares, new sinfull fires,
There being a turne perpetuall, and returne
'Twixt our repentance and profane desires;
  For senses to delights are wedded wholly,
  Which purchas'd, reason doth bewail their folly.

### On Time and Eternity

As death o'rthroweth man, and cuts his breath,
And fame most gloriously subdueth death;
So gourmandizing time doth fame o'rcome,
And to eternity time must succumb.

Sir Thomas Urquhart

## MAN AND GOD

As with the fire,
So with thy God do stand,
Keep not far off,
Nor come thou too near hand.

—Inscription on an Edinburgh<br>Chimney-piece, 17th Century

## CORNUCOPIA

If for one only Horne
  Which Nature to him gave
So famous is the noble Unicorne,
  What praise should that Man have
  Whose head a Ladie brave
Doth with a goodlie Paire at once adorne?

Drummond of Hawthornden

## SCEPTICISM

To save a maid St. George a dragon slew,
A brave exploit, if all that's said is true.
Some think there are no dragons—nay, 'tis said
There was no George: pray God there be a maid!

*Anon. (c. 1700)*

## POLITICS

Fools out of favour grudge at knaves in place,
And men are always honest in disgrace;
But, since preferment makes men knaves by course,
If those that's out were in, they would be worse.

*Anon. (early 18th century)*

## PEDIGREE

Here lies a man,
Com'd of Adam and Eve;
If any will climb higher,
I give him leave.

*Anon. (1703)*

## ON A LION ENRAGED AT SEEING A LAD IN HIGHLAND DRESS

Calm and serene the imperial lion lay,
Mildly indulging in the solar ray;
On vulgar mortals with indifference gazed,
All unconcerned, nor angry, nor amazed;
But when the Caledonian lad appeared,
Sudden alarmed, his manly mane he reared,
Prepared in fierce encounter to engage
The only object worthy of his rage.

*William Hamilton of Bangour*

171

## SUCCESS

*Here* continueth to rot
The body of FRANCIS CHARTERIS,
Who, with an *Inflexible Constancy*
and
*Inimitable Uniformity* of Life
*Persisted*
In spite of *Age* and *Infirmities*
In the practice of *Every Human Vice*,
Excepting *Prodigality* and *Hypocrisy*:
His insatiable *Avarice* exempted him from the first,
His matchless *Impudence* from the second.
Nor was he more singular
In the undeviating *pravity* of his manners
Than successful
in *accumulating Wealth*;
For, without *Trade or Profession*,
Without *Trust* of *Public Money*,
And without *Bribe-worthy* service,
He acquired, or more properly created,
*A Ministerial Estate*.
He was the only person of his time
Who could *Cheat* without the mask of *Honesty*,
Retain his primeval *Meanness*
When possessed of *Ten Thousand* a year,
And having daily deserved the *Gibbet* for what
he *did*,
Was at last condemned to it for what he *could* not *do*.[1]
Oh, indignant reader!
Think not his life useless to mankind!
*Providence* connived at his execrable designs,
To give to after ages
A conspicuous *Proof* and *Example*

[1] Colonel Charteris, rather late in life, was cast at the Old Bailey for rape and sentenced to death. He had interest enough, however, to procure a pardon.

Of how small estimation is *Exorbitant Wealth*
    In the sight of *God*
By His bestowing it upon the *Most Unworthy of All*
    *Mortals*.

                *John Arbuthnot, M.D.*

## THE WORLD

This is the best world that we can live in
To lend, to spend, and to give in;
But to borrow, or beg, or get a man's own,
It is the worst world that ever was known.

                      *Anon.*

## THE HAPPY WARRIOR

I murder hate by field or flood,
    Though glory's name may screen us;
In wars at home I'll spend my blood,
    Life-giving wars of Venus.

The deities that I adore
    Are social peace and plenty;
I'm better pleased to make one more
    Than be the death of twenty.

                      *Burns*

## ON A NOTORIOUS SHE-NAMESAKE

Cease, ye prudes, your envious railing,
    Lovely Burns has charms—confess.
True it is, she had one failing—
    Had a woman ever less?

                      *Idem*

## THE HENPECKED HUSBAND

Cursed be the man, the poorest wretch in life,
The crouching vassal to the tyrant wife!
Who has no will but by her high permission;
Who has not sixpence but in her possession;

Who must to her his dear friend's secret tell;
Who dreads a curtain-lecture worse than hell!
Were such a wife had fallen to my part,
I'd break her spirit or I'd break her heart;
I'd charm her with the magic of a switch,
I'd kiss her maids, and kick the perverse bitch.

*Idem*

## ON JOHN DOVE

Here lies Johnny Pigeon,
What was his religion?
    Whae'er desires to ken
To some other warl'
Maun follow the carl,
    For here Johnny Pigeon had nane!

*Idem*

## ON A GAY LAD

Lament him, Mauchline husbands a',
    He aften did assist ye;
For had ye staid whole years awa'
    Your wives they ne'er had missed ye.

Ye Mauchline bairns, as on ye pass
    To school in bands thegither,
Oh, tread ye lightly on his grass—
    Perhaps he was your faither!

*Idem*

## A BARD'S EPITAPH

Is there a man whose judgment clear
Can others teach the course to steer,
Yet runs himself life's mad career
        Wild as the wave?
Here pause—and, through the starting tear,
        Survey this grave.

*Idem*

## ON A SCHOOLMASTER

Mr Rhind is very kind,
He goes to kirk on Sunday.
He prays to God to give him strength
To skelp the bairns on Monday.

*Children's rhyme*

## LIFE

Like thee I once have stemm'd the sea of life,
Like thee, have languish'd after empty joys;
Like thee, have labour'd in the stormy strife;
Been grieved for trifles, and amused with toys.

*James Beattie*

## LAWS

Laws, as we read in ancient sages,
Have been like cobwebs in all ages.
Cobwebs for little flies are spread,
And laws for little folks are made;
But if an insect of renown,
Hornet or beetle, wasp or drone,
Be caught in quest of sport or plunder,
The flimsy fetter flies in sunder.

*Idem*

## THE QUESTION

Yes, yes, I grant the sons of earth
Are doom'd to trouble from their birth.
We all of sorrow have our share;
But say, is yours without compare?

*Idem*

175

## WOMAN

Could this ill warld hae been contrived
  To stand without mischeevous woman,
How peacefu' bodies might hae lived,
  Released frae a' the ills sae common!
But, since it is the waefu' case
  That man maun hae this teazing crony,
Why sic a sweet bewitching face?
  Oh, had she no been made sae bonnie!

James Hogg

## ON AN ABERDEEN FAVOURITE

Here lie the bones of Elizabeth Charlotte,
That was born a virgin and died a harlot.
She was aye a virgin till seventeen—
An extraordinary thing for Aberdeen.

Anon.

## STRICTURES ON THE ECONOMY OF NATURE

A' things created have their uses,
  This truth will bear nae doots,
As far as hauds to fleas and louses
  An' ither bitin' brutes.
I ken the use o' crawlin' clocks
  An' bugs upon you creepin';
But what's the use o' Barbara Fox?
  By jingo, that's a deep ane!

George Outram

## HERE LIES

Here lies of sense bereft—
  But sense he never had.
Here lies, by feeling left—
  But that is just as bad.

176

Here lies, reduced to dirt—
   That's what he always was;
Here lies without a heart—
   He ne'er had one, alas!

Here lies . . .
   He did so ere he died,
Then simply to begin, Here lies—
   But all his life he lied.
Death is a change, they say—
   Ye powers that rule the sky,
What change is here, I pray?
   For surely he did die.

                   *Idem*

## TWO EPITAPHS

### *On a Manufacturer*

Here lies lang-length-cut porpoise Dixon
Dished out for greedy mauks tae fix on,
Wha lang devoured his best bread wunners,
But noo devoured himsel' by hunners,
Whilk as they worry, grumlin' say—
Though fat, he's unco vulgar clay.

### *On a Country Gentleman whom the Author has seen passionately abuse, then liberally assist an Old Beggar*

Stop, beggar, stop—bedew this blighted sod
Wi' tears as het as e'er frae mourner flowed,
In him wha sleeps beneath its scanty grass,
(Though whan alive, mair tiger was than ass,)
Ye wad hae faund a brute the maist uncivil,
A furious, rampant, kindly kind o' deevil.

                *Roger Quinn, the elder*

177

## IN HOSPITAL

Fast came ye, sir, to me no weel,
A hunner students at your heel,
A hunner hands did ower me feel,
    Wi' Boreas blue.
I had nae fever then, but, deil,
    I hae it noo!

*Anon. (from Martial)*

## MAKE-BELIEVES

When I was young and well and glad
I used to play at being sad;
Now youth and health are fled away,
At being glad I sometimes play.

*R. F. Murray*

## ON A HIGHLAND FACTOR

Ged thachradh oighreachd mhór agad,
'S ged ghéill na sloigh fo d'smachd;
Tha 'm bàs 'us laghan geur aige,
'S gu feum thu géill d' a reachd.
Sud uachdaran a dh' òrduicheas,
Co-ionnan còir gach neach;
'S mar oighreachd bheir e léine dhuit,
'S dà cheum de thalamh glas.

.    .    .    .    .

'N sin molaidh a' chruimh shnàigeach thu,
Cho tàirceach 's a bhitheas d' fheoil;
'N uair gheigh i air do chàradh thu,
Gu sàmhach air a bòrd.
Their i, " 'S e fear miath 'tha 'n so,
Tha math do bhiasd nan còs,
Bho'n rinn e caol na ciadan,
Gus e féin a bhiathadh dhomh-s' ".

*Iain Mac A'Ghobhainn*

## SEASON'S GREETINGS

I remember, I remember
  Nothing further after that,
But I wakened in the morning
  On an alien lobby mat;
And I felt not unpersuaded
  (Though my reasons were not clear)
That I'd spent a Merry Christmas
  And a Prosperous New Year.
                    *George Fletcher, M.D.*


## SCOTS ORTHOGRAPHY

I know of a fellow called Menzies
About whom the peculiar thing is
    He incessantly chatters
    Political matters
And works himself up into frenzies.
                    *Archibald Browning*

## EFFICACY OF PRAYER

There was aince an auld body o' Sydney
Wha suffered from pains in the kidney.
    He prayed to the Lord
    That he might be restored,
And He promised He would—but He didnae.
                    *—Attributed to Neil Munro*


## THOUGHTS ON MY BOSS

Curse his new hoose, his business, his cigar,
His wireless set, and motor car,
Alsatian, gauntlet gloves, plus fours and wife,
—A'thing included in his life;
And, abune a', his herty laughter,
And—if he has yin—his hereafter.
                    *Hugh MacDiarmid*

179

## UP TO DATE

Christ, wha'd ha'e been Chief Rabbi gin he lik't!
Wi publicans and sinners did foregether,
But, losh! the publicans noo are Pharisees.
And I'm no shair o' maist the sinners either.

*Idem*

## SCOTLAND

Respectable Scotland! Land o' Grundy!—
Burns! and back-street pubs! and Sunday!—
(Of course it's no the pubs I mind:
But why the devil are they a' behind?)

*Roderick Watson Kerr*

## SECRETS

I had Smith's secrets, Robinson's I had;
To Jones I was a confidential brother:
My own I kept lest they should grow as bad
As those of Smith which Jones heard from the other.

*William Soutar*

## SURVIVAL OF THE FITTEST

With the Scots it was whisky or perish. And how
they have survived!—*Lawton Mackall*.

## OUR FRIEND

He had his faults, like all of woman born;
These and himself alike we deeply mourn.
They made of him a man we ill could spare—
It was his virtues that were hard to bear.

*Catherine Carswell*

# THE SABBATH DAY

*The Sabbath, whether we advert to its origin, its ultimate end, or its immediate effects, is calculated to excite admiration and gratitude in the bosoms of all who are susceptible of religious feelings or moral perception.*

JOHN STRUTHERS

*O quanta, qualia sunt ista Sabbata!*

ABELARD

# HYMN FOR SUNDAY

O BLEST Creator of the Light,
  Who bringing forth the Light of Days
With the first work of Splendor bright
  The World didst to Beginning raise;

Who Morn with Evening joyn'd in one,
  Commandest should be call'd the Day;
The foul Confusion now is gone,
  O hear us when with Tears we Pray;

Lest that the Mind with Fears full fraught,
  Should lose best Life's Eternal Gains,
While it hath no Immortal Thought,
  But is inwrapt in sinful Chains,

O may it beat the inmost Sky,
  And the Reward of Life possess;
May we from hurtful Actions fly,
  And purge away all wickedness.

Dear Father, grant what we intreat,
  And only Son who like Power hast,
Together with the Paraclete,
  Reigning whilst Time and Ages last.
                    *Drummond of Hawthornden* (?)


# EXHORTATION TO SOBRIETY

Another preaching against drunkenness, told the
hearers: There were four sorts of drunkenness.

1. To be drunk like a sow, tumbling in the mire
like many of this parish.

2. There is to be drunk like a dog.  The dog fills

183

the stomach of him and spues all out again, and thou, John Jamison, wast this way drunk the other day.

3. There is to be drunk like a goose. Of all drunkenness, Sirs, beware of the drunkenness of the goose, for it never rests, but constantly dips the gob (*beak*) of it in the water: You are all drunk this way, Sirs, I need name none of you.

4. There is to be drunk like a sheep. The sheep seldom or never drinks, but sometimes wets the mouth of it in the water, and rises up as well as ever; and I myself used to be drunk thus, Sirs.

But now, I see, *said he*, two gentlemen in the kirk; and, gentlemen, you are both strangers to me; but I must vindicate myself at your hands. I have here the cursedest parish that ever God put breath into; for all my preaching they will go into a change-house after sermon, and the first thing they'll get is a mickle capful of hot ale, and they will say, I wish we had the minister in the midst of it: Now, gentlemen, judge ye how I am rewarded for my good preaching.—*Robert Calder, Scots Presbyterian Eloquence Displayed.*

## WARNING TO SABBATH-BREAKERS

Open profaning the Sabbath is such a Sin, that sometimes hath been punished, by letting them fall into Crimes, that have brought them to a dismal End, as I have heard many of our Malefactors confess. One instance among many, that might be given, I cannot pass here, of the Lords very remarkably punishing the open Breach of the Sabbath, which I had from Mrs Hamilton that singular Christian in Donochadee in Ireland, when I was there, since gone to her Rest: When her Father, Mr Andrew Stewart, was Minister in that Place, he discharged all Boats or Barks to loose on the Sabbath; one Sabbath-morning, six brisk Gentlemen with fine Horses and Servants, they threatned the Seamen to take them in, and go off; they acquainted their Minister: He came to the Shore in his Night-gown, and spoke to them; one of them put his Hand to his Sword, and threatned him, giving him ill Names; he walked a little upon the Shore, and then said, Go ye off, but if God do not remarkably punish you for Contempt of his Day, and threatning me, He never spake by me. He advised the Seamen quietly, to take Ten Days Provision with them, for they would need it, and not let the Gentlemen know of it, otherways they would take it from them, when they came to a Strait; being a fair Gale, and 4 or 5 Hours sailing to Portpatrick, they took no Provision, neither for them-selves nor Horses: They went off, and were not out of Sight, when the Wind turned, and rose to a very great Height, and drove them up to the North-Seas of Scot-land, where they were in great Danger and Distress, more than eight Days; their Horses died for Hunger, and some of themselves; and the rest liv'd not long thereafter: Let our many Takers and Travellers of Journies, Foot and Horse, upon the Lord's Day (never so much Practised in Scotland, as at this Day, tho' common in England) take a Look of this frightful Beacon.—*Patrick Walker*.

## IN DARKEST LOCHABER

Should we go about here to give you an Account of the Religion of the People in this Country [Lochaber], it would be an unpleasant Work, and perhaps scarce seem to deserve credit; you would scarcely believe that in a Christian Island, as this is said to be there should be People found who know so little of Religion, or of the Custom of Christians as not to know a Sunday, or Sabbath from a Working Day, or the Worship of God from an ordinary Meeting, or Conversation: I do not affirm that it is so, and I shall say no more of it here, because I would not publish what it is to be hoped may in time find Redress; but I cannot but say that his

Majesty's Gift of £1000 annually to the Assembly of *Scotland* for sending Ministers or Missionaries for the propagating Christian Knowledge in the *Highlands*, is certainly one of the most needful Charities that could have been thought of worthy of a King, and well suited to that occasion; and if prudently apply'd, as there is Reason to believe it will be, may in time break in upon this horrible Ignorance, that has so far spread over this unhappy Part of the Country.

On the other hand, What shall we say to the Neglect, which for so many Years past has been the Occasion of this surprizing Darkness among the People, when the poor abandon'd Creatures have not so much as had the common Instruction of Christianity, so much as to know whether there was any such thing as a God or no, much less how to worship him. . . .— *Defoe.*

## THE SIN OF EUTYCHUS

Sleeping or drowsiness, in time of divine service, is a profanation of the Lord's Day, and hinders our profiting by the ordinances. Therefore guard against it. Many are watchful enough about the devil's service; they can spend whole nights in drinking, gaming, etc., without sleep; but cannot hold up their eyes half an hour in hearing a sermon. Consider what an evil custom it is, you who are chargeable with it, and reform it. How ridiculous were it for a man that came to the market to buy provision for himself and his family, to fall asleep in the market-place and so miss his errand! Do you not come on the Sabbath, which is heaven's market day, to the ordinances to get provision for your souls; and will you fall asleep in the meantime of the market, and so go home empty? What do you know but, while you slept, that truth was delivered that might have saved your souls? . . . Remember it will not always last with you, the Sabbath and sermon will quickly come that will be your

last; and who knows but this or the next may be it? . . .
God will ask, Where are the fruits of so many sermons?
It will be a fearful *item* in your accounts: "So many
sermons slipt away". How will you answer for it?

Again, Consider how provoking this practice is to
God. Would not a prince be displeased with a subject,
if he should fall asleep when he is speaking to him?
would not a judge be angry with a criminal, if he
should sleep when he were about to pronounce his
sentence? And have you not to do with the King of
Kings, and *Judge of the world*, when you are hearing
the word? . . . Remember what befell Eutychus when
he slept in time of sermon, Acts xx., it almost cost him
his life. God made him a monument of displeasure, for
a warning to all sleepers: He got a sad fall, but you
may get a worse; he fell to the ground, but you may
fall to the lowest hell, and there you will not get a
Paul to take you up as he got. Your sin is more aggravated than his; it was midnight when he slept, but
you sleep at midday; Paul had preached several hours,
but half an hour and less puts you asleep.—*The Rev.
John Willison.*


## O DAY OF REST AND GLADNESS!

The Lord knows the carnality and weariness that
our hearts are naturally prone to in the work of the
Sabbath; Wherefore, for remedy thereof, He hath
graciously appointed variety of exercises on the Sab-
bath-day, that, when we weary of one, another may
be our recreation. Are you weary of hearing? then
recreate yourselves with prayer: If of that, then recreate
yourselves with singing of God's praises: If of that,
then recreate yourselves in reading of God's Word,
and other good books: If of that, then recreate yourselves with meditation: If you weary of that, then
recreate yourselves with Christian conference, repeat-
ing the sermons, instructing your families, etc. If you

are weary of public duties, then go to private: If of
these, go to secret duties. Is there not here a delightful variety of pleasant spiritual employments, sufficient
to recreate ourselves with for one day? How think you
to spend a whole eternity in spiritual exercises, when
you weary so much of one day?—*Idem.*

## THE FAITHFUL SHEPHERD

(THOMAS PATERSON, MINISTER OF ST. CUTHBERT'S,
EDINBURGH. *Obiit* 1726)

He did not waste his lungs in froath and foam,
With heart and brains he press'd the conscience
    home.
No trifling tales with cant dropt from his mouth,
In manly words he stated solemn truth,
Was well acquaint with books and mankind too,
Of learning had an universal view,
Knew all the senseless jargon of the schools,
And by his life and sermons prov'd them fools,
For he joined truth with peace, and walk'd by gospel
    rules,
His reasoning was deep, yet very clear,
Gave knowledge to the soul, and charm'd the ear.
A pleasant temper 'mongst his gifts took place,
And shew'd good nature was ally'd to grace.
He liv'd in peace, and hated broils and din,
He never had a quarrel save with sin;
But when the wicked pled for what will damn us,
Oh then he was an unbelieving Thomas.
          *Alexander Pennecuik, the younger*

## SUNDAY CLOTHES

Being Sunday, we saw many women in and near
town, walking to church in their best apparel, and
really very neatly dressed. White gowns, shawl, black

velvet bonnet, gloves, and an umbrella, absolutely walking barefooted in the mud, very composedly, with their shoes and stockings in their hands. This custom is defended as clean, for they must wash their feet,—as wholesome, for they are sure of having dry shoes and stockings,—and it is certainly saving.— *Louis Simond* (1810).

## THE DAY OF REST

In Edinburgh two men have just been taken up for whistling in the street on Sunday, and in Glasgow a barber has been sent to jail for having dared to shave three men on that same day! Owing to the zeal with which these pious regulations are enforced you see the populace, driven from home by sheer boredom, thronging the pavements like citizens forced from their firesides by some public calamity. Their spiritual guides forbid not merely work for gain, but anything whatsoever in the nature of amusement. In other countries on holy days, the crowds in public places are out for recreation; but in Scotland all you see is a lot of people, religiously unemployed, wandering aimlessly about the town, and going home after a long "day of rest" thanking heaven that they will be back at work again on the morrow. Relaxation has been made so painful that fatigue comes as a blessed relief.—*The Marquis de Custine* (1822).

I shall say nothing of the terrible Scotch Sunday, beside which London's is a positive jollification. This day, consecrated to the honour of heaven, is the nearest thing to hell that I have ever seen on earth. Said a Scotchman to a French friend as they were returning from church: "Not quite so fast, or people will think we are taking a walk!"—*Stendhal*.

## PITY THE POOR FOREIGNER!

To make the best of a bad job and without thinking I started to amuse myself by humming and whistling. Suddenly in comes my old landlady with a sacred countenance. "Fie for shame," she said, "you're singing!"

Remembering Sosie in Molière's *Amphitryon*, I said to myself "Cette femme assurément n'aime pas la musique".

Then after a pause, for I was rather taken aback, "Why," I said, "what's the harm in singing?" "Sir," she answered, as she shut the window, "God forbid that anybody should sing on the Sabbath." Having a very modest opinion of my vocal powers, and being ignorant of the customs of the country, I supposed she had simply taken a polite way of telling me that I was a bad singer and was annoying her, which might very well have been the case, and that what her words really meant was "God forbid that anybody should sing so badly". I desisted accordingly, fearing there might be sick folk in the house.

I learned afterwards that on Sunday in Scotland one must not sing, whistle, dance or play, but one may drink, yawn and sleep, since when I have done my best to conform to the custom of the country. Presently I asked my worthy landlady to lend me a book, and she let me have a volume of the *Lives of the Presbyterian Saints*, which were not of much use to me, as they rival our own *Lives of the Saints* in soporific quality. To show her that I knew as well as she did that it was Sunday, I asked her if there was a Catholic chapel in the town. "Catholic!" she repeated, "Catholic!"—making such a face that you would think she had seen the Devil—"Catholic!" and left my room without another word. That made me want more than ever to find out if there was really a chapel in the town, and accordingly I went out and without much trouble was directed to one, where I had the pleasure of hearing an eloquent sermon in Gaelic, of which unfortunately I didn't understand a word but "the Virgin Mary".—*The Chevalier de Latocnaye.*

Sunday is indeed (in Scotland) a *dies non.* I have just seen my landlady, who has informed me that a very fine young man was drowned this morning, which, she added, "served him right for bathing on the Sabbath day!" I asked her if she thought it would serve me right to cut my throat for being shaved on a Sunday; she replied with an angry countenance, "I dinna ken, sir," indeed she looks upon me as lost mutton for singing on the Sabbath, and I have got warning to quit, for a musical transgression, by playing on the flute.—*Felix MacDonogh.*

We arrived at Edinburgh on a Sunday, that is to say, on one of those days of strict observance, when every house is closed, every shop is impenetrable, and everybody is at prayers. The solitude was immense, absolute, and the first feeling we had of Edinburgh was, that this prodigious city had been anciently built by a race of giants who had long since vanished from the earth.—*Charles Nodier.*

M. C. Nodier and his friends, said the consul, arrived here one Sunday morning. They had the misfortune to lose almost all their hats on the way; they had only one remaining among four. The observation of the Sabbath is so strict in Edinburgh that they could not get any hatter to open shop till late in the day; and in order to lose no time, each of the party in his turn wore the preserved hat, and took a solitary walk through the town!—*Amedée Pichot* (1822).

## ODOUR OF SANCTITY

The other fault [of Glasgow Cathedral] belongs to
the unclean part of the national character; for the
seats are so closely packed that any person who could
remain there during time of service, must have an
invincible nose. I doubt even whether any incense
could overcome so strong and concentrated an odour
of humanity.—*Southey* (1819).

## DR. CHALMERS

On Sunday I went to *Kirk* to hear the great lumin-
ary of this county, Dr. Chalmers, Professor of
Humā-nity at Glasgow, and an author upon many
subjects. He dined here on Saturday, and was treated
as a regular Jeroboam. His appearance on that day
was that of a very quiet, good kind of man, with very
dirty hands and nails; but on Sunday I never beheld a
fitter subject for Bedlam than he was. . . . The stuff
the fellow preached could only be surpassed by his
manner of roaring it out. I expected he would have
carried the poor Kirkaldy pulpit clean away. Then
his *Scotch* too! His sermon was to prove that the *manner*
of doing a kindness was more valuable than the matter,
in support of which I remember two notable illustra-
tions.—"If," said he, "you suppose a fā-mily to be
suddenly veesited with the ca-lā-mity of pō-verty, the
tear of a menial—the fallen countenance of a do-
mēstick—in such cases will afford greater relief to the
fā-mily than a speceefick sum of money without a
corresponding sympathy." A pretty good start, was
it not—for Scotland, too, of all places in the world!
but it was followed by a higher flight.—"Why," said
he, or rather shouted he, "Why is it that an *ep*ple
presented by an infant to its parent produces a greater
pleesure than an *ep*ple found by the raud-side? Why,
because it is the moral influence of the geft, and not

the speceefick quality of the *ep*ple that in this case constitutes the pleesure of the parent." Now what think you of the tip-top showman of all Scotland?— *Thomas Creevey.*[1]

## SUNDAY AT GOLSPIE

*August 2.*—Remained at Golspie, and, as it happened to be Sunday, we had an opportunity of observing, with a mingled feeling of respect and admiration, the deep devotional character of the Highland peasantry, who, however they may spend the other six days of the week, never fail to remember that the seventh day is the Sabbath, as the decency of their apparel, the staid and reverential expression of their countenances, and their constant observance of the sacred ordinances, abundantly testify. We also saw how much true piety may be generated in the bosoms of men whose avocations as shepherds lead them more particularly, in the awful solitudes of the hills, "to look through Nature up to Nature's God", or, as fishermen, teach them continual dependence upon His providence; and how naturally habits of reflection lead even untutored minds to seek with gladness the truths of the Gospel, and to embrace with thankfulness the blessings of religion.—*Beriah Botfield* (1829).

## THE CHURCHGOERS

Then forth they go, for now before the door
The short'ning shadow marks the hour of nine;

[1] Creevey was not only malicious, but ignorant. Dr. Chalmers was never a professor of Humanity and never a professor at Glasgow. At the date of this extract (1825) he was professor of Moral Philosophy at St. Andrews.—EDD.

And by the broomy hill are coming o'er
  Their village neighbours, glittering, clean and fine.
Upon the road, with neighbours, neighbours join,
  And converse sweet beguiles the tedious way,—
Some trace, in Nature's works, the hand Divine;
  Some through the flowery fields of Scripture stray,
And some, alas! retail the nonsense of the day.

*John Struthers* (1776–1853)

Some goes to church just for a walk,
Some go there to laugh and talk;
Some go there the time to spend,
Some go there to meet a friend;
Some go there for speculation,
Some go there for observation;
Some go there to doze and nod,
It's few goes there to worship God.

*Sir James Cameron Lees, D.D.*

## HAIL, SABBATH!

How still the morning of the hallowed day!
Mute is the voice of rural labour, hush'd
The ploughboy's whistle, and the milkmaid's song.

   .      .      .      .

Hail, Sabbath! thee I hail, the poor man's day:
The pale mechanic now has leave to breathe
The morning air pure from the city's smoke,
While wandering slowly up the river side,
He meditates on Him whose power he marks
In each green tree that proudly spreads the bough,
As in the tiny dew-bent flowers that bloom
Around the roots, and while he thus surveys
With elevated joy each rural charm,
He hopes (yet fears presumption in the hope)
To reach those realms where Sabbath never ends.

*James Grahame*

Hail! holy day, of heav'n the certain pledge
  And pleasing prelibation here below;
'Tis thine, Creation's groaning to assuage
  And bind with balmy hand her wounds of
      woe.
Rejoicing in the mornings ruddy glow,
  The labouring Ox, all wet with pearly dew,
The clover'd vale at will traverses slow
  While idly gleams upon the distant view,
Far o'er the fallow field, the glittering soil-worn
     plough.

Yea, e'en the simple Ass, the daily drudge
  Of yonder wandering ignominious train,
The thistle champs along the common's edge,
  And lightsome ease obliterates all his pain.
But chief, in freedom from the weary wain
  Exulting, roams at large the bounding Steed;
Light floats upon the breeze his flowing mane,
  He snorts, he paws, he skims the flow'ry mead,
The Sabbath day to him a day of joy indeed.

                    *John Struthers*

With silent awe I hail the sacred morn,
  That scarcely wakes while all the fields are still;
A soothing calm on every breeze is borne,
  A graver murmur echoes from the hill,
And softer sings the linnet from the thorn;
  The skylark warbles in a tone less shrill.
Hail, light serene! hail, sacred Sabbath morn!
  The sky a placid yellow lustre throws;
The gales that lately sighed along the grove
  Have hushed their drowsy wings in dead repose:
So soft the day when the first morn arose.

                    *John Leyden*

## EIGHTEEN-FORTY-THREE

The Free Kirk,
The wee kirk,
The Kirk without the steeple;
The Auld Kirk,
The cauld Kirk,
The Kirk without the people.

*Anon.*

## MORAL VALUES

There sometimes appears to have been in our countrymen an undue preponderance of zeal for Sabbath observance as compared with the importance attached to *other* religious duties, and especially as compared with the virtue of sobriety. The following dialogue between Mr M. of Glasgow, the celebrated artist, and an old Highland acquaintance whom he had met with unexpectedly, will illustrate the contrast between the severity of judgment passed upon treating the Sabbath with levity and the lighter censure attached to indulgence in whiskey. Mr M. begins: "Donald, what brought you here?" "Ou, weel, sir, it was a baad place yon; they were baad folk—but they're a God-fearin' set o' folk here!" "Well, Donald," said Mr M., "I'm glad to hear it." "Ou ay, sir, 'deed are they; an' I'll gie ye an instance o't. Last Sabbath, just as the kirk was skailin', there was a drover chield frae Dumfries comin' along the road whustlin', an' lookin' as *happy* as if it was ta muddle o' the week; weel, sir, oor laads is a Godfearin' set o' laads, an' they were just comin' oot o' the kirk—'od they yokit upon him, an' a'most killed him!" Mr M., to whom their zeal seemed scarcely sufficiently well directed to merit his approbation, then asked Donald whether it had been drunkenness that induced the depravity of his former neighbours? "Weel, weel, sir," said Donald, with some hesitation, "*may*be; I'll no say bit it micht." "Depend upon it," said Mr M., "it's a bad thing whiskey." "Weel, weel, sir," replied Donald, "I'll no say but it *may*"; adding in a very decided tone—"speeciallie *baad* whusky!"—*Dean Ramsay*.

## LET US ALL BE UNHAPPY ON SUNDAY

We zealots, made up of stiff clay,
  The sour-looking children of sorrow,
While not over jolly to-day,
  Resolve to be wretched tomorrow.
We can't for a certainty tell
  What mirth may molest us on Monday;
But, at least, to begin the week well,
  Let us all be unhappy on Sunday.

What though a good precept we strain
  Till hateful and hurtful we make it!
While though, in thus pulling the rein,
  We may draw it so tight as to break it!
Abroad we forbid folks to roam,
  For fear they get social or frisky;
But of course they can sit still at home,
  And get dismally drunk upon whisky.

*Lord Neaves*

## A POPULAR PREACHER

### 1. *The Congregation*

It turned out all as he pictured—the crush at the
  narrow door,
The screaming and fainting of women—but nobody
  cursed or swore—
The squeeze in the strait high pews, the crowd
  packed close in the aisles,
The blaze of peony faces, and glimmer of ghastly
  smiles,

The reeking and mopping of bald heads, the
 coughing and taking of snuff:
Yet they were grave too, and patient. It was God's
 house: that was enough.

．　　．　　．　　．　　．

## 2. *The Sermon*

... Mainly it was but a weft of Paley and woof of
 Paul
Calico-printed with anecdotes, wholly apocryphal,
On Shelley and Hume and Voltaire, set forth with
 manifest trick,
Clever enough in its way, of artfulest rhetoric.
Not that there were not at times touches of some-
 thing higher,
When the man's own soul broke out, with gleams of
 a central fire,
Through the crust of his pulpiteering; also there
 were some strokes
Of a grim satirical humour—they were not exactly
 jokes,
More like Elijah's burning scorn of the Prophets of
 Baal,
Or the ring of the spear of Ithuriel, smiting the
 steel-clasped mail
Of Satan. They were the bits of the sermon that I
 liked best:
I seemed to look on the devil discomfited then with
 a jest
Wholly sincere and natural. But that only came now
 and then;
And after a while I was wishing me home at mine
 inn again,
With that latest volume of Spencer's. . . .

*Walter Chalmers Smith, D.D.*

## WE ARE VERY STRICT IN THESE PARTS

Hanging over the low garden wall outside, his lower man clad in light trousers, and his upper part in a white shirt, across which a pair of braces are lightly stretched, is John M'Farlane, apparently having thrown himself across the parapet to dry. A flick of Bobtail's towel where the trousers are tightest awakens Mr M'Farlane to consciousness with a loud interjection. "Och, is it you, shentlemen; and are you really going to bathe the day? Don't you know this is the Sabbath? We are very strict in these parts. There was a shentleman from Manchester here last year, and he was taking a walk on Sabbath evening down the road yonder, and he met Lachlan M'Pherson (that's the elder that lives up there on the hull where the smoke is rising), and Lachlan rebuked him terrible heavy. "Why!" says the shentleman (a fine quiet man he was), "did not Jesus Christ walk in the fields on the Sabbath day?" "Oh, yes", says Lachlan, "but I never thought the petter of Him for it." You see, shentlemen, we are very strict in these parts; not like the South where I'm told people even play the piano on the Sabbath. So, if you please, just wash at home this day, and go to the kirk at the back of twelve. There's Free Church and Parish Church here. I goes to the Parish myself—Mr M'Rory, a very fine man: but wife goes to Free—it suits the women better, but it comes to the same on the other side of Jordan."—*Sir James Cameron Lees, D.D.*

### UNIVERSITY CHAPEL, ABERDEEN

The Chapel glories in its oak—
In part demolished
Which Covenantry vandals broke,
Then praised and polished,
They hew and hack,
And then hark back.

For many years the student went
In meagre numbers.
His Sunday morn was gladly spent
In happy slumbers.
He did not hear
The pulpiteer.

They scroll the wall with blazoned creeds.
A "Box of whistles"
Peals forth: a sort of curate reads
The great Epistles.
O, Master Knox,
These be your flocks!
*John Malcolm Bulloch*

200

# SONGS

*After some little time, the chief ordered one of them to sing me a Highland song. The bard readily obeyed, but in his going on, the chief (who piques himself upon his school-learning), at some particular passage, bid him cease, and cried out to me—"There's nothing like that in Virgil, or Homer!" I bowed and told him I believed so.*

BURT

# IF THE KIRK WAD LAT ME BE

REFRAIN. *Deliberately, Complainingly*

I'm a puir sil-ly auld man, — And hirp-ling ower a tree. — And fain, fain, kiss wad I, An' the kirk wad lat me be. — Gin a' my duds were aff, And guid new claes were on, — O! I could kiss a young lass — As weel as on-y man. —

When I was young on the fairms,
Wi' Susan and Maggie and Jean,
I'd whiles hae ane in my airms
An' ane o' the ithers atween.
I'm a puir, etc.

Some say that kissin's a sin,
But I think it's nane ava,
There's aye a kiss in the win'
When the whin has a flo'er i' the shaw.
I'm a puir, etc.

*Verses 2 and 3 by R. C. Buist.*

## HO-RO, MY NUT-BROWN MAIDEN

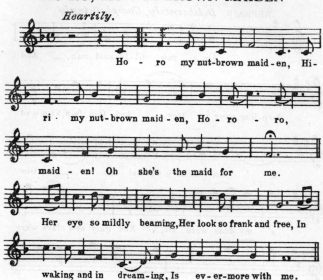

*Heartily.*

Ho - ro my nut-brown maid - en, Hi - ri - my nut-brown maid - en, Ho - ro - ro, maid - en! Oh she's the maid for me. Her eye so mildly beaming, Her look so frank and free, In waking and in dream-ing, Is ev-er-more with me.

O Mary, mild-eyed Mary,
By land, or on the sea,
Though time and tide may vary,
My heart beats true to thee.
 *Chorus.*

And since from thee I parted,
A long and weary while,
I wander heavy-hearted
With longing for thy smile.
 *Chorus.*

In Glasgow and Dunedin
Were maidens fair to see,
But never a lowland maiden
Could lure mine eyes from thee;
 *Chorus.*

Mine eyes that never vary
From pointing to the glen
Where blooms my Highland Mary
Like wild-rose 'neath the Ben.
        *Chorus.*

And when with blossoms laden
Bright summer comes again,
I'll fetch my nut-brown maiden
Down from the bonnie glen.
        *Chorus.*

## A SONG AFTER SUNSET

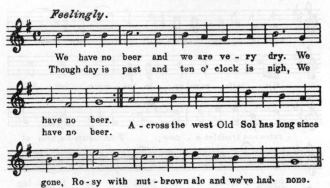

*Feelingly.*

We have no beer and we are ve-ry dry. We
Though day is past and ten o' clock is nigh, We

have no beer.    A - cross the west Old Sol has long since
have no beer.

gone, Ro-sy with nut - brown ale and we've had none.

We were not always thus nor could avow
        We'd had no beer.
Even as the owls we oft were screwed; but now
        We have no beer.
All day we have been sober; from our slate
Previous convictions, Lord, obliterate.

So long have we been thirsty, and so long
        We've had no beer.
We need a glass or two at evensong,
        Sad hearts to cheer.

And with the morn we shall go rolling home
To that same tavern which we started from.

*Robert Browning (Scotus)*

## JOHN GRUMLIE

*With energy.*

John Grum-lie swore by the light o' the moon And the
green leaf on the tree That he could dae mair
wark in a day Than his wife could dae in three.
His wife rose up in the morn-ing Wi'
cares and troubles e-now; "John Grum-lie, bide at
hame, John, And I'll gae haud the plow." Sing-ing
CHORUS
fal de lal lal de ral lal fal lal lal lal lal la "John
Grumlie, bide at hame, John, And I'll gae haud the plow."

"First ye maun dress your children fair,
And put them a' in their gear,
And ye maun turn the maut, John,
Or else ye'll spoil the beer.

And ye maun reel the tweel, John,
 That I span yesterday;
And ye maun ca' in the hens, John,
 Else they'll a' lay away."
    Singing, etc.


Oh, he did dress his children fair,
 And he put them a' in their gear;
But he forgot to turn the maut,
 And so he spoiled the beer.
And he sang aloud as he ruled the tweel
 That his wife span yesterday,
But he forgot to put up the hens,
 And the hens a' laid away.
    Singing, etc.


The hawkit crummie loot down nae milk;
 He kirned, nor butter gat,
And a' gaed wrang and nocht gaed richt;
 He danced wi' rage and grat.
Then up he ran to the heid o' the knowe,
 Wi' mony a wave and shout—
She heard him as she heard him not,
 And steered the stots about.
    Singing, etc.


John Grumlie's wife cam' hame at e'en
 And laughed as she'd been mad,
When she saw the house in siccan a plight,
 And John sae glum and sad.
Quo' he, "I gie up my housewife's kep,
 I'll be nae mair guidwife".
"Indeed", quo she, "I'm weel content,
 Ye may keep it the rest o' your life."
    Singing, etc.


"The deil be in that", quo' surly John,
 "I'll do as I've done before."

Wi' that the gudewife took up a stoot rung,
    And John made aff to the door.
"Stop, stop, gude wife, I'll haud my tongue,
    I ken I'm sair to blame;
But henceforth I maun mind the plow,
    And ye maun bide at hame."
        Singing, etc.
                        *Anon.*

# THE WIND BLEW THE BONNIE LASSIE'S PLAIDIE AWA'

*Heartily.*

Frae flesh-er Rab that lived in Crieff A
bon-nie lass-ie want-ed to buy some beef; He
took her in his arms and down she did fa', And the
wind blew the bonnie lass-ie's plai-die a-wa'.

CHORUS
Her plai-die a-wa', her plai-die a-wa', The
wind blew the bon-nie lass-ie's plai-die a-wa'; He
took her in his arms and down she did fa', And the
wind blew the bon-nie lass-ie's plai-die a-wa'.

The plaidie was lost and couldna be fund—
"The deil's in the plaid, it's awa' wi' the wind;
And what will I say to the auld folks ava?
I daurna say the wind blew the plaidie awa'".
    *Chorus.*

It wasna lang after the plaidie was lost,
Till the bonnie lassie grew thick about the waist,
And Rabbie was blamed for the hale o' it a',
And the wind blawin' the bonnie lassie's plaidie awa'.
    *Chorus.*

When Rabbie was summoned to answer the Session,
They a' cried out "Ye maun mak' a confession";
But Rabbie ne'er answered them ae word ava
But "The wind blew the bonnie lassie's plaidie awa'".
    *Chorus.*

The auld wife came in puir Rab to accuse,
The minister and elders began to abuse
Puir Rabbie for tryin' to mak' ane into twa;
But Rabbie said, "The wind blew the plaidie awa'".
    *Chorus.*

The lassie was sent for to come there hersel',
She look'd in his face, says "Ye ken hoo I fell;
And ye had the cause o't, ye daurna say na"—
But Rabbie said, "The wind blew the plaidie awa'".
    *Chorus.*

Rab look'd in her face and gied a bit smile,
He says, "My bonnie lassie, I winna you beguile;
The minister is here, he'll mak' ane o' us twa,
That'll pay for the plaidie that the wind blew awa'".
    *Chorus.*

The whisky was sent for to make a'thing right,
The minister and elders they sat a' the night,

And sang till the cock began for to craw,
"The wind blew the bonnie lassie's plaidie awa'".
    *Chorus.*

Now Rab and his lassie are hand in hand,
They live as contented as ony in the land;
And when he gets fou he minds o' the fa',
When the wind blew the bonnie lassie's plaidie awa'.
    *Chorus.*                "*Blind Rob.*"

*The author of the foregoing example of just printable Scots ribaldry was a blind fiddler who flourished in the Crief neighbourhood over a century ago. Those who feel that the words are unworthy of the tune of "The White Cockade" may sing the original verse, viz.:*

My love was born in Aberdeen,
The bonniest lad that e'er was seen:
But now he's made our hearts fu' sad,
He's ta'en the field wi' his white cockade.

#### Chorus

O he's a ranting roving blade!
O he's a brisk and bonny lad!
Betide what may, my heart is glad
To see my lad wi' his white cockade.

O leeze me on the philabeg,
The hairy hough and garter'd leg!
But aye the thing that blinds my e'e
Is the white cockade aboon the bree.
    *Chorus.*

I'll sell my rock, I'll sell my reel
My rippling-kame and spinning-wheel,
To buy mysel' a tartan plaid,
A braid sword, durk, and white cockade.
    *Chorus.*

I'll sell my rokelay and my tow,
My good grey mare and hawkit cow,
That every loyal Scottish lad
May take the field wi' his white cockade.
*Chorus.*                    *Anon.*

## PAWKIE PAITERSON'S AULD GREY YAUD

**With gusto.**

As Aw was gaun up Hawick Loan Yea Mon-an-day at morn __ Aw heard a puir auld grey meer Gi'e mon-y a hea-vy groan __ Gi'e mon-y a hea-vy groan, sir, And this she said to mei "Aw'm Paw - kie Pait-er-son's auld grey yaud, Sei how they're guid-in' mei! Aw'm Paw-kie Pait-er-son's auld grey yaud, Sei how they're guid-in' mei! __

CHORUS

211

The miller o' Hawick Mill bred mei,
   And that Aw du weel ken;
The miller o' Hawick Mill fed mei
   Wi' mony a sort o' corn.
But now the case is altered,
   And this ye plainly sei—
Aw'm Pawkie Paiterson's auld grey yaud,
   Sei how they're guidin' mei!

When a' the rest's set to the corn
   Aw'm sent oot to the fog;
When a' the rest's set to the haye
   Aw'm sent oot to the bog.
It's Aw gaed into Hawick Moss,
   'Twas like to swally mei—
Aw'm Pawkie Paiterson's auld grey yaud.
   Sei how they're guidin' mei!

And as for Nellie Harkness
   She ryses in the morn,
And cries 'O Godsake, uncle!
   The yaud's amang the corn'.
Hei tuik his muckle plow-staff than,
   And cam' and swabbled mei—
Aw'm Pawkie Paiterson's auld grey yaud.
   Sei how they're guidin' mei!

There's auld Rob Young o' the Back Raw,
   Hei's of'en shod ma clutes,
Sae Aw wull leave him ma shank banes
   To bei a pair o' butes.
If hei push his legs weel in them,
   They'll come up till his knei—
Aw'm Pawkie Paiterson's auld grey yaud,
   Sei how they're guidin' mei!

And as for Peggie Duncan,
   She is a bonnie lass,

Sae Aw wull leave her ma eyn holes
　To bei a keekin' glass—
To gar her eyn sei streichter,
　For they of'en stand aglei—
Aw'm Pawkie Paiterson's auld grey yaud,
　Sei how they're guidin' mei!

As for the minister o' Wilton,
　His coat it is worn thin,
And for to keep him thrae the cauld
　Aw'll leave him ma auld skin,
Wi' hide and hair, to keep him warm
　As lang as it's dune mei—
Aw'm Pawkie Paiterson's auld grey yaud,
　Sei how they're guidin' mei!

And as for Stonie Stewart,
　He's of'en scarce o' stanes,
And for to mend his auld fail dykes
　Aw'll leave him ma auld banes;
And a' the callants o' Hawick Loan
　Wull make banefires o' mei—
Aw'm Pawkie Paiterson's auld grey yaud,
　Sae that's the end o' mei!"

*George Ballantyne* (*fl. 1811*).

## THE TAYLOR HE CAM HERE TO SEW

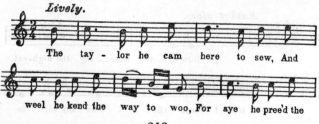

Lively.

The tay - lor he cam here to sew, And
weel he kend the way to woo, For aye he pree'd the

213

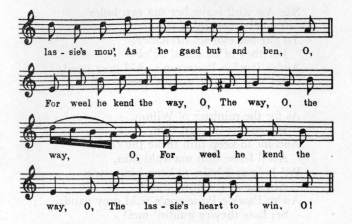

las - sie's mou', As he gaed but and ben, O,

For weel he kend the way, O, The way, O, the

way, O, For weel he kend the

way, O, The las - sie's heart to win, O!

The taylor rase and shook his duds,
The flaes they flew awa in cluds!
And them that stay'd gat fearfu' thuds,—
The taylor prov'd a man, O!
For now it was the gloamin,
The gloamin, the gloamin,
For now it was the gloamin,
When a' to rest are gaun, O!

*Burns*

## THE BOATMAN

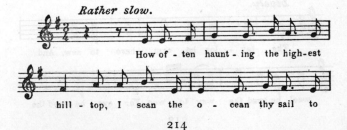

*Rather slow.*

How of - ten haunt - ing the high-est

hill - top, I scan the o - cean thy sail to

see! Wilt come to night, love, wilt come to-
mor - row, Or ev - er come, love, to com-fort me?
Fhir a bha - ta, no ho - ro ei - le, Fhir a
bha - ta, no ho - ro ei - le, Fhir a
bha - ta, no ho - ro ei - le, O fare thee
well, love, wher-e'er thou be.

There's not a hamlet, too well I know it,
Where you go wand'ring or stay awhile,
But all its old folk you win with talking,
And charm its maidens with song and smile.

    *Chorus.*

Dost thou remember the promise made me,
The tartan plaidie, the silken gown,
The ring of gold with thy hair and portrait?
That gown and ring I will never own.

    *Chorus.*               *Anon.*

# CHARLIE IS MY DARLING

*Joyfully.*

Oh! Charlie is my darling, my darling, my darling, Oh!

*Fine.*

Char - lie is my dar - ling, The young Chev - a - lier.

'Twas on a monday morn-ing, Right ear-ly in the year, When

Char - lie came to our town, The young Cheva - lier.

As he cam' marchin' up the street
The pipes played loud and clear,
And a' the folk came rinnin' out
To meet the Chevalier.

*Anon.*

# KATE DALRYMPLE

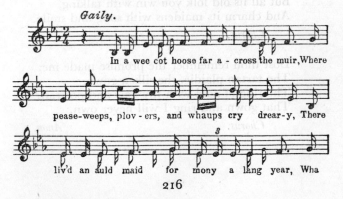

*Gaily.*

In a wee cot hoose far a - cross the muir, Where

pease-weeps, plov - ers, and whaups cry drear-y, There

liv'd an auld maid for mony a lang year, Wha

216

ne'er a woo-er did e'er ca' dear-ie. A
lane-ly lass was Kate Dal-rym-ple, A
thruf-ty quean was Kate Dal-rym-ple, Nae
mu-sic ex-cept-in' the clear burnie's wim-ple, Was
heard rovin' the dwellin' o' Kate Dal-rym-ple.

Her face had a smack o' the gruesome an' grim,
    That did frae the fash o' a' wooers defend her,
Her lang Roman nose nearly met wi' her chin,
    And brang folk in mind o' the auld witch o' Endor.
A wiggle in her walk had Kate Dalrymple,
A snivel in her talk had Kate Dalrymple,
An' mony a cornelian an' cairngorm pimple,
Did blaze on the dun face o' Kate Dalrymple.


But mony are the ups an' the douns in life,
    When the dice-box o' fate's jumbled tapsalteerie;
Sae Kate fell heiress to a rich frien's estate,
    An' nae longer for wooers had she cause to weary.
The squire cam' a wooin' syne o' Kate Dalrymple;
The lawyer, scrapin', bowin', fan' out Kate Dalrymple,
On ilk wooer's face was seen love's smiling dimple,
For noo she's nae mair Kate, but Miss Dalrymple.

She'd aftentimes thocht, when she dwelt by hersel',
  She could wed Willie Speedyspool, the surkin'
      weaver;
An' noo unto Will she the secret did tell,
  Wha for love or for int'rest, did kindly receive her,
He flang by his treadles sune for Kate Dalrymple,
He brunt a' his treadles doun for Kate Dalrymple,
Tho' his richt e'e doth skellie, an' his left leg doth
      limp ill,
He's won the heart and got the hand o' Kate
  Dalrymple.

*Anon.*

## I DINNA LIKE McFARLANE

*As speedy as the words permit.*

A - fore that I'd be terr-a-neezed as I this file hae
been, I'd rai-ther rin' frae here tae Birse wi'
peez in baith ma sheen, I'd rai-ther dee for
want o' breath than pine for want o' love, And it's
a' be-cause Mc - Far-lane mer-rit Sou - sie.
Sou-sie's kan-kert faith-er wi' mine could niv-er

gree, And aye fan I'd gang ower that gait he'd turn his dog at me. So I sent ma freen Mc - Far-lane doon to see fit he could dee, Mc - Far-lane o' the Sprots o' Bur-nie-boo-zie.

CHORUS.

I din-na like Mc - Far-lane I'm safe e-nough tae state. His lug wad cast a sha-dow ower a sax - fit gate. He's soft as on-y gob-lin' and slid-dery as a skate Mc - Far-lane o' the Sprots o' Burn-ie-boo-zie.

McFarlane spak nae wird for me but plenty for
    himsel',
He reesed the lassie's barley scones, her kebbick and
    her kail.
Her faither cried oot "Sprottie, man, ye should try
    yer luck yersel' ",

Tae M<sup>c</sup>Farlane o' the Sprots o' Burnieboozie.
Though M<sup>c</sup>Farlane is the grimmest chiel for twenty
    miles aroon,
Though they buy his fottygraph tae fleg the rottens
    frae a toon,
He kittled up his spunk at this and spiered gin she'd
    come doon
And be mistress o' the Sprots o' Burnieboozie.

### Chorus

I dinna like M<sup>c</sup>Farlane, I tell ye it's a fac';
He's a nose for splittin' hailstanes and a humphy
    back;
He's legs like guttaperka, ilka step his knees gang
    knack—
M<sup>c</sup>Farlane o' the Sprots o' Burnieboozie.

Oh, a dirl o' the teethache's nae particularly sweet,
Bit love's the only power on earth that iver gait me
    greet;
It's like kittlie chilblains roon yer heart instead o'
    yer feet—
They were aggravated wi' the sicht o' Sousie.
Noo freens and kind philosophers, ye've heard what
    me befell;
Niver lippen tae the middle man, bit dee yer work
    yersel',
Or I'll bet my hinmost sarkit ye're a day ahin the
    markit
As fan I sent Jock M<sup>c</sup>Farlane roon tae Sousie.

### Chorus

I dinna like M<sup>c</sup>Farlane, it's afa' bit it's true;
A pewter speen wis tint in Jock M<sup>c</sup>Farlane's moo.
He couldnae weel be grimmer, sups his brose wi' the
    skimmer—
M<sup>c</sup>Farlane o' the Sprots o' Burnieboozie.

*G. Bruce Thomson*

## WIDOW TWANKEY'S SONG

(Edinburgh Pantomime Ditty)

*Philosophically.*

I yince was young and fresh and fair, But
noo I'm auld an' yelly I
crossed the sea tae marry ma Joe, wha'd
set-tled out in In-dy; But fand him mairrit when
I got there, Sae there was a bit o' a shin-dy,
Lil-ly-loo-ral loor-al-lay lil-ly loo-ral li-do.

Scot-land is ma nat-ive place, I was
born in Por-to-bel-ly

But I showed him that for his sake
I wasna goin' to turn dwiny,
So I took a place as a nursery maid
Wi' a faimly goin' to Chiny.
I wished him joy o' his dusky dear,
Frae now till Kingdom come, sirs,
And hoped he might hae a dizzen weans
And every yin black as the lum, sirs.
      Lilly, looral, etc.

I hadna been in Chiny lang
When I received attention
Frae a gentleman wha garments made
Which I divna like tae mention.
Mr Mustapha wis his name,
A decent, honest man, sirs,
And his pigtail it was siccan a length
It measured a yaird and a span, sirs.

      Lilly, looral, etc.


Mr Mustapha had but ae faut,
An' that was smokin' opium.
O sirs, I flighted wi' him tae quat
Or else I widna stop wi' him.
Whenever he went awa' frae hame
I was vexed aboot his business,
He intae an opium public-hoose,
Syne in a state o' dizziness.

      Lilly, looral, etc.


Mr Mustapha, ye must stop these ways
And try yer ways tae mend, man,
Or Mr Mustapha, ye can tak' ma word
Ye'll hae a maist a'fa end, man.
An' sae it happened as ae nicht
I was sittin' at ma tea, sirs,
He was brocht hame deid, and noo I'm left
A widda, as ye see, sirs.

      Lilly, looral, etc.

*Words ascribed to Kenneth Maitland*

# THE LUM HAT WANTIN' THE CROON

*With spirit.*

The burn was big wi' spate, An' there cam' tum-blin' doon Tap-sal-tee-rie the half o' a gate, An auld fish hake, an' a great muckle skate, An' a lum hat wantin' the croon ———

The auld wife stood on the bank
As they gaed soomin' roon,
She took a guid look, and then, says she,
"There's food an' there's raiment gaun to the sea,
An' a lum hat wantin' the croon".

So she gruppit the branch o' a saugh,
An' she kickit aff ane o' her shoon,
An' she stuck oot her fit, but it caught in the gate,
An' awa' she went wi' the great muckle skate,
An' the lum hat wantin' the croon.

223

She floated fu' mony a mile,
Past cottage and village and toon,
She'd an awfu' time astride o' the gate,
Though it seemed to 'gree fine wi' the great muckle
    skate,
An' the lum hat wantin' the croon.


A fisher was walkin' the deck,
By the licht o' his pipe and the moon,
When he sees an auld body astride o' a gate,
Come bobbin' alang in the waves wi' a skate,
An' a lum hat wantin' the croon.


"There's a man overboard", cries he;
"Ye leear", quo' she, "I'll droon.
A man on a boord? It's a wife on a gate,
It's auld Mistress Mackintosh here wi' a skate
An' a lum hat wantin' the croon".


Was she nippit to death at the Pole?
Has India bakit her broon?
I canna tell that, but whatever her fate,
I'll wager ye'll find it was shared by a gate,
An' a lum hat wantin' the croon.


There's a moral attached to my song,
On greed ye should aye gie a froon,
When ye think o' the wife that was lost for a gate,
An' auld fish hake and a great muckle skate,
An' a lum hat wantin' the croon.

*David Rorie, M.D.*

224

# FLAT-FOOTED JEAN

*Sentimentally.*

The first time I met my Jean, she was

on - ly sev - en - teen, That's the

age that's so po - et - i - cal - ly

sweet; In my eyes she'd no' a fault, Tho' she

walked a wee bit hault For the

want o' on - y in - steps to her feet.

**CHORUS.**

Jean, Jean, my bon - ny bon - ny Jean,

Come to my airms ance a - gain, For they

say your feet are flat, but you're

nane the waur o' that, You're my

225

I

bon - ny blue - eyed Scotch las - sie Jean.

'Twas in Edinburry toon that we spent wer honey-
    moon,
    And I wantit Jeannie's photo taen in state,
But the artist said it must no' be full length, but a bust,
    For he couldna get her feet intae the plate.

        *Chorus.*

As the roads was mud and glaur, we took a tramway
    caur
    For to get a wee bit hurl alang the street;
The conductor said, "My lass! gin I'm to let ye pass
    Ye mun tak' twa extra tickets for your feet".

        *Chorus.*

Jeannie's far ower auld a tike for to learn to ride a
    bike,
    And I always tell her that it's just as weel,
For the bike would soon be roupit, as she'd get maist
    awfu' coupit
    From her feet aye gettin' tangled in the wheel.
        *Chorus.*

Noo my Jeannie's auld and worn, and her weddin'-
    goon is torn
    A' in pieces for to mak' the bairns neat,
But this I'll say to you, "If your lass is guid and true,
    Weel, ye needna fash yersels aboot her feet".

        *Chorus.*

                    *R. T. Boothby*

# WAE'S ME FOR PRINCE CHARLIE

*With sentiment.*

A wee bird cam' to our ha' door, He war-bled sweet and clear-ly: And aye the o'er-come o' his sang, Was "Wae's me for Prince Char-lie."

Oh! when I heard the bonnie, bonnie bird! The tears came drap-pin' rare-ly: I took my bon-net aff my head For weel I lo'ed Prince Char-lie.

Quoth I, "My bird, my bonnie, bonnie bird,
  Is that a tale ye borrow?
Or is't some words ye've learnt by rote,
  Or a lilt o' dool and sorrow?"
"Oh! no, no, no!" the wee bird sang,
  "I've flown since morning early;

But sic a day o' wind and rain!—
　　Oh! wae's me for Prince Charlie.

"Dark night cam' on, the tempest howl'd
　　Loud o'er the hills and valleys;
And where was't that your Prince lay down,
　　Whase hame should be a palace?
He row'd him in a Highland plaid,
　　Which cover'd him but sparely,
And slept beneath a bush o' broom—
　　Oh! wae's me for Prince Charlie."

*William Glen*

# THE HEN IT IS A BONNY BIRD
## A Round for four Voices

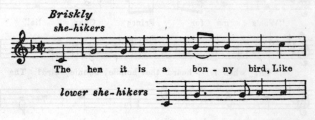

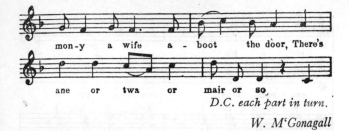

mon-y a wife a - boot the door, There's

ane or twa or mair or so,

*D.C. each part in turn.*

*W. M'Gonagall*

## HORNIE GOLLOCH

Round parts for two sopranos or two tenors: *faux bourdon* for
two basses or a tenor and a bass

*Grimly.*

I.

The

II.

Hor - nie gol-loch, hor - nie gol-loch,

hor - nie gol-loch's an awe-some beast

The hor - nie gol-loch's an

hor - nie gol-loch, hor - nie gol-loch,

# DAILY PRESS

an' a for - ky tai - lie

han tle o' feet an' a

hor - nie golloch.

The

for - ky tai - lie

Ah! For - ky tai - lie

*Repeat last bar, as often as you like, fading away.*

*Anon.*

## DAILY PRESS

Round for four Voices entering two bars apart

*Loud and urgent.*

Dun - dee Post, Post! Dun - dee Post, Post! Evening

News! Even - ing News! Times, Times! Times,

Times! Glasgow Her - ald! Glasgow Her - ald!

# LE BOURDON

Round for four voices entering two bars apart

*Bell-like.*

Le bourdon dit à la clochet - te, "tais toi donc,

mé - chan - te so - net - te Boum - bon, boum - bon!"

La clo - chet - te lui ré - pond din - don, din - don, din - don.

# WHEN THE KYE COMES HAME

*Joyously.*

Come, all ye jol - ly shep - herds, That

whis - tle through the glen, I'll

tell ye o' a se - cret that

cour - tiers din - na ken. What

is the great - est bliss That the

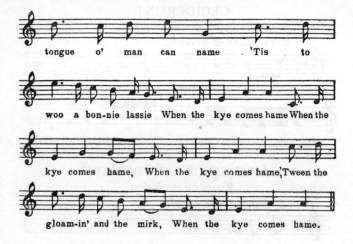

tongue o' man can name 'Tis to
woo a bon-nie lassie When the kye comes hame When the
kye comes hame, When the kye comes hame,'Tween the
gloam-in' and the mirk, When the kye comes hame.

'Tis not beneath the burgonet
Nor yet beneath the crown,
'Tis not on couch o' velvet,
Nor yet on bed o' down ;
'Tis beneath the spreading birch,
In the dell without a name,
Wi' a bonnie, bonnie lassie,
When the kye comes hame.

Awa' wi' fame and fortune,
What comforts can they gi'e?
And a' the arts that prey upon
Man's life and libertie!
Gi'e me the highest joy
That the heart o' man can frame,
My bonnie, bonnie lassie,
When the kye comes hame.

*James Hogg*

233 I₂

## CECIDERUNT

Round for four Voices entering a bar apart

*With marked accents.*

Ce - ci - de - runt in pro - fun - dum,

summum A - ris-to - te-les Pla-to et Eu-ri - pi - des.

## GAILY SINGS THE DONKEY

### Round for two Voices

*Sadly but not slowly.*

Gai - ly sings the don-key As he goes to grass,

If you don't sing sweeter, then you are an ass, Hee-

haw! Hee-haw, hee - haw, hee-haw, hee-haw.

## CAULD BLAWS THE WIND

*Slow and complaining.*

Cauld blaws the wind frae east to west, The

drift is dri - ving sair - ly, Sae

loud and shrill I hear the blast I'm

, sure it's win - ter fair - ly.

CHORUS.

Up in the morn - ing's no' for me,

Up in the morn - ing ear - ly! When

a' the hills are covered wi' snaw, I'm

sure it's win - ter fair - ly.

The birds sit chittering in the thorn,
   A' day they fare but sparely;
And lang's the night frae e'en to morn—
   I'm sure it's winter fairly.

*Burns*

## O MAY THY MORN WAS NE'ER SAE SWEET

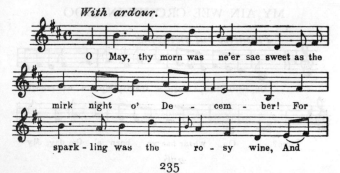

*With ardour.*

O May, thy morn was ne'er sae sweet as the

mirk night o' De - cem - ber! For

spark - ling was the ro - sy wine, And

235

pri - vate was the cham - ber:

And dear was she I dare - na name, But

I will ay re - mem - ber: And

dear was she I dare - na name: But

I will ay re - mem - ber.

And here's to them that, like oursel,
    Can push about the jorum;
And here's to them that wish us weel—
    May a' that's guid watch o'er them;
And here's to them we dare na tell,
    The dearest o' the quorum!

*Burns*

## MY AIN WEE CROODLIN' DOO

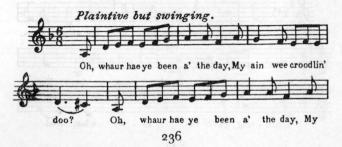

*Plaintive but swinging.*

Oh, whaur hae ye been a' the day, My ain wee croodlin'

doo? Oh, whaur hae ye been a' the day, My

# MY AIN WEE CROODLIN' DOO

ain wee crood-lin' doo? —  Oh, I hae been to my

Step - Mith - er: Mak' my bed, Mam - my,  noo, —

**CHORUS.**

Mak' my bed, Mam - my,  noo. ——

Oh, what did your stepmither gie to you, } *(bis)*
　My ain wee croodlin' doo?
She gied to me a wee, wee fish;
　Mak' my bed, mammy, noo. *(bis)*

Oh, what did ye do wi' the banes o' the fish, } *(bis)*
　My ain wee croodlin' doo?
I gie'd them to a wee, wee doug;
　Mak' my bed, mammy, noo. *(bis)*

Oh, what did the wee, wee douggie do, } *(bis)*
　My ain wee croodlin' doo?
It boo'd its heid, lay doon and dee'd
　As I fu' sune maun do.
　Mak' my bed, mammy, noo.

*Old Ballad*

237

# THE BARNYARDS O' DELGATY

**Decisively.**

In New Deer parish I was born, A
child of youth to Meth - lick came; And
gin' ye'll no be - lieve my word the
sess - ion clerk will tell the same.

CHORUS.

Lin - ten ad - ie, toor - in ad - ie,
Lin - ten ad - ie toor-in ae, Lin - ten, lour - in,
lour - in, lour - in, lin - ten lour-in, lour-in lee.

To bide upon my father's farm,
  That was never my intent;
I lo'ed the lasses double weel,
  And aye the weary drap o' drink.

  *Chorus.*—Linten adie, toorin adie, etc.


As I cam' in by Netherdale,
  At Turra market for to fee,

I fell in wi' a farmer chiel
  Frae the Barnyards o' Delgaty.
    *Chorus.*


He promised me the ae best pair
  I ever set my e'en upon;
When I ga'ed hame to Barnyards
  There was naething there but skin and bone.
    *Chorus.*


The auld black horse sat on his rump,
  The auld white meer lay on her wime,
And a' that I could hup and crack,
  They wouldna rise at yokin' time.
    *Chorus.*


Meg Macpherson mak's my brose,
  An' her and me we canna gree;
First a mote and then a knot,
  And aye the ither jilp o' bree.
    *Chorus.*


I can drink and nae be drunk,
  I can fight and nae be slain,
I can court anither's lass,
  And aye be welcome to my ain.
    *Chorus.*


My can'le noo it is brunt oot,
  The snotter's fairly on the wane;
Sae fare ye weel, ye Barnyards,
  Ye'll never catch me here again.
    *Chorus.*

            *Anon.*

## DRUMDELGIE

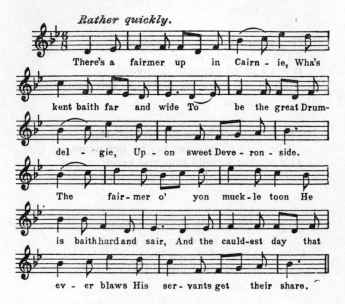

*Rather quickly.*

There's a fairmer up in Cairnie, Wha's
kent baith far and wide To be the great Drumdelgie, Upon sweet Deveronside.
The fairmer o' yon muckle toon He
is baith hard and sair, And the cauldest day that
ever blaws His servants get their share.

At five o'clock we quickly rise
  And hurry doon the stair;
It's there to corn our horses,
  Likewise to straik their hair.
Syne, after working half an hour
  Each to the kitchen goes,
It's there to get our breakfast,
  Which generally is brose.

When daylicht does begin to peep,
  And the sky begins to clear,
The foreman he cries out, "My lads,
  Ye'll stay nae langer here!

There's sax o' you'll gae to the ploo,
  And twa will drive the neeps,
And the owsen they'll be after you
  Wi' strae raips roun' their queets."


But when that we were gyaun furth,
  And turnin' out to yoke,
The snaw dang on sae thick and fast
  That we were like to choke.
The frost had been sae very hard,
  The ploo she wadna go;
And sae our cairting days commenced
  Amang the frost and snow.


Our horses being but young and sma'
  The shafts they didna fill,
And they aft required the saiddler
  To pull them up the hill.
But we will sing our horses' praise,
  Though they be young and sma',
They far outshine the Broadlands anes
  That gang sae full and braw.


Sae fare ye well, Drumdelgie,
  For I maun gang awa;
Sae fare ye weel, Drumdelgie,
  Your weety weather and a'.
Sae fareweel, Drumdelgie,
  I bid ye a' adieu;
I leave ye as I got ye—
  A maist unceevil crew.

*Anon.*

# THE BONNIE WEE TOBACCO BOYS

**Marching time.**

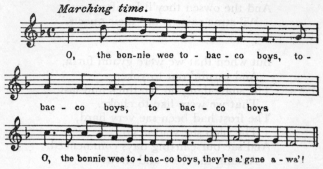

O, the bon-nie wee to-bac-co boys, to-
bac-co boys, to-bac-co boys
O, the bonnie wee to-bac-co boys, they're a' gane a-wa'!

*Glasgow Street Ballad.*

# JOHNNIE SANGSTER

**In walking time.**

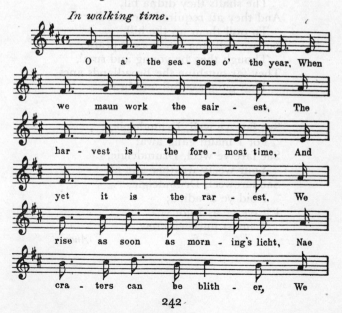

O a' the sea-sons o' the year, When
we maun work the sair-est, The
har-vest is the fore-most time, And
yet it is the rar-est, We
rise as soon as morn-ing's licht, Nae
cra-ters can be blith-er, We

buck - le on our fing - ers steebs And
fol - low oot the Scyth - er.

CHORUS.

For you John - nie, you John - nie,
you John - nie Sang - ster, I'll
trim the gav - el o' my sheaf, For
ye're the gal - lant band - ster.

A mornin' piece to line oor cheek
    Afore that we gae forder,
Wi' clouds o' blue tobacco reek,
    We then set oot in order.
The sheaves are risin' thick and fast,
    And Johnnie he maun bind them;
The busy group, for fear they stick,
    Can scarcely look behind them.

        *Chorus.*—For you, Johnnie, etc.

I'll gie ye bands that winna slip,
    I'll pleat them weel and thraw them,
I'm sure they winna tine the grip,
    Hooever well ye draw them.
I'll lay my leg oot ower the sheaf,
    And draw the band sae handy,

Wi' ilka strae as straucht's a rash,
   And that will be the dandy.

     *Chorus.*—For you, Johnnie, etc.


If e'er it chance to be my lot
   To get a gallant bandster,
I'll gar him wear a gentle coat,
   And bring him gowd in handfu's.
But Johnnie he can please himsel',
   I wadna wish him blinket;
Sae aifter he has brewed his ale
   He can sit doon and drink it.

     *Chorus.*—For you, Johnnie, etc.


A dainty cowie in the byre,
   For butter and for cheeses;
A grumphie, feedin' in the sty,
   Wad keep the hoose in greases;
A bonnie ewie in the bucht
   Wad help to creesh the ladle,
And we'll get ruffs o' cannie woo'
   Wad help to theek the cradle.

     *Chorus.*—For you, Johnnie, etc.

                    *Anon.*


# THE SOUTERS O' SELKIRK

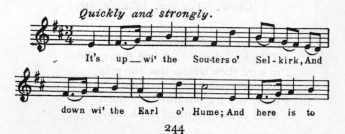

*Quickly and strongly.*

It's up wi' the Souters o' Selkirk, And down wi' the Earl o' Hume; And here is to

244

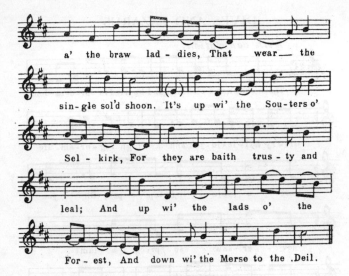

a' the braw lad-dies, That wear— the sin-gle sol'd shoon. It's up wi' the Sou-ters o' Sel-kirk, For they are baith trus-ty and leal; And up wi' the lads o' the For-est, And down wi' the Merse to the Deil.

It's fye upon yellow and yellow,
And fye upon yellow and green;
But up wi' the true blue and scarlet,
And up wi' the single sol'd shoon.
It's up wi' the Souters o' Selkirk,
For they are baith trusty and leal;
And up wi' the men o' the forest,
And down wi' the Merse to the deil.

O mitres are made for noddles,
But feet they are made for shoon,
And fame is as sib to Selkirk
As licht is true to the moon.
There sits a souter in Selkirk,
Wha sings as he draws his thread,
There's gallant souters in Selkirk,
As lang's there's water in Tweed.

*Anon.*

# DIVES AND LAZARUS

*With conviction.*

There once was a rich man, and he lived in Jer-u-sa-lem,

Glo - ry hal-le-lu-jah and a high rog-er-am. He

wore a shin-ing top-per, Oh you

nev-er saw so spruce a lum!

Glo - ry hal - le-lu-jah and a high rog-er-am.

CHORUS.

High rog-er-am! Low rog-er-am!

Skin-a-ma-link-a-doo-dle, and a high rog-er-am!

To the rich man's door there came a human wreckium,
    Glory, hallelujah, etc.
With a hooker-doon and a grauvat round his neckium,
    Glory, hallelujah, etc.
        *Chorus.*

The poor man humbly begged a jelly-piecium
The rich man swore at him and sent for the policium,
        *Chorus.*

The poor man died and he went up to Heavenium,
And canoodled with the angels till a quarter past
    elevenium.

> *Chorus.*

The rich man died, but he didn't fare so wellium—
He fell in with a chemist who was liquefying helium.

> *Chorus.*

The rich man was thirsty and loudly rang the bellium,
But Satan up and yelled at him, "This isn't an
    hotelium!"

> *Chorus.*

The rich man begged for some whisky to consolium,
But Satan's only answer was to shovel on more
    coalium.

> *Chorus.*

The moral of my song is that riches are as smokium,
So let us thank our stars that we're all stoney-
    brokium.

> *Chorus.*                                          *Anon.*

## CA' THE EWES TO THE KNOWES

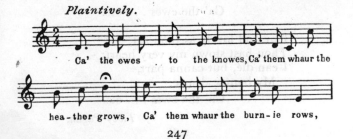

*Plaintively.*

Ca' the ewes to the knowes, Ca' them whaur the
hea-ther grows, Ca' them whaur the burn-ie rows,

My bon-nie dear-ie: Hark the Mav-is
ev'n-in' sang, Sound-in' Clu-den's woods a-mang;
Then a fauld-in let us gang, My bon-nie dear-ie.

We'll gae down by Cluden side,
Through the hazels spreading wide,
O'er the waves that sweetly glide
    To the moor sae clearly.

        Ca' the ewes . . . etc.

Yonder Cluden's silent towers,
Where, at moonshine midnight hours,
O'er the dewy bending flowers
    Fairies dance sae cheerie.

        Ca' the ewes . . . etc.

Ghaist nor bogle shalt thou fear;
Thou'rt to love and heaven sae dear,
Nocht o' ill may come thee near,
    My bonnie dearie.

        Ca' the ewes . . . etc.

Fair and lovely as thou art,
Thou hast stown my very heart;
I can die, but canna part,
    My bonnie dearie.

        Ca' the ewes . . . etc.

*Tibby Pagan.*

248

# YE BANKS AND BRAES O' BONNIE DOON

*As usually.*

Ye banks and braes o' bon-nie Doon, How can ye bloom sae fresh and fair? How can ye chant ye lit-tle birds And I sae wea-ry fu' o' care? Ye'll break my heart, ye war-bling bird That war-bles on the flow-'ry thorn Ye mind me o' de-part-ed joys, De-part-ed nev-er to re-turn.

Oft ha'e I roved by bonnie Doon,
By morning and by ev'ning shine,

249

To hear the birds sing o' their loves
As fondly once I sang o' mine.
Wi' lightsome heart I stretched my hand
And pu'd a rose-bud from the tree;
But my fause lover stole the rose
And left, and left the thorn wi' me.

*Burns*

## AULD LANG SYNE

*With feeling.*

Should auld acquaintance be forgot, And never brought to mind? Should auld acquain-tance be forgot, And days o' lang syne? For auld lang syne, my dear, For auld lang syne; We'll tak' a cup o' kind-ness yet, for auld lang syne.

We twa ha'e run about the braes
And pu'd the gowans fine,
But we've wander'd mony a weary foot,
Sin' auld lang syne.

*Chorus.*

250

We twa ha'e paidelt in the burn,
 Frae morning sun till dine;
But seas between us braid ha'e roared
 Sin' auld lang syne.
  *Chorus.*


And surely ye'll be your pint-stoup,
 And surely I'll be mine;
And we'll tak' a cup o' kindness yet,
 For auld lang syne.
  *Chorus.*


And here's a hand, my trusty fere,
 And gi'es a hand o' thine;
And we'll take a richt gude willie-waught,
 For auld lang syne.
  *Chorus.*

       *Burns*


## MAGGIE LAUDER

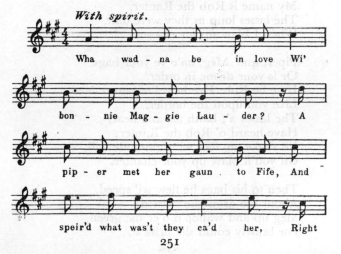

**With spirit.**

Wha wad - na be in love Wi'
bon - nie Mag - gie Lau - der? A
pip - er met her gaun to Fife, And
speir'd what was't they ca'd her, Right

251

scorn - ful - ly she an - swer'd him, "Be -
gone ye hal - lan - sha - ker! Jog
on your gate, ye blad - der - skate, My
name is Mag - gie Lau - der."

Maggie, quo' he, an by my bags,
I'm fidgin' fain to see thee;
Sit down by me, my bonnie bird,
In troth I winna steer thee:
For I'm a piper to my trade,
My name is Rob the Ranter,
The lasses loup as they were daft,
When I blaw up my chanter.

Piper, quo' Meg, ha'e ye your bags?
Or is your drone in order?
If ye be Rob, I've heard of you,
Live you upon the border?
The lasses a', baith far and near,
Have heard o' Rob the Ranter;
I'll shake my foot wi' right gude will,
Gif you'll blaw up your chanter.

Then to his bags he flew wi' speed,
About the drone he twisted;
Meg up and wallop'd o'er the green,
For brawly could she brisk it,

Weel done! quo' he—play up! quo' she;
Weel bobb'd! quo' Rob the Ranter;
'Tis worth my while to play indeed,
When I ha'e sic a dancer.

Weel ha'e you play'd your part, quo' Meg,
Your cheeks are like the crimson;
There's nane in Scotland plays sae weel,
Since we lost Habbie Simson.
I've lived in Fife, baith maid and wife,
These ten years and a quarter,
Gin ye should come to Anster fair,
Speir ye for Maggie Lauder.

*Ascribed to Francis Semple*

## BREAD AND CHEESE AND ONIONS

*With conviction.*

Take a toddle for a nice long walk in the
coun-try ev-'ry morn-ing, O-pen your mouth and
swallow all the air and when you're tired and
yawning, Step in-to a quiet lit-tle pub, sit
down and rest your bun-ions Call for a pint of
mild and bitter and some bread and cheese and on-ions.

*Anon.*

253

## ANDRO WI' HIS CUTTY GUN

*Dancingly.*

Blithe, blithe and mer-ry was she, Blithe was she but and ben; And well she lo'ed a Haw-ick gill, And leugh to see a tappit hen. She took me in and set me down And heght to keep me law-ing free; But, cunning carline that she was, She gart me birl my baw-bee.

We lo'ed the liquor well enough;
But waes my heart my cash was done,
Before that I had quench'd my drouth,
And laith I was to pawn my shoon.
When we had three times toom'd our stoup,
And the niest chappin new begun,
Wha started in to heeze up our hope,
But Andro wi' his cutty gun.

The carline brought her kebbuck ben,
With girdle-cakes weel toasted brown,
Well does the canny kimmer ken,
They gar the swats gae glibber down.
We ca'd the bicker aft about;
Till dawning we ne'er gee'd our bun,
And aye the cleanest drinker out,
Was Andro wi' his cutty gun.

He did like ony mavis sing,
And as I in his oxter sat,
He ca'd me aye his bonnie thing,
And mony a sappy kiss I gat.
I hae been east, I hae been west,
I hae been far ayont the sun;
But the blithest lad that e'er I saw,
Was Andro wi' his cutty gun.

*Anon.*

## CORN RIGS

*Lyrically and rather fast.*

It was u-pon a Lam-mas night, When corn___ rigs are bon-nie, O, Be-neath the moon's un-cloud-ed light, I held___ a-wa' to___ An-nie,___ O; The time flew by___ wi'___ tent-less heed, Till 'tween the___ late and ear-ly,___ O, Wi' sma' per-sua-sion she a-greed___ To

see me— thro' the bar - ley, — O.

Corn — rigs, and bar - ley rigs,

Corn — rigs are bon - nie — O, I'll

ne'er for - get that hap - py— night, — A-

mang the— rigs wi'— An - nie, — O.

The sky was blue, the wind was still,
    The moon was shining clearly, O:
I set her down wi' right good will,
    Amang the rigs o' barley, O:
I kent her heart was a' my ain;
    I loved her most sincerely, O;
I kissed her ower and ower again,
    Amang the rigs o' barley, O.

    *Chorus.*

I lock'd her in my fond embrace!
    Her heart was beating rarely, O:
My blessings on that happy place,
    Amang the rigs o' barley, O!
But by the moon and stars so bright,
    That shone that hour so clearly, O!
She aye shall bless that happy night,
    Amang the rigs o' barley, O.

    *Chorus.*

256

I hae been blithe wi' comrades dear,
   I hae been merry drinkin' O;
I hae been joyfu' gath'rin gear;
   I hae been happy thinkin', O:
Bu a' the pleasures e'er I saw,
   Tho' three times doubled fairly, O,
That happy night was worth them a',
   Amang the rigs o' barley, O.

    *Chorus.*

        *Burns*

# GREEN GROW THE RASHES, O!

*With conviction.*

There's nought but care on ev-'ry han', In
ev-'ry hour that pass-es, O; What
sig-ni-fies the life o' man, An'
'twere na for the lass-es, O.

CHORUS.

Green grow the rash-es, O!
Green grow the rash-es, O! The

257          K

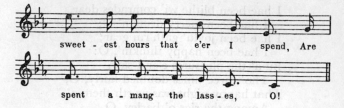

sweet - est hours that e'er I spend, Are

spent a - mang the lass - es, O!

The warldly race may riches chase,
    An' riches still may fly them, O;
An' though at last they catch them fast,
    Their hearts can ne'er enjoy them, O.

*Chorus.*

Gie me a cannie hour at e'en,
    My arms about my dearie, O;
An' warldly cares, an' warldly men,
    May a' gae tapsalteerie, O.

*Chorus.*

For you sae douce, wha sneer at this,
    Ye're nought but senseless asses, O;
The wisest man the warld e'er saw,
    He dearly lo'ed the lasses, O.

*Chorus.*

Auld Nature swears, the lovely dears,
    Her noblest work she classes, O;
Her 'prentice han' she tried on man
    And then she made the lasses, O.

*Chorus.*

*Burns*

## THE FLOWERS OF THE FOREST

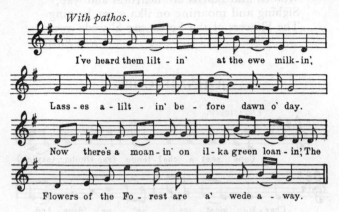

*With pathos.*

I've heard them lilt - in' at the ewe milk-in',
Lass - es a - lilt - in' be - fore dawn o' day.
Now there's a moan-in' on il - ka green loan-in', The
Flowers of the Fo - rest are a' wede a - way.

At buchts, in the morning, nae blythe lads are
    scorning,
The lasses are lonely, and dowie, and wae;
Nae daffin', nae gabbin', but sighing and sabbing,
Ilk ane lifts her leglin and hies away.

[In hairst, at the shearing, nae youths now are jeering,
The bandsters are lyart, and runkled, and grey;
At fair, or at preaching, nae wooing, nae fleeching—
The Flowers of the Forest are a' wede away.

At e'en, at the gloaming, nae swankies are roaming
'Bout stacks, wi' the lasses at bogle to play;
But ilk ane sits drearie, lamenting her dearie—
The Flowers of the Forest are a' wede away.

Dule and wae for the order, sent our lads to the Border!
The English, for ance, by guile wan the day;
The Flowers of the Forest, that foucht aye the fore-
    most,
The prime o' our land, are cauld in the clay.]

259

We hear nae mair lilting at our yowe-milking,
Women and bairns are heartless and wae;
Sighing and moaning on ilka green loaning—
The Flowers of the Forest are a' wede away.

*Jean Elliot*

## JOHNNIE COPE

*Derisively.*

Cope sent a chal-lenge frae Dunbar, (saying)
Char-lie, meet me an' ye daur, And
I'll learn you the art o' war, If you'll
meet me in the morn - ing.
O Hey! Johnnie Cope are ye wauk-in' yet? Or
are your drums a beat - in' yet? If
ye are wauk-in' I would wait to
gang to the coals in the morn - ing.

When Charlie look'd the letter upon,
He drew his sword the scabbard from,
Come, follow me, my merry men,
And we'll meet Johnnie Cope i' the morning, O
Hey! etc.

Now, Johnnie, be as good as your word,
Come, let us try baith fire and sword,
And dinna flee like a frighted bird
That's chased frae its nest i' the morning.
Hey! etc.

When Johnnie Cope he heard of this,
He thought it wadna be amiss
To ha'e a horse in readiness,
To flee awa' in the morning.
Hey! etc.

Fye now, Johnnie, get up an' rin,
The Highland bagpipes mak' a din;
It's best to sleep in a hale skin,
For 'twill be a bluidie morning.
Hey! etc.

When Johnnie Cope to Dunbar came,
They speir'd at him where's a' your men?
The deil confound me gin' I ken,
For I left them a' in the morning.
Hey! etc.

Now, Johnnie, troth ye were na blate,
To come wi' the news o' your ain defeat,
And leave your men in sic a strait,
So early in the morning.
Hey! etc.

In faith, quo' Johnnie, I got sic flegs
Wi' their claymores and filabegs,

If I face them, deil break my legs,
So I wish you a' good morning. Hey! etc.

*Ascribed to Adam Skirving*

## A BRISK YOUNG LAD

*Lively.*

There cam' a young man to my dad-die's door, My dad-die's door, my dad-die's door, There cam' a young man to my dad-die's door, A-seeking me— to woo.— And wow! but he was a braw young lad, A brisk young lad, and a braw young lad, And wow! but he was a braw young lad, Cam' seek-ing me— to woo.—

But I was baking when he cam',
When he cam', when he cam',
I took him in and ga'e him a dram,
To thowe his frozen mou'.

                    And wow! etc.

I set him in beside the bink,
I ga'e him bread and ale to drink
But ne'er a blythe styme wad he blink,
Until his wame was fou'.

          And wow! etc.


"Gae, get you gane, ye cauldrife wooer,
Ye sour-looking, hungry wooer";
I straightway showed him to the door
Saying, "Come nae mair to woo".

          And wow! etc.


A deuk-dub lay before the door,
Before the door, before the door,
A deuk-dub lay before the door,
And there fell he, I trew.

          And wow! etc.


Out cam' the gudeman and high he shouted,
Out cam' the gudewife, and laich she louted;
And a' the toun-neighbours were gathered about it,
And there lay he, I trew.

          And wow! etc.


Then out cam' I and sneered and smiled,
"Ye cam' to woo, but ye're a' beguiled,
Ye've fa'en i' the dirt, and ye're a' befyled;
We'll ha'e nae mair o' you".

          And wow! etc.


Yet, wow! but he was a braw young lad,
A brisk young lad, and a braw young lad;
And gay and gallantly was he clad,
Cam' seeking me to woo.

          And wow! etc.

                    *Anon.*

263

# AN ERISKAY LOVE LILT

dith.___ 'Na mo chlàr-saich cha robh
thee.___ Thou'rt the mus-ic of my

ceòl 'Na mo mheoir-ean cha robh àgh Rinn do
heart Harp of joy oh cruit mo chridh Moon of
iuil thuanns an oidhch Tha mo

phòg-sa mo leon, Fluair mi Eòl-as an
guid-ance by night, Strength and light thou'rt to
dhruidh-eachd ad shuil. Tha mo chiurr-adh ad

dain. Bheir mi o-ro bhan o Bheir mi
me. Vair me o-ro van o Vair me
loinn.

a-ro bhan i Bheir mi o ru o ho 'Smi tha
o-ro van ee Vair me o ru o ho Sad am

bron-ach's tu'm dhith._____
I with-out thee._____

*Adapted by Mrs Kennedy Fraser*
(By special permission)

## THE COCKLE GATHERER

*Quickly, as if humming.*

Ee-tl a doo veel Ee-tl a doo ho ro
I dal a du vil I dal a du ho ro

Ee - tl a doo veel Blythe I gather cockles here,
I dal a du vil 'Strusaidh mi na coil-leag-an,

Ee - tl a doo veel Ee - tl a doo ho ro
I dal a du vil I dal a du ho· ro

Ee - tl a doo veel Blythe I gather cockles here.
I dal a du vil 'Strusaidh mi na coil-leag-an.

Joy scream o' sea gulls Down on the skerry there,
Roic aig an-fhaoileag Shios anns na sgeirean ud,

Joy scream o' sea gulls While I gather cockles here.
Roic aig an-fhaoileag 'Strusaidh mi na coil-leag-an.

Joy scream o' sea gulls on the skerry there,
Roic aig an-fhaoileag anns na sgeirean ud,

Joy scream o' sea gulls While I gather cockles here.
Roic aig an-fhaoileag 'Strusaidh mi na coil-leag-an.

Ee - tl a doo veel Ee - tl a doo ho ro
I dal a du vil I dal a du ho ro

Ee - tl a doo veel While I gather cockles here.
I dal a du vil 'Strusaidh mi na coil-leag-an.

# THE COCKLE GATHERER

Ee – tl a doo veel  Ee – tl a doo ho ro
I  dal a  du  vil   I  dal a  du ho ro

Ee – tl  a doo  veel While I gather cockles here.
I  dal a  du  vil 'Strusaidh mi na coil-leag-an.

Laugh-ter of sea waves  Down  on the skerry there,
Gair aig an fhair-ge  Shios anns na sgeirean ud,

Laugh-ter of sea waves While I  gather cockles here.
Gair aig an fhair-ge 'Strusaidh mi na coil-leag-an.

Laugh-ter of sea waves  Down  on the skerry there,
Gair aig an fhair-ge  Shios  anns na sgeirean ud,

Laugh-ter of sea waves While I  gather cockles here.
Gair aig an fhair-ge 'Strusaidh mi na coil-leag-an.

Ee – tl  a doo veel  Ee – tl a doo ho ro,
I  dal a  du vil   I  dal a  du ho ro,

Ee – tl  a doo veel While I  gather cockles here.
I  dal a  du vil  'Strusaidh mi na coil-leag-an.

Ee – tl  a doo veel  Ee – tl a doo ho ro,
I  dal a  du vil   I  dal a  du ho ro,

Ee – tl a doo veel    Still I gather cockles here.
I dal a du vil    'Strusaidh mi na coil-leag-an.

*Kenneth Macleod*
(By special permission)

## LEWIS BRIDAL SONG

*Arr. from Lewis tune by*
*D. N. Morison*

*Gay but steady and rhythmical.*

I'd sail with you to Mia – vig in Uig,

Even tho' in twi – light, even tho' in twi – light.

I'd sail with you to Mia – vig in Uig,

Even thro' the dark and the sea-mist. How shall we fare when the

wind's in the sail, and storm clouds ga – ther,

storm clouds ga – ther? How shall we fare in the

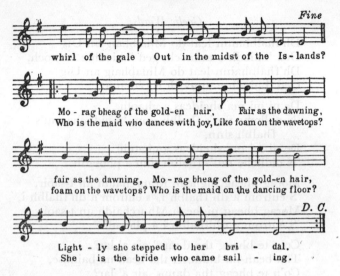

whirl of the gale    Out   in the midst of the   Is - lands?

Mo - rag bheag of the gold-en   hair,    Fair as the dawning,
Who is the maid who dances with joy, Like foam on the wavetops?

fair as the dawning,   Mo - rag bheag of the gold-en hair,
foam on the wavetops? Who is the maid on the dancing floor?

Light - ly she stepped to her   bri - dal.
She   is   the bride   who came sail - ing.

How shall we fare when the wind's in the sail,
And storm-clouds gather, storm-clouds gather?
How shall we fare in the whirl of the gale,
Out in the midst of the Islands?

Morag bheag of the golden hair,
Fair as the dawning, fair as the dawning,
Morag bheag of the golden hair,
Lightly she stepped to her bridal.

Who is the maiden who dances with joy,
Like foam on the wave-tops, foam on the wave-tops?
Who is the maid on the dancing floor?
She is the bride who came sailing.

*Hector M'Iver*

269

## Gaelic Words

Dh'fhalbhainn leat do Mhiabhaig an Uig
Ged 'bhiodh e anmoch, ged 'bhiodh e anmoch,
Dh'fhalbhainn leat do Mhiabhaig an Uig
Ged 'bhiodh e anmoch is ceo ann.

De ni mi ma sheideas a ghaoth
'N oidhche mu's fhalbh sinn, 'n oidhche mu's
    fhalbh sinn,
De ni mi ma sheideas a ghaoth
'N oidhche mu's fhalbh sinn a phosadh.

Morag bheag nighean Mhurchaidh an t-saoir,
'S eutrom a dh'fhalbh i, 's eutrom a dh'fhalbh i,
Morag bheag nighean Mhurchaidh an t-saoir,
'S eutrom a dh'fhalbh i a phosadh.

Co'n te bheag tha danns' air a' lar?
Tha bean-na-bainnse, tha bean-na-bainnse,
Co'n te bheag tha danns' air a' lar?
Tha bean-na-bainnse, 's cha mhor i.

## AN T-EILEAN MUILEACH
### (The Isle of Mull)

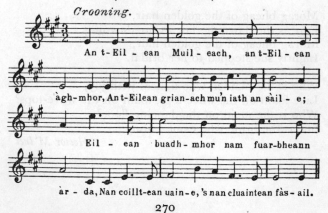

Crooning.

An t-Eil - ean Muil - each, an t-Eil - ean àgh-mhor, An t-Eilean grian-ach mu'n iath an sàil - e; Eil - ean buadh - mhor nam fuar-bheann àr - da, Nan coillt-ean uain - e, 's nan cluaintean fàs - ail.

270

B'e'n sòlas-inntinn leam a bhi 'g eisdeachd
Ri còisir bhinn-ghutach, ghomn a' Chéitein,
A'seinn gu sunndach an dlùth's nan geugan—
A' chorll' fo liath-dhealt, 's a' ghoran ag éirigh!

Chlaon gach sòlas dhiu siod mar bhouadar,
'S mar bhristeadh biulgein air bhàrr nan stuadh-
thonn;
Ach soraidh slàn leis gach loinn 'us buaidh
A bh'air eilean àghmhor nan àrd-bheann fuara.

*Dugald Macphail*

## THE ROAD TO THE ISLES

*Patuffa Kennedy-Fraser*

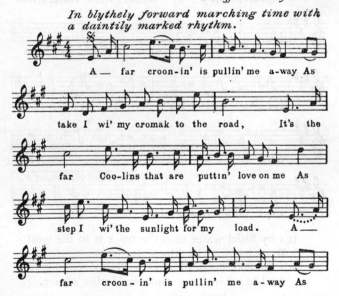

*In blythely forward marching time with a daintily marked rhythm.*

A — far croon-in' is pullin' me a-way As take I wi' my cromak to the road, It's the far Coo-lins that are puttin' love on me As step I wi' the sunlight for my load. A— far croon-in' is pullin' me a-way As

take I wi' my cromak to the road, It's the far Cool-ins that are puttin' love on me, As

CHORUS.

step I wi' the sunlight for my load. Sure, by Tummel and Loch Ran-noch and Loch ab-er I will go, By heather tracks wi' heaven in their wiles; If you're think-in' in your in-ner heart (swank is), swaggers in my step, You've never smelt the tangle o' the Isles. Oh, the far Cool-ins are puttin' love on me, As

1st 2nd Verses | 3rd V.

step I wi' my cromak to the Isles. D.S. Isles.

It's by Shiel water that the track is to the west
By Ailort and by Morar to the sea,
It's the cool cresses I am thinkin' o' for pluck
And bracken for a wink on Mother's knee.
*Chorus.*

272

It's the blue Islands that are pullin' me away
  Their laughter puts the leap upon the lame,
It's the blue Islands from the Skerries to the Lews
  Wi' heather honey taste upon each name.

    *Chorus.*

                  *Kenneth Macleod*
                (By special permission)

# I WISH I WERE WHERE GADIE RINS

CHORUS.

I wish I— were where Ga-die rins, Where Ga-die rins, where Ga-die— rins, I— wish I— were where Ga-die rins At the back o' Ben-a-chie. Ance mair to hear the wild birds sang, To wan-der birks and braes a-mang, Midst friends and fav-'rites left sae lang, At the back o' Ben-a-chie.

Oh mony a day in blithe springtime,
Oh mony a day in simmer's prime,
I've wand'ring wiled awa the time,
At the back o' Benachie.

Oh there wi' Jean, on ilka nicht,
And baith our hearts were young and licht,
We've wander'd, when the moon was bricht,
At the back o' Benachie.

Oh fortune's floors wi' thorns are rife,
And wealth is won wi' toil and strife,
Ae day gie me o' youthfu' life,
At the back o' Benachie.

## WE'VE GOT A HOME UP YONDER

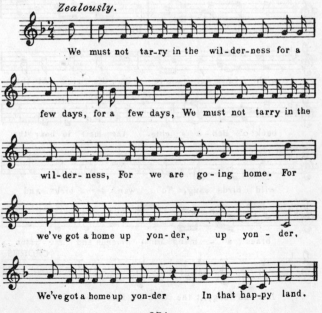

*Zealously.*

We must not tar-ry in the wil-der-ness for a few days, for a few days, We must not tarry in the wil-der-ness, For we are go-ing home. For we've got a home up yon-der, up yon-der, We've got a home up yon-der In that hap-py land.

King David the Psalmist often got tight
    For a few days—
A circumstance that affected his sight
    When he was going home.
And that explains how we read in the Psalms
    For a few days,
That he saw the mountains skipping like lambs
    As he was going home.
         Now he's got a home up yonder, etc.

*Anon.*

[Other verses, dealing with the matrimonial troubles of Solomon and Potiphar and other less edifying portions of the Old Testament narrative, are in oral circulation.]

## MY LOVE, SHE'S BUT A LASSIE YET

*Fairly quick.*

My love she's but a lass-ie yet, My love she's but a lass-ie yet, We'll let her stand a year or twa, She'll no be half sae sau-cy yet. I rue the day I socht her, O, I rue the day I

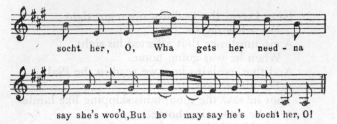

socht. her, O, Wha gets her need - na

say she's woo'd, But he may say he's bocht her, O!

Come, draw a drap o' the best o't yet,
Come, draw a drap o' the best o't yet
Gae, seek for pleasure where ye will,
But here I never miss'd it yet.
We're a' dry wi' drinkin' o't,
We're a' dry wi' drinkin' o't;
The minister kiss'd the fiddler's wife,
And couldna preach for thinkin' o't.

*Burns*

## THE PIPER O' DUNDEE

*Quickly.*

The pi - per came tae oor toon, tae

oor toon, tae oor toon, The

pi - per came tae oor toon, And

he played bon - nie - lie. He

played a spring, the laird to please, A
spring brent new frae yont the seas; And
then he gae'd his bags a heeze, And

**CHORUS.**

play'd an-i-ther key. And was-na he a ro-guey, A
ro - guey, a ro - guey, And
was-na he a ro-guey, The pi-per o' Dun-dee?

He play'd "The Welcome owre the Main",
And "Ye'se be fou and I'se be fain"
And "Auld Stuarts back again",
    Wi' muckle mirth and glee.
He play'd "The Kirk", he play'd "The Queen",
"The Mullin Dhu", and "Chevalier",
And "Lang awa', but welcome here"
    Sae sweet, sae bonnilie.

    *Chorus.*

It's some gat swords, and some gat nane,
And some were dancing mad their lane,
And mony a vow o' weir was ta'en
    That night at Amulrie.

277

There was Tullibardine and Burleigh,
And Struan, Keith and Ogilvie,
And brave Carnegie, what but he,
　　The piper o' Dundee?

*Chorus.*　　　　　　　　　　　　　*Anon.*

## EASTGATE

Be-hold how good a thing it is,

And how be - com - ing well___

To-gether such as breth-ren are, In　un-i-

ty　to　dwell, In　un-i - ty　to　dwell.

Like precious ointment on the head
　　That down the beard did flow,
Ev'n Aaron's beard, and to the skirts
　　Did of his garments go.

As Hermon's dew, the dew that doth
　　On Sion' hills descend:
For there the blessing God commands,
　　Life that shall never end.
　　　　　　　　　　　　*Psalm cxxxiii*

278

## COLESHILL

O Thou my soul, bless God the Lord;

and all that in me is

Be stir - red up His ho - ly name

To mag - ni - fy and bless.

Bless, O my soul, the Lord thy God,
   and not forgetful be
Of all his gracious benefits
   he hath bestow'd on thee.

All thine iniquities who doth
   most graciously forgive :
Who thy diseases all and pains
   doth heal, and thee relieve.

Who doth redeem thy life, that thou
   to death may'st not go down;
Who thee with loving-kindness doth
   and tender mercies crown:

Who with abundance of good things
   doth satisfy thy mouth;
So that, ev'n as the eagle's age,
   renewed is thy youth.

*Psalm ciii*

279

# DRUMCLOG

The Lord doth reign, and cloth'd is he with
ma-jes - ty most bright His works do show him
cloth'd to be, And girt a - bout with might.

The world is also stablished,
 that it cannot depart.
Thy throne is fix'd of old, and thou
 from everlasting art.

The floods, O Lord, have lifted up,
 they lifted up their voice;
The floods have lifted up their waves,
 and made a mighty noise.

But yet the Lord, that is on high,
 is more of might by far
Than noise of many waters is,
 or great sea-billows are.

Thy testimonies ev'ry one
 in faithfulness excel;
And holiness for ever, Lord,
 thine house becometh well.

*Psalm xciii*

## BALLERMA

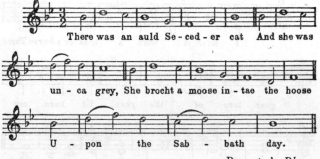

There was an auld Se-ced-er cat And she was un-ca grey, She brocht a moose in-tae the hoose U-pon the Sab-bath day.

*Precentor's Rhyme*

## BANGOR

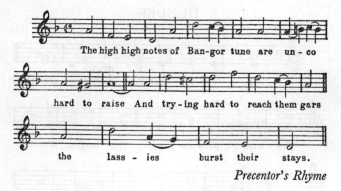

The high high notes of Ban-gor tune are un-co hard to raise And try-ing hard to reach them gars the lass-ies burst their stays.

*Precentor's Rhyme*

## CRIMOND

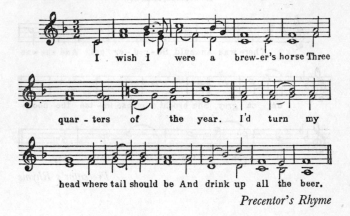

I wish I were a brew-er's horse Three quar-ters of the year. I'd turn my head where tail should be And drink up all the beer.

*Precentor's Rhyme*

## DUNDEE

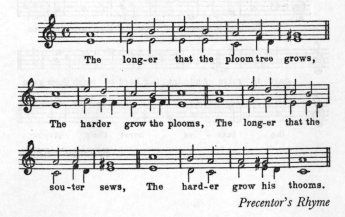

The long-er that the ploom tree grows, The harder grow the plooms, The long-er that the sou-ter sews, The hard-er grow his thooms.

*Precentor's Rhyme*

## MARTYRS

A weaver said un-to his son The day that he was born,

"My blessings on your curly pow, You'll rin wi'pirns the morn".

*Precentor's Rhyme*

## SUILEAN DUBH

### (Mouth music for dancing)

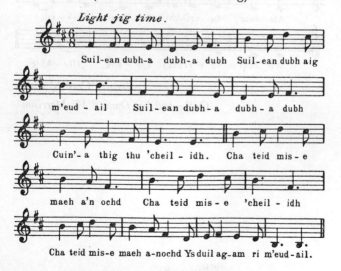

*Light jig time.*

Suil-ean dubh-a dubh-a dubh Suil-ean dubh aig

m'eud – ail Suil-ean dubh-a dubh-a dubh

Cuin'-a thig thu 'cheil – idh. Cha teid mis-e

maeh a'n ochd Cha teid mis-e 'cheil – idh

Cha teid mis-e maeh a-nochd Ys duil ag-am ri m'eud-ail.

# PORT-A-BEUL

## (Mouth music for dancing)

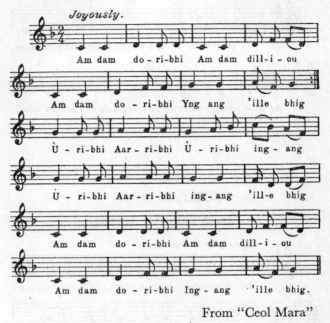

*Joyously.*

Am dam do-ri-bhi Am dam dill-i-ou

Am dam do-ri-bhi Yng ang 'ille bhig

Ù-ri-bhi Aar-ri-bhi Ù-ri-bhi ing-ang

Ù-ri-bhi Aar-ri-bhi ing-ang 'ill-e bhig

Am dam do-ri-bhi Am dam dill-i-ou

Am dam do-ri-bhi Ing-ang 'ille bhig.

From "Ceol Mara"
Collected by *Duncan M. Morrison*

# MIRTH AND DANCING

There s some folk like *Macfarlane's geese: they*
*like their play better than their meat.*

OLD SAW.

*Hornpipes, jigs, strathspeys and reels*
*Put life and mettle i' their heels.*

BURNS

# OUTDOOR GAMES

How fine is the muscular action—
So highly conducive to health—
Oh! Hygeia's glances are sweeter
Than all the caresses of wealth.

So, in 1836, wrote a pusillanimous London Scot, a
baker at Blackheath, concerning the national pastime
of shinty. Already by that time, you will mark, the
game had been deprived of its immemorial money
prize to the winner. And, as if this were not bad
enough, it had degenerated from a game that was full
of ill-feeling and practically destitute of rules, so that
it corresponded to the *palio* of Siena, into a carefully
umpired contest of equal numbers subjected to gentle-
manly regulations and imbued with what is known in
England as "the proper sporting spirit". Originally fit
alike for beggars and for kings, conducted with
"banners flying, bagpipes playing", upon a field that
had "the appearance of a battle scene", while "souls of
heroes floated on the breeze", it enlisted indefinite and
unequal numbers, up to forty or so on each side, and
was played all day, new players stepping now and again
from an ambush at favourable moments. The ball was

of wood—a man might run a mile with it in his hand
if he wasn't stopped—and if you felt like changing your
stick midway for a Lochaber axe there was nothing to
hinder you. The more knots you had on your stick the
better, so that the game was sometimes called "knotty"
or "shinny"—the latter with reference to the other
fellow's shins, for if you didn't see the ball you could
let fly at the other man. A favourite expedient for cold
Sundays on the road to church and back, the first nail
was put in its coffin by the Sabbatarians of the late
eighteenth century. After that it was fit only for week-
days and Anglo-Scots, with stereotyped sticks, a ball
of leather or wool and nothing but honour for the best
men.

Other famous Scotch ball-games required a river in
which the players were immersed for the greater part
of the time. Those good old days are past. For a cold
day out-of-doors in Scotland, however, there are still
a few warming, fairly risky games that have escaped
revision and may be played by fit persons without
bothering too much about rules and with impromptu
arrangements for counting. Here are some of them.

## BAB THE BOWSTER,

also known as *Hunch-Cuddy-Hunch*, is played by equal
sides chosen by counting out. The "oots" then choose
a captain, who is the *Bowster* because he must stand
with his back against a wall, while the others form a
cuddy by bending down as for leap-frog, one at the
tail of the other, the nearest planting his head in the
Bowster's belly. The "ins" queue up about 30 feet
away, and, led by their captain, run, one by one, place
their hands on the endmost bent player's back, and
leap as far as they can towards the Bowster. If, during
the process, the cuddy breaks under the strain, it must
reform and allow the game to start as before. If, on
the other hand, the "ins" jump so feebly that there is

not room for the last of them, they must become cuddy. If the cuddy stays firm and all are landed on it, the last jumper calls out, "Bab, bab, bab the Bowster!" during which remark the cuddy does its best to throw its riders without itself falling down. If it succeeds, the "loupers" have to be cuddy next time. If it fails it must be cuddy again. Often this game leads to argument.

## HOT PIES

"Baker" stands with his back to the other players or "customers", who are queued up. He keeps calling "Hot pies!" and moving his arms stiffly from his sides to the level of his shoulders and back again. He may do this at any speed he likes, and may use both arms together or alternately, but he must never bend his arm at the elbow. The customers run forwards in turn, trying to dodge under his upraised arm without being touched. The one who is touched becomes baker.

## JINKS

Players choose pseudonyms, most commonly Sunday, Monday, Tuesday, etc., or names of fruits. The player counted "out", by any of the well-known rhymes, throws a ball high against the gable of a house or other wall and shouts "Tuesday, Jinks" or any other name. Tuesday may catch the ball as it descends and throw it up again, calling the pseudonym of another player. If he fails to catch the ball before it touches the ground, or if he deliberately lets it bounce, he then attempts to strike another player with the ball. The players should shout "Jinks!" otherwise they must stand still immediately the "out" man catches the ball. "Out" tries to forestall them by shouting "Nae jinks!" but he must not do so until the ball is in his grasp. Anyone whom he beats to it must stand still and

289                                                      L

"out" has a pot shot at him. If they all get their "Jinks" out first, he must throw at them on the run. The player struck by the ball is then out. If he fails to put anyone out, the last player to throw throws once more after having the others lined up. "Out" then has another shot and this goes on until he succeeds.

## KIRN—DUNOON—INNELLAN—ROTHESAY

Player who is "down" stands on one side of the roadway with his back to the other players who are lined up across the road. He recites "Kirn—Dunoon—Innellan—Rothesay", porter fashion, at any speed he chooses, or at various speeds. While he is chanting, all the other players must keep moving towards his side of the road. At the last syllable he wheels round and tries to catch one of the others on the move. Anyone challenged has now to attempt to reach the other side by running and dodging the porter. If caught he is out of the game. Meanwhile the others stand still. Porter recommences. If all the passengers are caught before the porter's wall is reached by anyone, the porter becomes a player for next game and first passenger caught becomes porter. If any remain uncaught, they have now to get back to the other side in the same manner. This goes on until all the passengers are caught. If they have not all been caught in one journey, it is the *last* to be caught who becomes porter.

## COCK-A-ROOSTY

Cock-a-Roosty is a hopping game. The person counted out chooses one player from the others lined up against a wall or along the side of a road. The challenged one must hop from the moment of leaving his den until he reaches the other side of the road or whatever space is marked off as Home. He may choose to fight the challenger (who also hops) or to dodge him. If he succeeds in making the challenger touch ground with both feet, he may cross the road on both his own; but if he dodges across he is equally "free". If he is upset he takes his stand along with the challenger and both jointly oppose the next person challenged. The game continues until everyone is upset. If, however, a challenged person should upset all the challengers in one encounter, then all those except the original challenger become free, and the challenger has to begin afresh.

## COCK-FIGHTING

Cock-fighting is the same game carried out on either side by hoppers carrying a passenger.

# PEEVER GAMES

Peever is so peculiarly a Scottish game that the English call it Hopscotch. It is also sometimes known as Beds. But Peever is still the proper, as it is the old name. It is essentially a pavement game, as the lines between flagstones create natural "beds", and a hard smooth surface is best for the "scliffing" of the peever or *pierre*, which, along with a piece of chalk, is all the apparatus required. It can, however, be played in a large room or on hard earth, the beds on earth being scored in. The different sizes of paving stones may be utilised by players to create a stimulating unevenness which demands the utmost skill and judgment in hopping. But beginners or male players had better content themselves with regular beds. Those who regard the pastime as feminine—*i.e.* effeminate—had better try it first before expressing this opinion aloud. They will probably go back to its table variant, Shove-halfpenny, which is not only less strenuous but has the advantage over Peever in always being played to an accompaniment of beer.

The peever (*pierre*) is a roughly rounded flat disc of marble, stone or pipe-clay about 2 inches in diameter and ⅜ of an inch thick. A piece of tile will serve.

I

A diagram is marked out thus:

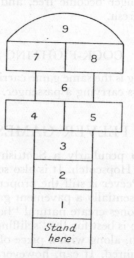

Order of play is decided by mutual agreement, fight or counting-out rhyme. Player A stands in space marked and "scliffs" the peever into Bed 1. If it does not come to rest in bed without touching a line, this is a "loss" and A retires until all the others have played. If peever lands fairly, A hops from Stand to 2 with one hop, from 2 to 3, then lands with one hop into 4 and 5, a foot in each; into 6 on one foot; 7 and 8, one foot in each; into 9 on one foot. Player turns round and comes down the row similarly.

## II

A stops on one foot in Bed 2, picks up peever from Bed 1, hops into 1, thence into Stand. To fall, touch a line with foot, land twice in one space, or indeed to infringe any rule of procedure constitutes a "loss" and retirement. If A has got through this ordeal successfully, he scliffs the peever into Bed 2, hops into 1, over 2 into 3, and then continues as before. After that he does his "Threesie Up", "Foursie Up", etc., to 9, which he does twice, then returns down the line— "Eightsie Down", etc. If he gets through these 18 rounds successfully he marks his initials on any space he chooses. This space must not be trespassed on by any player thereafter. It is definitely forbidden ground. A is rewarded for success by another turn. This time instead of hopping he jumps with both feet simultaneously. Of course, he has to do 4 and 5, 7 and 8 successively, instead of together as before. He does the "up and down" series. Note that there will be only 16 rounds this time, since a bed is initialled. He may be a "loss" at any time during this part of the game, but his initials remain; that is his point for the whole game. If he has succeeded in the jumping round, he has to walk the beds with eyes shut, taking one step and one step only to each bed and missing initialled beds. At 4 and 5 and at 7 and 8, he must come astride (unless one of these is initialled). This round finishes A, generally in both senses of the word. As soon as A has had a loss or gets three spaces initialled, B commences and acts exactly as A has done, except of course that he must avoid all initialled beds from the beginning. The game is finished when all the beds are initialled, and the winner is the player with most beds to his credit.

## III

Draw the same diagram as for Game A. First

player from Stand scliffs the peever into Bed 1, hops up to it on right foot, then with a tap with the side of the right foot knocks it into Bed 2. He approaches it again by hops (as many as he likes, but never landing on a line) and knocks it as before into Bed 3, then into 4, 5, 6, 7, 8, 9, 9, 8, . . . 1, Stand. Thus "Onesy Right" is completed. Now begins "Onesy Left", which is the same programme, but hopping on the left foot and kicking with it. If he has not made a loss, he scliffs peever into Bed 2 and does his "Twosy Right", then "Twosy Left" and so on. If he gets right through his ordeal, finishing at "Ninesy Left", he has to go through the whole process once more, but allowing himself only one hop from bed to bed. This should kill him off; but, should he survive, he does the business once more with eyes shut and taking any number of hops to each bed but knocking the peever into the appropriate bed with one kick. It is unlikely that any player will finish the course. Next player begins, and whoever has gone furthest in the sequence is, of course, winner.

## IV

Discouraged or less ambitious players may use this diagram:

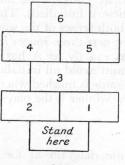

294

# V

Another less ornate fashion of the game is played with this diagram:

| 7 | 8 |
|---|---|
| 6 | 5 |
| 3 | 4 |
| 2 | 1 |

*Stand here*

# VI

Draw on the ground the following diagram:

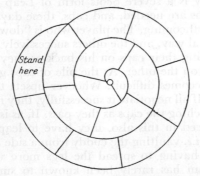

*Stand here*

Player A from the Stand scliffs the peever into the first bed, approaches it by one hop, kicks it with the side of the hopping-foot into second bed, approaches it by one hop again and knocks it into third bed, and so on till he reaches the centre. He then initials any one bed, and on his next round is entitled to rest as he pleases in that bed. This continues till he makes a "loss". Player B has to repeat A's performance, but he

295

has to skip A's initialled beds, *i.e.* he must scliff the peever straight into the following bed and hop into it right over A's initialled bed. Game continues until every player in succession makes a loss. Player with most initialled beds wins.

This game may be played without a peever, players merely hopping.

## BALL BEDS

Any game of "Peevers" may be transformed into a game of Ball Beds by substituting a ball for the peever. After the ball is picked up it must be bounced once and caught in each succeeding bed.

## BUNNETY

Bunnety is a severe Scots form of Leap Frog, for which caps are needed, and caps, these days, are not always forthcoming. The player who is "down" stoops in the usual way, and the others successively leap over him, placing their caps on his back as they go, each cap piled on the other. As the pile of caps grows, the placing becomes difficult. Whoever upsets the pile is "down". If all negotiate it successfully, they repeat the jump, touching the caps as they pass. If, as is unlikely, they succeed in this also, they have to leap the pile sideways, *i.e.* vaulting the cuddy from a side approach and thus having to spread the legs more widely. A whole team has rarely been known to survive this round, but should they do so, the next test is to leap from the side approach but without touching back or caps. Some boys can do this.

## WRANG SOO BY THE LUG

A player stands with his hands clasped behind his head, fingers interlocked. The others stand behind him. One of them hits him a smack on the hands with his open palm and he wheels round as quickly as he can and tries to spot the player who smacked him. This gives all the players an opportunity for acting. The one who is accused of the smack challenges his accuser by saying, "What have I to do?" The accuser orders any penalty (such as standing on his hands and smoking a cigarette through) he likes, but he does so in the knowledge that if he has not caught the right man he must himself undergo the punishment he prescribes. In addition to this he must go on in his original rôle till he catches somebody out, who takes his punishment and his place. Of course, instead of a smack, players can touch gently. Anything is allowed that aids deception and puts the standing member on the wrong tack.

[N.B.—The same game can be played with caps tied on to strings, the caps being used instead of hands for touching or walloping. It is then called *Buff the Bear*.]

# BOOL GAMES

Bools, as you must be aware, is the Scotch for marbles (from the French, *boule*), and the Scottish varieties, besides being large, differ in some respects from those prevalent in England. Here are some of them.

## DOBBLERS

Any number of players place one bool each in a row, If the row is more than four or five, they may make two or three rows, one behind the other. They fix their rotation by whatever method suits them, generally by rolling towards a goal. Each player in turn throws his plunker (Anglice, *taw*) and picks up as many bools as he displaces. He leaves his plunker lying and subsequent players may aim at it. Each time his plunker is hit he has to put a bool into the row.

## ONE-STEP

The bools are placed as before. The range is larger. Each player takes one step and must throw his plunker without pausing. He may either hit the bools direct or strike the ground, bounce on to the wall behind and catch them in this way from behind on the rebound. If he succeeds either way, he is entitled to throw now from his new position in a stationary posture, *i.e.* without the handicap of taking a step. But if his plunker strikes a bool from the wall in the rear, the stroke does not count unless he shouts "Back licks" before an opponent has time to shout "Nae back licks". This, besides introducing a little characteristic metaphysics, avoids flukes.

## TWO-STEPS

Same as *One-Step*, but with a still longer range and taking two steps instead of one.

## FIVE-O'S

A circle of about 18 inches in diameter is described with heel or chalk and each player places a bool within it; or, in the variant which gives the game its name, a square is drawn and the bools are placed at the corners and centre at the discretion of each player. In rotation each throws his plunker in an attempt to dislodge one or more out of the base. Each bool knocked out becomes the property of that player. Each plays his first throw from a fixed line and subsequent throws from wherever his plunker has come to rest on the previous throw. If the plunker comes to rest within the base, there it must stay and be treated as one of those originally staked, and the player who has forfeited it continues to play with another, if he has it. When all the bools within the base have been won, the game goes on, the players aiming at one another until one sole victor remains. But no player must aim at an opponent's bool until the base is empty.

## THREE-HOLEY

Three-Holey is the same as *Five-O's*, except that the bools are arranged in three holes in a row. It is more difficult to dislodge them from a hole or hollow than from the level.

## PLUNKERS

Plunkers is a simple game-device for shortening a dull tract of road, such as the one to school. Each throws his bool and the next player aims at it. Next again aims at any bool ahead of him. Each bool struck is pocketed by the striker, and the defeated has to put down another bool or retire.

## SPANGY

Draw a diagram on the ground thus:

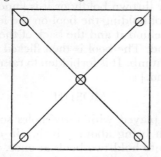

A bool is placed by each player in one of the positions indicated. If more than five play, other bools may be placed at intervals along the marked lines. Players

299

line up about fifteen yards from the diagram. In turn they "knuckle" their taws as described below, aiming at any one of the targets. Any bool knocked out of the diagram is appropriated by the player. Each knuckles in turn and leaves the taw lying. If he comes near enough a bool within the diagram he may at his next turn attempt to capture it by "spanging", *i.e.* by placing a thumb on his taw and a finger on the bool and knocking them together by a sharp jerk; he must not draw them together. No bool may be knuckled within the diagram; if a player cannot win the bool inside the diagram by spanging, he must at his next turn return to the starting-line. But if he fails in his attempt to win by spanging and yet leaves his taw within the diagram, he may on his next turn make another attempt. Taws may be spanged by opponents in any position within or outside the diagram, and in that case the player whose taw has been spanged takes taw back to starting-line and gives winner one bool.

[*N.B.*—It will be noted that we always talk of "throwing" the bool or plunker. Any one of the games described can be played by rolling instead of throwing or knuckling; but rolling in Scotland is regarded as a pansy proceeding unworthy of the manly player. The bool is either thrown boldly or it is knuckled. Knuckling consists of holding the bool on the forefinger with the thumb behind it and the back of the hand resting on the ground. The bool is then flicked forward by a skite of the thumb. It is forbidden to raise the knuckles off the ground.]

## MOSHIE

Moshie is played with three holes scooped in the ground, each being about 2 inches in diameter and deep enough to hold two bools at once. Some players arrange the holes in a straight row with about an arm's-length between them: others prefer them to define the points of an isosceles triangle of which the base would measure a couple of arm's-lengths (or the out-stretched arms from finger-tips to finger-tips), while the sides would each measure an arm's-length.

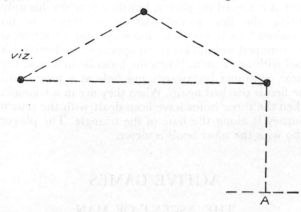

*viz.*

A

Whether the holes be in a row or a triangle, the players—usually three in number—have their stance opposite to the hold that is furthest to the right at about the same distance from it as it is from the hole nearest to it (see A).

A bool is put in each hole to begin with, each player contributing one, and the players all throw or roll in turn, aiming at the nearest hole. If a player gets into the hole the lying bool is his, to take out, but he does not immediately have an extra shot. He merely cries, "I'm a moshie!" If none go in, the next round is led by the player who has come nearest to the hole, and he tries to knuckle the most conveniently-lying bool of another player into the hole, *not to go in himself.* Any-body who succeeds in this takes the potted bool for his own.

The next round is led by the player who went in his first shot into the hole, *i.e.* by the "moshie", or failing this, by the first who knuckled in one of his opponents, and the shots are played either from a line drawn through the first hole, or from the standing position of a bool, the aim being the next nearest hole. Players are allowed to cannon themselves in by striking the lying bool of a preceding player, but they may do this only during the first round. After that there are no "moshies", as it would be too easy, and all attempts are confined to knuckle in an opponent by hitting his bool with one's own. When the holes lie in a row, the game continues backwards, one hole at a time, until the first is reached again. When they are in a triangle, when the three holes have been dealt with the return journey is along the base of the triangle. The player who wins the most bools is victor.

# ACTIVE GAMES

## THE ASCENT OF MAN

The Ascent of Man is so called because it was invented by Henry Drummond, though with characteristic modesty he described it as merely a non-fatal adaptation of a game that he came across in the Western States of America, where it is played with bowie-knives. You need for it a fairly large pitch-dark room, and the less furniture there is the better for everybody and also for the furniture. The procedure is simplicity itself. Each player tries to capture another by leaping on his back. In Drummond's time the game was for men only, but nowadays girls may join in provided they are active enough and suitably clothed.

## CARROT, CARROT, NEEP!

The one who is "out" stands with his face to a wall, while the others line up in readiness to cross the road or the room. So long as he cries out "Carrot, carrot!" they may move, but when he says "Neep!"

they must try to stop, for he is then allowed to wheel round and to send back any whom he detects moving. The first across wins and takes his place at the wall instead of the other.

## TRIALS OF SKILL

Stand up, put your head forward, and lay an empty wine- or beer-bottle across the back of your neck. Without touching it at any time with your hands, go down on your hands and knees and pick up with your teeth a cork conveniently placed on the floor. Rise to your feet again without dislodging the bottle. It has often been done.

Lay a round bottle, *e.g.* a screw-stopper beer-bottle or a lemonade bottle, end-wise on the floor. Competitors line up: referee is armed with a watch with a second-hand. First competitor is given a pencil and a sheet of paper with a board or other backing surface. He sits on the bottle with a hip on either side and the neck of the bottle pointing towards his feet. His legs must be kept crossed with his heels touching the floor. No part of his legs must touch the floor and he must not lay his feet flat. At the word "Go!" he begins to write a sentence agreed upon at the start. Referee times him. Both hands must be clear of the ground. If one touches he must stop writing till it is clear again. In thirty seconds the referee calls "Stop!" Each competitor takes his turn and the referee decides the winner according to the number of letters written and the legibility of the writing. This is an exercise in balance, and it will generally be found that cyclists have a slight advantage.

## HUSBANDS AND WIVES

Husbands and wives is the active parlour game *par*

*excellence* for middle-aged or even elderly men and women. It is very comforting to both sexes, as it provides each with an opportunity for jeering at the other.

1. *Wives look on and Laugh.*—Four chairs are placed in the four corners of the room, marked respectively "handkerchiefs", "ties", "coats" and "shoes". (If desired more chairs may be provided for "socks", "waistcoats", etc., etc. The men line up and at the word "Go!" leave their handkerchiefs and other articles of attire at the proper places. Then, *without stopping*, they do a second round, retrieve their things and put them on decently and in order. Each must recognise even his own handkerchief.

2. *Husbands look on and Laugh.*—Each woman is given two folded sheets of newspaper (a sheet is four pages). She must stand on one, spread out the other in front of her, step on to it, pick up the first sheet, now behind, and put it down for the next step, and in this way progress from one end of the room to the other without stepping on anything but her newspapers. By this time it is hoped that she may be convinced of the inefficiency of newspapers as a protection of spring-cleaned floors against a visit by the sweep or other entering male.

3. *Wives and Husbands look on and Cheer.*—A pile of assorted garments is put in a basket or on a chair, and a clothes-line is stretched across the room. Players in turn are furnished with clothes-pegs and timed in hanging up all the clothes neatly on the line. Or two players with two equal piles may race.

## RINGMASTER, OR THE CIRCLE OF CHALK

You must have a chalkable floor. Any number of players stand in a circle on one foot, with arms folded. The chalk circle is drawn round them. At "Go!" everybody starts trying to shove somebody else out of the circle, and hence out of the game. He who unfolds his arms or allows both feet to touch the ground is also out. The survivor is ringmaster.

The game can also be played by opposing teams in which a chalk line is drawn across the floor between them. It is then called *Jebusites and Perizzites*.

## RING A-ROUND THE JACKETS

Without necessarily being rough, this game is a tester of stamina. The players pile up their jackets and, having joined hands round the pile, endeavour to make each other touch it. They must not leave go of one another's hands. Whoever touches the jackets (with feet, face or any part of himself) is put out of the circle. The final "singles" is interesting to watch.

## BLIND MAN'S PUFF

Put a lighted candle somewhere about the level of the players' mouths (preferably and for obvious reasons not on the mantelpiece when the fire is alight); blind-fold one player so that he cannot see any light through, round or over the bandage, and turn him round three times on the spot where the bandaging was done—*i.e.* about three yards from the candle and facing it. His job (or hers) is to walk up to the candle and blow it out. It is an exceptional player who walks in the right direction and blows in the right place.

## BRIEF CANDLES

Brief Candles is amusing at any time, but it ought to be played over coffee and dessert, when it gets better and better as the decanter goes round. One of the table candles is extinguished and placed, along with a box of matches, before one of the company, who must then strike a match, light the candle, blow out the candle, re-light it, blow it out again—and so on as long as light of match or candle lasts. As a rule you will light the candle from the match, but it is equally permissible to light the match from the candle. It is only when both are out that you are out. Then you pass candle and matches to your left-hand neighbour, and so the game goes round the table. With the average match a skilled player can light about fifty brief candles.

## PASSING PENNIES

The players sit in two rows on chairs opposite to each other, each row being a "side". At either end, on a chair set between the rows and looking down them, sit A and B, who belong to neither side. A has a penny, or other object of which two are identical in size and shape, in each hand. At the word "Go!" he hands in the same moment the one in his right hand to the left hand of the end player on his right, and the one in his left hand to the right hand of the end player on his left. Each end player passes it to his neighbour, who must use the same hand as the one who passes it to him, and so on down the rows, racing. When the end is reached the last player in the row touches the hand of B that lies nearest to him, then he transfers the object to his other hand and passes it to his neighbour, who takes it with the same hand—*i.e.* with the reverse hand from the one used in the other journey. The side that gets the object back into A's nearest hand without mishap or cheating, has won. If there is cheating or dropping on either side, the race on that side has to start afresh from the beginning. It is the business of A and B to act as umpires in case of dispute.

# TABLE GAMES

## I

A bare table is wanted for these three simple but

strenuous and hilarious games. Should the table be rounded at the ends but oblong, the chances are all the more varied. Should it be round the players can range themselves all round it, with a chalk tick or a strip of stamp-paper to mark where the diameter comes, dividing the sides. If the table is rectangular the players must confine their beginnings to either end.

A scrap of stamp-paper is stuck in the centre. Each player has two draughts (black one for one side, white for the other) or, if there are no draughts available, one side plays with two halfpence apiece, the other with two pennies (or superior players may resort to sixpences and shillings, or even to half-crowns and florins). Colours or coins are first tossed for, then there is a second toss for the start. The draughts or coins are ranged, two at a time on either side as if on a shove-halfpenny board, each one being only half on the table. Everybody plays their two in turn, side and side about. Thirteen points is game. Anybody making a bull— *i.e.* covering or partly covering, but not merely touching the stamp-paper, scores 13 for his side. Failing this, the side that comes nearest to the stamp-paper counts one for that counter *and for every other counter that is nearer than any of the other side's*, but not for any counter that has a successful rival on the other side. This means that while only one side scores, it may be kept from scoring more than a single point in one game. When coins are used they change sides with each game.

## II

Goals are chalked at either end of the table and a marble is put on the centre sticking-plaster. The players kneel behind the goals (as many as the table will accommodate, or singly) and try to make a goal by blowing the marble.

## III

Four players stand at the four corners of a rectangular table that has a coin placed on sticking-paper in the centre. They bounce an old tennis-ball transversely across the table, trying to dislodge the coin, while the man at the other corner catches the ball and has his try in returning it. If possible there should be two tennis balls, one for each pair of cross corners, as this saves passing the ball from hand to hand and makes the game faster. An alternate shot and return is allowed to each pair of cross-players, these being partners. Or each man may play for himself, the score being thirteen.

# FLOOR GAMES

## I

The same as above, but the coin, preferably a shilling, is placed on the floor at one end of the room, while the players, divided into two sides, take their stand at the other end and try to dislodge the coin with the ball. Only one tennis-ball is needed for this.

## II

Instead of the coin, put a cap or hat in the middle of the room, range the players at equal distances round it and give them either two playing-cards or two coins apiece. These they try to throw into the hat, one at a time as the turns pass. Or one player may deal with a whole pack of cards at a time, taking, of course, each card singly.

# SEDENTARY GAMES

## HAPPY FAMILIES (NEW STYLE)

This is an unsuspectedly instructive (and, we hope, amusing) game which is one of several that have been invented specially for users of this book. It derives from the saddening reflection that, marry whom we will and try as we may, we cannot endow our offspring with the temperaments, gifts or characters which our own experience of life tells us would be the best with which to go through life without discredit or despair. We may attend pre-natal clinics in the hope that the unborn Jock or Jean will inherit the qualities of our own favourite uncle or our admired sister-in-law, but for all that we and the scientists can do, the little wretch may come into the world with the mental outfit of cousin Tom, with his ticket-of-leave, or of great-aunt Sarah, who did not drink herself into the grave until she had driven the rest of her family into it. Worst of all, it may have its parents' most regrettable faults in an aggravated form and without their compensating virtues. The most we can achieve is to wait and hope—and see, trusting that, if we have got a sow's ear, large sums of money spent on the latest psychological treatment will turn it into a piece of useful, decent leather. *Happy Families* enables us to imagine for a short time that we are controllers of destiny.

Each player has paper and pencil and 100 points to distribute between the ten listed qualities for an imaginary boy or girl to whom we should most gladly be parents. Alternative lists can be substituted if the two here given seem to fall short. But whatever the ten you decide upon they must in any single game be common for the boy and the girl and to all the players.

*N.B.*—The condition of good health has been omitted from both our lists as being of course.

| | |
|---|---|
| Looks and/or Charm | Stupidity |
| Intellect | Conceit |
| Athleticism | Conventionality |
| Artistic gifts | Hardness |
| Sensibility | Sex appeal |
| Wit and/or humour | Selfishness |

| | |
|---|---|
| Will-power | Ambition |
| Affection | Good spirits |
| Religious feeling | Enthusiasm |
| Wisdom | Swank |

Players may put noughts for any qualities they think their child would be better without. But they must make up for this by increasing points for the qualities they consider desirable and, when added up, the points must reach 100, even should the 100 be confined to one quality. The process is completed first for Jock, then for Jean, and the finished paper is passed on to the right-hand neighbour who reads it silently and awards marks, taking 100 as the maximum and judging according to the merits as a whole. The papers are passed on from hand to hand till all are thus marked by each person, their own excepted. They are then all read aloud in turn by one player. The person who has the highest general marks is winner.

## A MARRIAGE HAS BEEN ARRANGED

Each person writes down his or her name at the top of a long slip of paper and hands it on to his or her neighbour on the right. One player, who is in charge of the game, then reads out the first "quality" on our list (or on any list invented for the occasion) and the players write down *at the bottom of the paper* what measure, etc., of this quality he would prescribe for a mate were he Providence intending a happy marriage for the name at the top of the paper. He then folds over the lower end of the slip, so that the next player, to whom he passes it in turn, will not see his opinion. The next player, aware only of the name at the top, plays Providence again by appending his reply to the second question as this is read out. And so on, until each paper has been the round, without, however, returning to the named person. The named persons then receive their own papers back and each in turn reads out the description of his or her mate. After this the papers once more go the round, each player (except the one named at the top) recording his or her opinion of the match as a whole—with a view to its prospects of a happy married life—by allotted marks, with 10 as the full mark. The player in charge then re-reads all the papers aloud, in each case giving the added-up marks. The person who, in the estimation of the company, is most satisfactorily mated, is the winner.

*N.B.*—Our list allows for ten players. If there are fewer it must be cut to the required length; if more, additional qualities must be added.

| | |
|---|---|
| Social estimation | Age |
| Temperament | Tastes |
| Worldly goods | Nationality |
| Profession or position | Will-power |
| Appearance | Talents |

## SIMON SAYS

Being the silliest of all round games, this is fittest for a tedious railway or coach journey when cards and other distractions have palled. Somebody takes the lead by cocking his thumb up on his knee and saying "Simon says thumbs up!" Everybody does the like. Other commands are "Simon says thumbs down", "Simon says trot-trot-trot" (which means that the players must keep jigging the downturned thumb while the leader repeats the words) and "Simon says stop trotting". But the name of power is Simon. If it is omitted the command is bad, and he who obeys it is out.

*N.B.*—The only merit of this game is that it can be played for money. Any average punter can think of a dozen ways of doing this, but the simplest is to have a kitty into which everybody puts a chip to start with, and then a leader is chosen by lot. A player who falls out can buy himself in three times at a chip a time, and can take the bank (become leader) on payment of two chips. Should two or more players wish to take the bank at the same time they must bid against each other, the highest bidder winning. The leader may not bid. The game goes on until only two are left in, one being leader. At this stage no player can buy in except the one who is left, which means that leader and player can change places as often as they like by the player paying in two chips. The leader who catches the player out wins the kitty.

## THE SHIP'S ALPHABET

A captain is chosen. He asks the first player the name of the letter and the answer is A: (1) Name of ship, (2) of captain, (3) of cargo, (4) where from? (5) whither bound? (6) B: and so on. Promptitude is essential, and if the answer is not forthcoming while the other players count three aloud the defaulting player loses a life. Three lives lost eliminates him from the game.

## SPELLING BEE

Each player tries not to complete a word but to force somebody else to do so, the round proceeding letter by letter. A person so forced loses a life, but has three lives.

## THE TABOOED LETTER

The Yezidis of Iraq, a simple and logical people, argue that as the Devil is admittedly an influential personage in human affairs, one ought to do nothing that might offend him. Accordingly they not only refrain from pronouncing his name (Sheitan) but all words beginning with *sh*. This complicates their lives

—how much so can be tested in any company. Let the company agree that a certain letter of the alphabet (or combination of letters) is taboo and that no word containing it may be used. Then, strictly observing the taboo, let A ask B a question, which B answers, also observing the taboo, after which B fires a question at C, who in turn does his best. And so on. Any player who utters a taboo word or fails to answer while avoiding it throughout three seconds counted by the others, is out, but this does not prevent him from putting his question to the next player.

There are other variants of this game. Quite a good one is:

## GUILTY OR INNOCENT

One of the company assumes any sort of fantastic dress that may be handy and calls himself the Old Man of the Woods. The other players assume the names of wild animals—lion, tiger, bear, etc. Each in turn is asked by the Old Man of the Woods what he has been hunting and what he has eaten to-day, and answers any nonsense that occurs to him. If the answer contains a letter that the Old Man of the Woods has secretly decided to be taboo, then the player is pronounced "guilty" and pays a forfeit for each time the forbidden letter occurs in his answer.

## TENS

Several categories—persons, things, etc.—are chosen, and a letter of the alphabet. Each player, subject to a time limit, is to write down ten names in each category beginning with the chosen letter. Score one for each person who has got a name not written by anybody else. (There are many variations of this game, and new ones can always be devised.)

## "I SHOULD SMILE!"

This is a sit-round-the-fire game in which the players wear their glummest Sabbatical faces—excepting one, who grins all he knows how. After a moment or two this obliging idiot passes his hand across his face "to wipe off the grin", which he then throws with a gesture at another player, who in turn does his smiling best—and so on. Any player who smiles without being thrown a smile or who fails to stop smiling, having thrown his smile away, is out.

## NICKNAMES

Read out a list of famous nicknames, allowing ten seconds for the players to write down the true name of each person alluded to: *e.g.* the Swan of Avon (Shakespeare), the Great Lexicographer (Dr. Johnson), *Ursa Major* (Dr. Johnson), the Stagirite (Aristotle), etc.

## CROSS QUESTIONS AND CROOKED ANSWERS

A asks his left-hand neighbour B some fool question, to which B gives what answer he can, not being a mere yes or no. In the same way B questions C, and C questions D, etc. When the round is complete each player has to repeat (*a*) the question he had from his *right-hand* neighbour and (*b*) the answer he had from his *left-hand* one.

## DUMB CLUBS

This is a good game for players who are shy of speech. Two players go out as for ordinary "clubs", while those in the room decide upon something they think will be difficult to guess, such a "a hair of the dog that bit you". The players who come in are to try which of them can make the discovery first. They go round in opposite directions, asking questions as fast as they can, but are answered only by nods, becks and wreathing smiles, or by shakes of the head. *They* may speak as much as they like, but all answers must be in dumb show and, although gesture in moderation is allowed—as, for example, rough measurements given with the hands—there must be no employment of the dumb alphabet. The questioner who elicits the secret first has won, and the one from whom he had the final clue goes out next time with the unsuccessful player. Or it may be played with a number of small clubs, the successful questioner always joining the club which gave him the clue until the largest club wins. In this case the unsuccessful questioner must go out in the company of one player from the unsuccessful club in which he finds himself at the end.

## DRAWING WITH DOTS

Each player has a piece of paper upon which he puts five dots disposed as he pleases. The slips are then mixed in a hat, nobody being allowed to draw his own. When redistributed a drawing has to be made on each slip which shall touch all the points in its outline. The drawings may be confined to animals or human beings or faces. When finished they are passed round for marking, five marks being the maximum. All the marks are added up at the end and the highest-marked drawing wins.

## PUBLIC SPEAKING

One player starts addressing the company as provocatively as possible, having reference to the various known prejudices of members of the audience! At every pause in the discourse every member of the audience must say "Hear, hear!" with enthusiasm, either real or realistically simulated. If any member of the audience either fails to utter the response within an appreciable interval or with manifest lack of enthusiasm, the speaker notes the fact and passes on the speaking to that one to continue. And so it goes on. Each person who thus has to become speaker loses one life, and each speaker who passes on the post gains two lives. To begin with, each player has five lives. The one who first gains ten lives has won.

## FAMOUS NAMES

Two go out. Those who remain in the room choose the name of some famous man or woman, the number of letters in the name corresponding to the number of players in the room. They sit in any order (though if you want to make the game easier they may sit in the proper order for the spelling of the name). The two who come in put questions, racing all the time, to the sitting players, each of whom has chosen, in addition to the common name and unknown to the rest, some other famous name beginning with the letter assigned to him. The questioning player who first discovers the common name has won.

# LITERARY GAMES

For those who are vain about their literary gifts there are limericks, clerihews, *bouts-rimés* and bellocrimes.

## LIMERICKS

Everybody thinks he knows how to write these, but few can. The limerick is a peculiarly subtle form, as difficult as a five-act tragedy, and in structure not unlike it. The theme is stated in the first line, is expanded in the second, develops into action in the

316

third and fourth, and in the fifth attains the catas-
trophe, which must be as inevitable as it is shocking,
or at least surprising.

## CLERIHEWS

The "clerihew" is not so difficult as the limerick, yet
is by no means so easy as it looks. The correct formula
is

> Dante Alighieri
> Seldom went to the dairy.
> He wrote the Inferno
> On a bottle of Pernod.

Avoid the vicious practice that has crept in recently
of metrically mutilating the last line, *e.g.*

> He wrote the Inferno
> On Pernod.

This is the negation of clerihew art.

### *BOUTS-RIMÉS*

Everybody knows these and can make something of
them—a couple of rhyming words, or several couples,
being given on which to build as sensible verses as
you can.

### BELLOCRIMES

These are a sort of mixture of *bouts-rimés* and consequences. Imperfect couplets, consisting of the first line,
or the first line and a bit, are written down suitably
spaced. Players have to complete the couplets. The
paper is folded so that each player sees only his own
task.

*E.g.*, the italicised passages in brackets being the completions—

> There was a man called Peter Pole
> *(Who disapproved of birth control)*.
> He doted on his family life,
> *(He very seldom beat his wife)*.
> He ne'er had letters from the bank
> Marked "Private", *(for he never drank)*.
> His wife, a large and lovely woman,
> *(Regarded him as barely human)*.

And so on. Of course the average will not be up to the level of this noble fragment. But you can try.

# A FEW PROBLEMS

## THE LITTLE BRIDESMAIDS

When Jean and Ailie were bridesmaids at the wedding of their only aunt, Jean was but a fifth of the present age of Ailie, but has now reached twice the age that Ailie was then. If the sum of Jean's and Ailie's ages at the time of the wedding was fifteen years, how long has the aunt been married?

## THE ROPE TRICK

A rope is hung over a pulley and an Englishman and a Scot, of equal weights, are given the two free ends. They are told that the first to reach the pulley and touch it will receive a prize. The Englishman is the better rope-climber and tries, while the Scot is dour and does not try, but he wins. Why?

## THE MASSACRE OF MACPHERSON

Macpherson spent the first third of his life in Scotland, and then went to Canada to live there for six years. War broke out, and for the next four years Mac was a soldier. He then married, and spent a ninth of his life with his wife as his chief companion, when a son was born to share his affection. The boy, much to his parents' regret, died when he had only attained a third of the age that his father reached five years later when he passed away. How old was Macpherson when he died?

## THE GENEROUS FATHER

A man decided to give each of his children, nephews and nieces, assembled to celebrate his silver wedding, a present of twenty-five shillings. Unfortunately the calls on his purse that day had left him in the position of being ten shillings short of the requirements. He was, therefore, reluctantly compelled to change his mind, and make his present a pound. By doing so he found himself with twenty-five shillings left. What had he at first and how many recipients were there?

## THE NOBLEST PROSPECT

Four brothers decided to leave Glasgow to start work in London and all adopted different means of travel. Ronald paid 120s. to proceed by aeroplane in 5½ hours; Hamish took the train and did the journey in 8 hours at a fare of 50s. 3d.; Ian went by coach, being charged 30s. for an adventure taking 15½ hours; and Gordon chose the steamer, which meant a train journey from Glasgow of an hour's duration costing 5s. 10d. and a fine sea trip from Edinburgh of 36 hours costing 32s. 6d. What would you suggest as being the relative values of the brothers as Scotsmen, and, putting that consideration aside, what relative values do you consider they put on their time, if, and it is a very questionable if, the comfort and other considerations were the same?

## NORTH AND SOUTH

An express train left London for Glasgow, a distance of $401\frac{1}{2}$ miles, at the same time as a parliamentary train left Glasgow to do the opposite journey. The express travelled at an average speed of sixty miles per hour and the other train at half that rate. Which was the nearer to London when they met?

## CAPITAL

A merchant finds that his capital grows each year by one-third of what is left after he has taken £1000 out of the business each year for his personal expenses. If, at the end of three years' trading, he discovers that his capital has doubled, what sum had he to commence operations?

## THE HOSPITAL

A hospital showed an increase of 3 per cent in the total number of patients treated during the year. The change was not uniform in the different sections, for the number of in-patients fell by 12 per cent while the out-patients increased by 5 per cent, due to the change in road risks. What was the ratio of the two types of patients?

## RAILS

In railway lines the lengths of metal are not closely butted together, but gaps are left between them. The reason is that allowance must be made for the expansion due to rise of temperature. On the other hand, *tramway* rails are laid without any such provision and, indeed, are often welded together. Why?

## CAMPBELL, PERKINS AND MURPHY

If it takes Campbell 50 per cent longer to do a job of work than Perkins and Murphy could do it in working together, and if it takes Perkins twice as long on the same job as Campbell and Murphy working together, how many times the period taken by Campbell and Perkins in partnership, would it take Murphy to accomplish the job on his own?

*N.B.*—This is not meant to be funny. It is quite a nice problem.

## RATS!

If anyone told you that he was pursued by rats so big that every dimension was one hundred times the normal, and even though you could see them yourself, you would know they were not real, because no such creatures could ever exist in Nature. Why should they be so regarded?

*N.B.*—This is a serious question.

## THE THREE BALLS

If you were told, and it seems to be a fact, that a bullet leaving a rifle does not attain its maximum velocity until it has got a certain number of feet upon its journey, and yet a golf-ball leaves the club and a football leaves the foot on a free kick with the highest speed they ever have in their flight, how would you account for the difference?

# AN EXAMINATION PAPER

## I. HISTORY

1. Who said, and in what circumstances, the following?—
   (*a*) "I'll mak siccar."
   (*b*) "I will bell the cat."

    (c) "It came with a lass, and it will go with a lass."

    (d) "The monstrous regiment of women."

    (e) "Better bairns greet than bearded men."

2. What do you know or (a) Margaret Logie, (b) the Wolf of Badenoch, (c) Jingling Geordie, (d) the Guidman of Ballengeich, (e) Sawney Bean, (f) Toom Tabard?

3. What was Robert the Bruce's mother tongue, and do you know anything of his linguistic attainments or limitations?

4. "Berwick-on-Tweed is an English town which gives its name to the adjacent Scottish county." Discuss this statement with a wealth of historical detail.

5. Who was Captain Green, and what is his importance in the history of Scotland?

6. Who was the "Admirable Crichton", where was he born, and what did he do?

7. Why was the Battle of Bannockburn?

## II. CHURCH

1. Say why the following dates are memorable in the history of Scotland, viz.: 1638, 1643, 1679, 1690, 1712, 1843, 1903, 1931.

2. Who were (a) the Cameronians, (b) the Burghers and the Anti-Burghers, (c) the Glassites, (d) the Morisonians?

3. Who were (a) Jupiter Carlyle, (b) the Apostle of the North, (c) Rabbi Duncan, (d) the Great Norman, (e) "Orwell", (f) A. K. H. B.?

4. What is "moderating in a call"?

5. When you read in the newspapers that "the Rev. Mungo Mucklebairn preached the church vacant" you do not understand anything derogatory to the man of God's pulpit powers. What do you understand?

## III. LAW

1. Why is a fiscal so called?
2. Why do clever people go to Scotland to commit suicide?
3. How many judges are there in (*a*) the Court of Session, (*b*) the High Court of Justiciary?
4. Distinguish between (*a*) a law-agent, (*b*) a procurator, (*c*) a solicitor, (*d*) a Solicitor of the Supreme Court, (*e*) a writer, (*f*) a Writer to the Signet.
5. What, if anything, do you understand by *stellionate* and how would you distinguish it from (*a*) *hamesucken*, (*b*) *stouthrief* and (*c*) *spulzie*?
6. What is a "paper lord"?

## IV. LITERATURE

1. The following familiar quotations are all from Scottish authors. Identify.

    (*a*) " 'Tis distance lends enchantment to the view."
    (*b*) "Uncertain, coy, and hard to please."
    (*c*) "Oh, what a tangled web we weave,
        When first we practise to deceive!"
    (*d*) "Let me make the songs of a nation, and I care not who makes the laws." (Think twice before answering this: there is a catch.)
    (*e*) "Great Nature's plan."
    (*f*) "Britannia rules the waves."
    (*g*) "My name is Norval."
    (*h*) "Only for telling a man he was wrong,
        Two lovely black eyes!"

2. Name the author of the quotation in Misc. 1, below.
3. What do you know of (*a*) Mansie Wauch, (*b*) Johnny Gibb of Gushetneuk, (*d*) Jeems Kaye?

## V. GEOGRAPHY

1. Pronounce the following place-names so as not to excite the derision of the natives: (a) Milngavie, (b) Buckhaven, (c) St. Ninians, (d) Friockheim, (e) Polmadie, (f) Stonehaven, (g) Mallaig, (h) Monzie.
2. Identify as nearly as you can the following districts of Scotland: (a) Kyle, (b) Angus, (c) Lennox, (d) Mearns, (e) The Merse, (f) Cunningham, (g) Buchan, (h) The Stewartry.
3.            "O who be ye would cross Loch Gyle,
              This dark and stormy water?"
   Where is Loch Gyle? And—though this does not, strictly speaking, belong to this section—do you see anything in the boatman's question to suggest that he was the local idiot?

## VI. BURNS

1. Translate *accurately* into standard English:
   (a) "A daimen icker i' the thrave."
   (b) "His lyart haffets."
   (c) "I on the question targe them lightly."
   (d) "Tirl the hallions to the birses."
   (e) "Painch, tripe, or thairm."
   (f) "The swats sae ream'd in Tammie's noddle,
        Fair play, he cared na de'ils a boddle."
2. Quote any passage from Burns indicative of his views on Sabbath observance.
3. See page 84 and give a conjectural restoration of the line that Burns somehow couldn't remember.

## VII. MISCELLANEOUS

1. "Cam' ye by Athol, lad wi' the philabeg." What precisely is a philabeg?

2. Spell *without hesitation* the name that is pronounced Cohoon. (For a written answer the time allowed is 5 seconds.)

3. (*a*) Name the Universities of Scotland in order of seniority.

 (*b*) Is there anything in its history or constitution that distinguishes Edinburgh from the other Scottish Universities?

4. When did Scotland begin to play golf?

5. What is a schooner of beer?

6. What are (*a*) a Banavie flea, (*b*) a Glasgow magistrate?

7. "I'm sair hadden doon wi' a bubbly-jock." Does this convey any meaning to you, and if so what, and explain why and all about it?

8. In the seventeenth, eighteenth and nineteenth centuries respectively Scotland had three transcendent mathematicians: (*a*) The first made the modern methods of calculation, but thought nothing of that. He believed his life's work was his demonstration that the Pope was Antichrist. (*b*) The second made discoveries in geometrical theory equal to Euclid's, but during the 'Forty-five Rebellion he had to apply his science to the art of fortification, and ultimately died from the effects of the privations he suffered during the campaign. (*c*) The third was the greatest physicist of his age, but he declined to join the Royal Aeronautical Society on the ground that flight by means of a heavier-than-air machine was a demonstrable impossibility. Can you name the three men?

9. When and where was the first Rugby international played between Scotland and England, and who won?

10. You are, perhaps, nobody in particular, but it has fallen to you to preside at a public dinner in Edinburgh, to which a number of important

people have been invited. You have on either side of you at the chairman's table the Secretary for Scotland (a commoner), the Earl of Mar, the Earl of Derby, Mr Bertrand Russell, the Lord Provost of Edinburgh, the Lord President of the Court of Session and two Lords-Ordinary, the Sheriff of the Lothians, the Sheriff of Lanarkshire, the Lord-Advocate, the Moderator of the General Assembly, the Minister of St. Giles', and the Principal of Edinburgh University, who is, of course, a knight. Indicate according to the subjoined plan, how you should find them placed?

| 13 | 11 | 9 | 7 | 5 | 3 | 1 | CHAIR | 2 | 4 | 6 | 8 | 10 | 12 | 14 |
|---|---|---|---|---|---|---|---|---|---|---|---|---|---|---|

# DANCING

We differ from the English in respect of sport and games. Though we like to shoot and fish—especially to fish—we do not pride ourselves upon being a nation of sportsmen, nor on the moral attributes which such pride implies. Though we love to fish, especially when there's a bit of good poaching to be had, no Scot has found it worth while to sit down and write a book like Isaac Walton's. And though we are not bad at "Rugger" and make rather a point of golf, being capable of rivalling in the art of boredom on that subject the most enthusiastic of English cricketers, the national bent has always been for games like shinty, where fair play and rules are both less important than being the best man and getting the other man down. In three words, we don't see the need to make a song and dance of our games.

But we make good songs about other things and, as a race, we are dancers. Some of our songs are in this book. Our national dance of the reel, in its various forms, is as strenuous and as complicated and demands as much of athleticism and of grace as the national dances of the Russians. The reel cannot be taught by book, and English people find it hard to learn, even when they can pay for lessons. It is to be hoped that parties of holiday-makers will be able to form and go through Foursomes and Eightsomes of their own accord, and that they will often feel like doing so. Nothing is more warming of a cold night or more limbering to the tired muscles after a day's tramping. At the end of a shinty match the players always danced before they went to bed.

## Some Simple Scottish Dances

For those who do not dance the reel, however, or for mixed companies containing some who do not, we give here clear (we trust) directions for eight Scottish country dances, which are the next best thing. They are all great fun, not least when differences of opinion arise as to correctness of procedure during their progress. In case anybody has a mouth-organ, tin whistle, fiddle, accordion, or comb rolled in tissue paper, we have given the correct tunes at the end of our musical anthology.

### THE DUKE OF PERTH

AIR: *The Duke of Perth*, or *The Brownie's Reel*.
TIME: As for any reel.

Three couples form the dance, any number of sets of three facing each other down the room, men facing women 6–7 feet apart.

**Duke of Perth.**

Bars

1st man and woman link arms in centre and swing once round. The woman then goes down behind and between the 2nd and 3rd men, and at same time the 1st man goes down behind and between the 2nd and 3rd women . . . . 6

1st couple link left arms in centre and swing once round . . . . . . . . 2

1st man links right arm with 1st corner woman, swinging half round. At same time she swings 2nd corner man half round . . . . 2

1st couple link arms in centre and swing once round 2

1st man links right arm with 2nd corner woman and swings half round. At same time she swings 1st corner man half round . . . . 2

1st couple link left arms in centre and swing half round . . . . . . . . 2

Set to corners with *Pas de Basque* (see notes). 1st

328

woman sets to 2nd corner man and swings half
round. At same time 1st man sets to 1st corner
woman and swings half round . . . 4
Repeat the setting, turning at opposite corners . 4
1st woman dances Reel of Three (see notes) between 2nd and 3rd men. At same time 1st man
dances Reel of Three between 2nd and 3rd women.
The two sets of Three are danced simultaneously 8

The first couple go to places to repeat the whole,
one couple down the line, and so on to the end.

## PETRONELLA

Air: *Petronella.*
Time: 8 bars = 8 seconds.

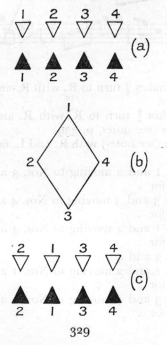

M 2

Women with R. hand to top of Room.⎫ In lines 6 to
Men with L. hand to top of Room.  ⎬ 7 feet apart.

**Petronella.**

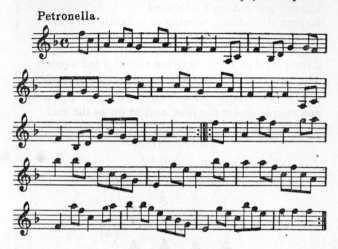

Bars

1st woman makes $\frac{3}{4}$ turn to R. with R. and L.
*Pas de Basque.*

1st man makes $\frac{3}{4}$ turn to R. with R. and L.
*Pas de Basque* (see notes, p. 339) . . 1–2

*Pas de Basque* (see notes) with R. and L. facing
each other . . . . . 3–4

Repeat bars 1 and 2 moving to Nos. 3 and 1
(see Fig. b) for . . . . . 5–6

Repeat bars 3 and 4 moving to Nos. 4 and 2
(see Fig. b) for . . . . . 7–8

Repeat bars 1 and 2 moving to Nos. 4 and 2
(see Fig. b) for . . . . . 9–10

Repeat bars 3 and 4 . . . . 11–12

Repeat bars 1 and 2 moving to Nos. 1 and 3
(see Fig. b) for . . . . . 13–14

Repeat bars 3 and 4 moving to Nos. 1 and 3
(see Fig. b) for . . . . . 15–16

1st couple holding R. hands move down the
centre . . . . . . 17–20
1st couple holding R. hands move up the
centre . . . . . . 21–24
1st and 2nd couples *Poussette* (see notes) . 25–32

1st couple repeat bars 1 to 32 moving down one
couple each time until they reach the bottom of the
set.

Couples Nos. 2, 3 and 4 repeat the whole of above
in turn, all finishing in original positions.

*Note.*—The couple below the leading couple is the
couple that *Poussettes* during bars 25–32.

## FLOWERS OF EDINBURGH

Air: *Flowers of Edinburgh.*

Time: 8 bars = 6–8 seconds.

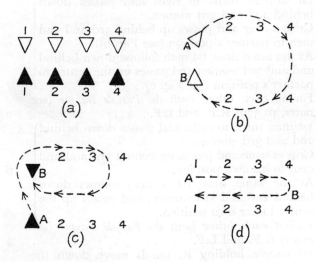

### The Flowers of Edinburgh.

<table>
<tr><td></td><td>Bars</td></tr>
</table>

1st woman turns to right and passes down
behind 2nd and 3rd women.

Crosses over and passes up behind 3rd and 2nd
men to partner's position (see Fig. b).  } 6

At the same time 1st man follows down behind
2nd and 3rd women and passes up the centre to
partner's position (see Fig. c).

Facing each other both do *Pas de Basque* (see
notes, p. 339) R.F. and L.F.  .  .  .  2

1st man turns to right and passes down behind
2nd and 3rd women.

Crosses over and passes up behind 3rd and 2nd
men to his own position.  } 6

At the same time 1st woman follows down
behind 2nd and 3rd women, and passes up the
centre to her own position.

Facing each other both do *Pas de Basque* (see
notes) R.F. and L.F.  .  .  .  2

1st couple holding R. hands move down the

332

centre (see A, Fig. d) . . . . 4
1st couple holding R. hands move up the centre
(see B, Fig. d) . . . . . 4
1st and 2nd couples *Poussette* (see notes), 2nd
couple takes the place 1st couple had in the line,
and *vice versa* . . . . . 8

———

32

1st couple repeat bars 1 to 32, beginning at 2nd couple's place and moving down one place each 32 bars till they reach the bottom of the set.

Couples Nos. 2, 3 and 4 repeat the whole of above in turn, all finishing in original positions.

*N.B.*—The couple below the leading couple is the one that *Poussettes* (see notes) during bars 25 to 32.

## STRIP THE WILLOW

AIR: Any 9/8 Jig Tune.

TIME: 8 bars = 9–10 seconds.

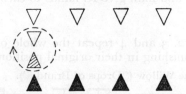

*N.B.*—Throughout this dance your partner always receives your right hand, hence you move clockwise with your partner: any other dancer receives your left hand, when you move counter-clockwise.

Bars

1st couple give R. hands and turn each other . 4
Woman moving down, partner ready to turn her:
1st woman gives L. hand and turns with 2nd man 2
   ,,   ,,  R.  ,,   ,,  partner . 2
   ,,   ,,  L.  ,,   ,,  with 3rd man 2
   ,,   ,,  R.  ,,   ,,  partner . 2

|                                                                      | Bars |
|----------------------------------------------------------------------|------|
| 1st woman gives L. hand and turns with 4th man                       | 2    |
|   ,,   ,, R.  ,,   ,, partner      | 2    |

Man moving up, partner ready to turn him:

|                                                                      | Bars |
|----------------------------------------------------------------------|------|
| 1st man gives L. hand and turns with 4th woman                       | 2    |
|   ,,   ,, R.  ,,   ,, partner      | 2    |
|   ,,   ,, L.  ,,   ,, with 3rd woman | 2  |
|   ,,   ,, R.  ,,   ,, partner      | 2    |
|   ,,   ,, L.  ,,   ,, with 2nd woman | 2  |
|   ,,   ,, R.  ,,   ,, partner      | 2    |

At same time:

|                                                                      | Bars |
|----------------------------------------------------------------------|------|
| 1st woman and 1st man give L. hands to 2nd man and woman and turn    | 2    |
| 1st woman and man give R. hands and turn each other                  | 2    |
| 1st woman and man give L. hands to 3rd man and woman                 | 2    |
| 1st woman and man give R. hands to each other                        | 2    |
| 1st woman and man give L. hands to 4th man and woman                 | 2    |
| 1st woman and man give R. hands to each other                        | 2    |

$$\overline{\phantom{xxxx}}$$
40

Couples 2, 3 and 4 repeat the whole of above in turns, all finishing in their original positions.

Strip the Willow ("Drops of Brandy").

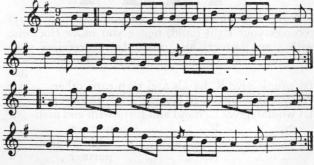

334

# CIRCASSIAN CIRCLE

AIR: *Circassian Circle.*

TIME: 8 bars = 8 seconds.

*Eight couples*

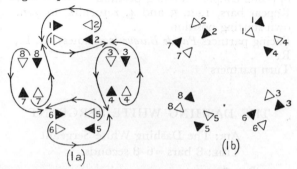

(1a)     (1b)

Couples form in sets of four, as if for *Lancers*, but without sides, and all start together (see Fig. 1a).

Circassian Circle.

*First Figure: Rights and Lefts.*                                              Bars

Women change with the men opposite, passing
them on the right   .   .   .   .   .   2

Partners change places, so that they are in the
opposite couple's starting position   .   .   2

Repeat bars, 1, 2, 3 and 4, returning to your
own starting position   .   .   .   .   4

Facing partners *Pas de Basque* (see notes) R., L.,
R.   .   .   .   .   .   .   .   4

Turn partners   .   .   .   .   .   4


# THE DASHING WHITE SERGEANT

AIR: The Dashing White Sergeant
TIME: 8 bars = 6–8 seconds.

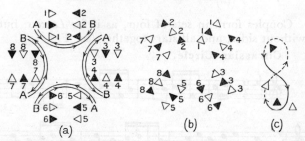

(a)               (b)               (c)

With a full tale of dancers this is a fine romp.

                                                                Bars

Each set joins hands all at once and dances half
round to L. (see A, Fig. a)   .   .   .   .   4

Still holding hands each set dances half round to
R. (see B, Fig. a)   .   .   .   .   .   4

The centre dancer sets to the one on his or her R,
and they turn   .   .   .   .   .   .   2

The centre dancer sets to the one on his or her L.
and they turn   .   .   .   .   .   .   2

Reel of Three (see notes) with the dancer on each
side of him or her (Fig. c)   .   .   .   .   8

Each set advances and retires in threes . . 4
Advance, passing through the opposite three . 4

Repeat *ad lib* with the three that are advancing to meet you (see Fig. b).

*N.B.*–Always move in the direction you are facing at the start.

**The Dashing White Sergeant.**

# THE MEDLEY, OR WALTZ COUNTRY DANCE

AIR: Any old waltz tune.

TIME: Fast waltz time.

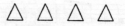

|  | Bars |
|---|---|
| 1st woman and 2nd man change places waltzing, and passing on the right . . . | 8–8 |
| 1st man and 2nd woman do the same . | 8–8 |
| Repeat, returning to former places . . | 16–16 |
| 1st couple waltz down the middle and up again . . . . . . | 32–8 |
| 1st couple *Poussettes* (see notes) . . | 40–16 |

# WALTZ COTILLION

AIR: Any waltz tune.

TIME: Not too fast.

The couples line up, each one side by side facing the other couples.

|  | Bars |
|---|---|
| 1st couple waltz inside the figure . . | 16 |
| 1st and opposite woman waltz singly, changing places . . . . . . | 8 |
| 1st and opposite man do the same . . | 8 |
| All couples repeat the figure, except first couple, who remain where they are . . | 16 |

1st couple waltz back to places . . . 8

All other couples do the same together . . 8

Each takes his partner's right hand, they balance with a waltz step; the man then passes the woman under his right uplifted arm, twirling her to the next man and he to the next woman. They then repeat this figure until all regain their places . 32

The men give their arms to their partners and march round to waltz step . . . 16

All waltz round to original places . . 16

## NOTES ON TERMS USED

*Pas de Basque* (or *Setting Step*, as it ought to be called in Scottish country dances) is known to anybody who can dance at all. It is performed first from right to left and then from left to right, first giving a small spring into the "second position" with the right foot, (*a*) bringing the left foot in front to the 5th position, (*b*) and beating the right foot behind, (*c*) all while you say "One-and-two", after which the same is repeated beginning with your left foot.

Naturally if you are reel dancers and have a *Pas de Basque* movement lasting 8 bars, you will introduce for the sake of variety not less than 4 "points", "shuffles", or "high cuts" into the last two bars. But in the dances given here this is not necessary, although of course you can do it if you like, and the more who do it the merrier you will be.

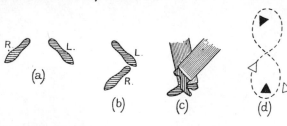

*Poussette.*—This is a means of couples changing places. The leading couple moves down on the man's side and the couple moving up pass on the woman's side. Holding partners' hands, women begin with their right foot, men with their left foot, and all turn four times with eight *Pas de Basques*, arriving at the desired position and ready to start again.

*Reel of Three.*—One woman dances this, circling first round the man opposite and then round her partner, and setting opposite to each in turn as she goes in this order (see Fig. *d*).

In all the diagrams, men are in black, women in white. But dancers may wear what colours they please, so long as they dance.

# BOTTLE AND WALLET

*O! braw times for the guts!*
DUGALD GRAHAM.

*Leeze me on drink!*
BURNS.

# BOTTLE AND WALLET

"THE diet of the Scots", wrote John Chamberlayne in the eighteenth century, "is agreeable to their estates and qualities. No people eat better, or have greater varieties of flesh, fish, wild and tame fowl, than the Scots nobility and gentry in their own country, where they can furnish their tables with ten dishes cheaper than the English can provide three of the same kinds; and of their wines, the French themselves did not before the Union drink better, and at very easy rates. The tradesmen, farmers and common people are not excessive devourers of flesh, as men of the same rank are in England. Milk-meats and oatmeal, several ways prepared, and kale and roots dressed in several manners, is the constant diet of the poor people (for roast-meat is seldom had but on gaudy-days); and with this kind of food they enjoy a better state of health than their more southern neighbours, who fare higher".

Some of this pleasant picture of Scots food and drink is out of date. We may, however, draw attention to the fact that to-day the best roast beef in England, the sweetest mutton, the finest as well as the cheapest sorts of fish, and most of the game that's worth while— not to speak of the highest grades of oatmeal and of strawberries—come from north of the Tweed. Sometimes, as with lobsters, the native products do not reach our tables except *via* the London markets. Perhaps this is one reason among many for the sad declension in Scotland to that low form of feeding known as the high tea. Where at one time in a simple household you would sit down to a dish of cock-a-leekie broth, a hot partan pie, or a juicy mutton one (and even now there are no mutton pies to compare with those of Scotland), with a glass of wine, ale or whisky, to-day you are as often as not presented with a bewildering choice, all on the board at once, of breads, scones, cakes, cheese, potted-head and pickles, and asked to help yourself to all in turn, while you are expected to wash the barbarous medley down with gobs of tea. If we no longer enjoy a better state of health than our more southern neighbours, this is, no doubt, accountable for it. Our palates are rather French (or anyhow, European) than Yorkshire, and our own native ways of preparing our native products for gustation are decidedly not English. Some, such as the milk-meats and oatmeal dishes mentioned by Chamberlayne, are manly as Cossack cookery. Others show a delicate discrimination (proved long ago by our discovery of braxy mutton) which presupposes the true culinary instinct. Better any day a single dish of well-prepared high mutton, high venison or high grouse than a multiple high tea.

Here it will be enough to note some of our most characteristic foods and the dishes made from them, first in the form of broths, then proceeding naturally through vegetables, fish and shell-fish, game, meat dishes, cheese and egg dishes, to scones, oatcakes, shortbread, butter-scotch and Edinburgh rock. There was a Scottish saying, quoted by Burt, that "if you would live well on the Sabbath, you must eat an episcopal dinner and a presbyterian supper". We may take it that the first was composed mainly of strong meats and fishes, the second of farinaceous and milk foods. So all tastes will be served. And if some feeders are so abandoned as to mix the two, their stomachs must be upon their own heads.

*N.B.*—For the traveller with a short purse, a couple of mutton pies bought in any shop is a good way out of a meal. A tablespoonful of water should always be added to each pie before heating it in the oven. This makes gravy. Mutton pies should be eaten hot.

## *Broths*

Like the Russians, we believe in the kailyard school for our broth, and if everybody in Scotland were to stick to the old custom, still preserved among French peasants and bourgeois and Russian workers, of relishing every day a pint of liquid containing the innumerable salts of the commonest green-stuff, Scotland would be the better for it.

### KAIL BROSE

This old cottage recipe requires half an ox head or a cow heel, a cabbage or a head of greens of any sort, a teacupful of oatmeal, and salted water.

Cover the meat in a large saucepan with three quarts of salted water. Boil till the fat floats on the top. Add the green-stuff, having first well washed it and cut it up small. Toast the oatmeal with a little salt in it, press it into a bowl, add a teacupful of the boiling fat liquor from the pot, and stir. It will form knots, which is what you want, or ought, in this case, to want. Put it into the broth, stir for a moment or two, removing, if you like, superfluous fat from the surface. Serve, with or without the meat, according to appetite. If you have been up Schiehallion beforehand you will want the ox head. If not it will serve as the basis of a barley broth for next day.

### POWSOWDIE, OR SHEEP'S HEAD BROTH

This is an excellent specific for those who have been driven back from attempting Glencoe by the famous "hunger-bunk" which haunts that pass for foot passengers. It demands a sheep's head, as large, as young and as fat as possible, and a sheep's trotters, all of which the blacksmith will singe for you the day before without charging you anything, as they must be

345

soaked overnight. Before soaking get somebody else—
perhaps the blacksmith's wife—to scrape and brush
these members and to remove the glassy part of the
eyes. She may also consent to split the head with a
cleaver, lay the brains aside, clean the gristly parts,
slit the trotters and take out the tendons. Every good
Scotswoman knows how to do such necessary things.
Thus prepared you have only to wash every bit once
more and put them in water before earning a night's
repose.

First thing in the morning pour off the water and
put the solids with rather more than a gallon of fresh
water in a lordly pot, adding from two to three pounds
of scrag or trimmings of sweet fresh mutton, a cupful
of barley, two cupfuls of fresh green or soaked white
peas and some salt. Take off the scum as it rises, and
when it has boiled more than an hour add some sliced
carrots and turnips and onions. Continue the boiling
while you are challenging Glencoe, having left in-
structions that after three hours or so it is to be
allowed merely to simmer. A ram's head ought to boil
longer than a wether's, and the older the sheep (the
blacksmith will have told you its age if the butcher was
reticent) the longer must it both boil and simmer. Before serving add a generous heap of chopped parsley.
Glencoe and all, you will eat no more that night. But
you may safely sit and drink.

## HOTCH-POTCH

For this you want the kitchen garden at its best and
some neck of lamb or mutton. You may either make
the stock the day before, removing the meat before
you make the broth, or you can cut up the meat and
serve all together. Either way, success depends upon
long, slow and gentle cooking.

Three pounds of meat go to two and a half quarts
of water. When the liquor is strong enough (*i.e.* after

an hour and a half of boiling) add every kind of vegetable you like and can get, cutting them up first and
putting in the most easily softened ones later than the
harder roots. Be generous with your onions. Some
people like the inclusion of a sprig of mint. The proportion of vegetables is as much a matter of taste as
the kinds are of convenience. If the main body of meat
has been taken out of the stock, small pieces of beef
and/or mutton, cut up as for a pie, ought to be added.
A shake of white pepper is allowed last thing before
serving, when the broth should be thick and creamy.
Three hours is not too long for the cooking of the
vegetables and the added meat. Before adding the
vegetables the stock should be well skimmed and any
added meat should be lean.

## COCK-A-LEEKIE

This asks for a fowl if you can afford it. If not,
some beef or veal stock will serve, but it must be good
and strong. If you are really rich, or awfully greedy,
you will put the trussed bird into the meat stock.
Whatever you do in this respect you will need from
six to a dozen leeks, one dozen prunes and some
Jamaica pepper. If the leeks are big winter ones you
should discard the coarsest of the green parts. Also
you may choose between cutting up the leeks finely
or putting them through a sieve when soft. Everything,
except the prunes, put in together with some salt in
the water, must first come to the boil and then simmer
by the side of the fire for four hours at least, with
occasional skimmings. Half an hour before serving,
take out the fowl, and cut up and return the flesh.
At the same time add the pepper and prunes. Or
the prunes may be cooked separately and handed
round on a dish by themselves, to be incorporated
with the soup or not as your guests see fit. You can
judge of your guests' characters by their behaviour

when confronted with the prunes. If they refuse or grimace, they are not worth cooking for, anyhow not cooking cock-a-leekie for (sometimes spelled cockie-leekie). If the maker of the broth has been considering one of her guests as a possible husband, this prune test is well-nigh infallible. If he rejoices in the prunes he will be an appreciative husband. If he turns away from them he will be an easy one to feed, and married felicity on tins, with an occasional chop, may be embarked upon with confidence.

## BARLEY BROTH

There are many ways of making barley or "Scotch" broth, and all of them are good. One may start off with stock, made from a sheep's head, a fowl, shin of beef or scrag or neck of lamb. Or one may start cooking the harder vegetables with any of these and take the meat out before serving the broth. In the good old days the meat so treated did for the servants' dinner. Now it is good enough for ours as a second course or next day. The barley ought to be Scotch, as this is better and more glutinous than English pearl barley. The vegetables are carrots, turnips (more of the former than the latter), celery, onions, a little chopped greens if wanted, and some chopped parsley before serving. There are two ways of dealing with the onions. They can either be cut up and fried in butter till golden before pouring on the stock or adding the water and meat, or they can be added whole with the other vegetables, when they should be removed still whole before the stuff is served. Half a cupful of the barley is enough for five people. If the stock is first made, the vegetables should boil for three hours; if meat and vegetables are put in together, it will want two hours longer. Do not season till near the end, then add some cream or the yolk of an egg and stir, but do not let it boil again. Some people leave a turnip in whole, remove it when soft, mash it and put it back. Much time and trouble will be saved when making this or any of the other vegetable broths, if the vegetables are only roughly sliced to start with. Then, when they are soft, if the broth is poured through a colander, the vegetables can be easily and quickly cut up small while still in the colander by using two knives, one in each hand and working with them crosswise. A lump of sugar and another of butter should be added to all the barley broths, the sugar at the beginning, the butter at the end.

Grouse, pheasant, partridge, hare and rabbit soups are all better in Scotland than elsewhere. But those who want hare or rabbit soup usually know how to make it, and those who can come by the game birds have usually come also by some attendant who can dress them for the tureen. The bird soups are improved, if thick, by a final addition of cream; if thin, by a glassful of sherry or red wine; a bouquet of herbs is absolutely necessary. Brown bread crumbs cast upon the soup at the last are correct, but some people prefer sago, as brown bread may make the liquid curdle. The sago must be added an hour before serving, and must be carefully stirred. Unlike oatmeal, it has no virtue in its knots.

## Fish and Shell-fish Soups

These are among the best and the most characteristic that Scotland has to offer, and as they are rarely to be met with elsewhere in the British Isles outside of the most expensive restaurants for French fare, half a dozen sorts are included here.

### CULLEN SKINK

Cullen Skink is a cottage recipe from the shores of the Moray Firth.

Skin a Findon haddock (the same as a "Finnan haddie") and just cover it with boiling, unsalted water in a pan. When it is well boiling add a chopped onion, and when the fish is cooked, which will be in a very few minutes, take it out and remove all the bones. Put the bones back in the stock, adding some water, and boil for an hour. Strain, throw away the bones and bring again to the boil. Add a pint of boiling milk, the flaked fish, and salt if necessary. When this has boiled for a few minutes thicken with mashed, cooked potatoes, and add a tablespoonful of butter and a good dollop of coarse black pepper. You will notice that this soup is quickly made.

## FISH SOUP ("FISH-AND-SAUCE")

This is made from any kind, or several kinds together, of white sea-fish, so it suggests itself when you have come home with a mixed catch. Make a stock with the heads, tails and bones, throwing in any small fish whole, but skinned. Keep the flesh of the better ones for fillets to add later. With the stock boil some green onions, parsley, chives and whole pepper for an hour. When strained, thicken with butter kneaded in browned flour or with cornflour and butter; add the fillets and cook them. Flavour with catsup or anchovy, and chopped parsley, and before serving add a little cream. It may well be served with heaped-up boiled rice.

The best fresh haddock soup is made with a stock taken from skate and ling, which give their flavour, while none but the haddock fillets appear at table. Beef stock instead of fish stock makes a change.

## PARTAN BREE

A partan is strictly a crab, but may be a lobster. Pick the flesh from two cooked crabs or lobsters, keeping aside the parts from the claws. Boil five or six ounces of rice in slightly salted milk till soft, but not mushy, and pass with the crab meat through a hair sieve. Stir till perfectly smooth with a wooden spoon, and add, gradually, as much white, unseasoned stock as you will need for your company, taking care that the result is thinner than a purée. Season with salt, white pepper and anchovy. Re-heat and add the claw-meat, but do not boil. Pour into a tureen that has some cream in it.

## COCKLE OR MUSSEL BROSE

Scrape well the shells and wash in several waters, leaving under the tap in a colander till the water runs clear. Then steep for two hours. When drained out put them in a closely covered iron saucepan and shake over the fire till the shells open. Remove at once, strain the liquor off into a basin, and take the mussels out of the shells, throwing away the beards and black parts. Put on the liquor to boil with milk and water or stock made from uncooked fish bones or fresh fish. When this boils, add the mussels and go on boiling, but not for longer than ten minutes. Toast a handful or so of oatmeal and mix with it some of the boiling bree, as with *Kail Brose*, put the knotted oatmeal into the soup, and when well heated through serve very hot.

## SALMON SOUP

They never dare make this with fresh salmon in England and it is not so good with tinned. But if you have fishing or poaching friends you may eat of it in Scotland. Prepare a stock with the head, bones, fins and skin of a salmon, the bones of one or two fresh whiting (the whiting makes all the difference) and a few root vegetables, boiling all for half an hour. Strain and remove all the fat and oil. Thicken with a little potato flour or mashed, cooked potato. Add chopped parsley, some scallops of the uncooked salmon and some brown bread crumbs. As soon as the salmon is cooked the soup is ready. This is provided in heaven for good Scots.

## WINKLE SOUP

Scotland is full of winkles which are easily gathered at low tide. They can be cooked in a pot of fresh water on the beach and eaten in the English manner with a pin, or—far better—they can be made into soup with the addition of fish stock or milk and water, and oatmeal, much in the same way as the cockles or mussels. But they still have to be extracted with a pin, and the water they are first boiled in needs careful straining before it is added to the other stock as it is apt to be sandy. Be sure not to add any salt to either stock or water. In winkle soup the oatmeal should not be knotted, but rained smoothly and steadily, a little at a time from the left hand into the boiling stock, while stirring continuously with a wooden spoon in the right hand. The object is to get the consistency of a thin gruel, which is then cooked for about twenty minutes before the cooked winkles are added, after which you allow it to go ahead for ten minutes longer before you eat it.

## SHELL-FISH SOUP

In the Hebrides, where the long shell-fish called razor-fish is common, they use it for soup, either alone, chopped up small, or mixed with any other kinds of shell-fish there may be. The same recipe is followed, except that more milk is needed, together with a good dollop of butter and extra pepper, and the thickening is often done with cornflour instead of with oatmeal, this being mixed in smoothly. When shell-fish is scarce, or people are poor, the first washings of the naked shell-fish are re-strained and used in the stock, as much of the delicacy of flavour is lost in freeing them from sand. But if you do not want the sand along with the delicacy of flavour the straining has to be done several times through a fine mesh.

# Vegetables

## COLCANNAN

Colcannan is a Highland dish made from two or three good red carrots, eight or ten potatoes, and two turnips, all well boiled. When cooked, chop the cabbage finely and mash the other vegetables. Melt a big lump of butter in a stew-pan, put in the vegetables and mix thoroughly. Season with salt, pepper and a head of mignonette (if you can get any). Add a tablespoonful of brown sauce before serving as hot as may be.

## KAILKENNY

Kailkenny comes from Aberdeen and therefore is economical, especially if you have a cow that gives cream. Mash equal quantities of boiled cabbage and potatoes (observe that you may thus use up yesterday's leavings). Stir in a cupful of cream, season with pepper, salt and chopped parsley; mash and mix well and serve hot.

## CLAPSHOT

This is an Orcadian variant of the same dish, omitting the cream, using mashed turnips instead of the cabbage, and brightening the whole with chopped chives, a piece of dripping and a suspicion more of pepper and salt. It is served just as hot or hotter than Colcannan.

## RUMBLEDETHUMPS

Rumbledethumps, or, as Christopher North called it, "decent rumbledethumps", is the same as Colcannan, but it comes from the Borders and does without the cream or dripping, substituting an extra beating, as you mix in layers the potatoes and cabbage, with a beetle, or wooden potato pestle, and allowing an extra allowance of common black pepper. You cannot, however, do without the butter to help things out, even in the Borders.

## STOVIES

Stovies are potatoes of the best quality cooked in a pot with just enough water to cover the bottom. We always add onions ourselves, but some people prefer the potatoes alone. Salt is sprinkled on them and dabs of butter, and they are closely covered and very gently simmered till all is soft and melted. Milk added, as the water is absorbed, is a great help to this delicious and filling dish. But butter is always better for Stovies than dripping. Some wise women begin by frying the onions gently in the butter before adding the potatoes and water. Others put scraps of left-over meat with the vegetables when these are half cooked. This is less wise, but more economical.

## BANFFSHIRE POTATOES

In spite of their name these can be prepared anywhere in Scotland. Beat to a cream an ounce of butter; add the yolk of an egg and go on beating, then mix in three ounces of bread crumbs, a pinch of powdered sweet herbs, some chopped parsley, pepper and salt, and three-quarters of a gill of milk. Have seven unpeeled potatoes beheaded and hollowed out. Stuff them with the mixture; put their heads on again, bake

354

in a quick oven and serve hot in a napkin. Grated cheese may be added instead of or with the bread crumbs.

## TURNIP PURRY

Turnip Purry, or mashed turnip, is good by itself or with most meats. Pare off all the woody or stringy parts with the skins of some turnips or swedes. Boil them in unsalted water for an hour, or, if they are old, two hours. Drain, and mash well with a wooden spoon, passing them through a sieve if you have the energy. Put the mash back in the stew-pan and warm up with fresh butter, black and white pepper, and salt. Stir in some cream before serving. To be truly Scottish the turnips ought also to have the addition of a very little powdered ginger, and even less powdered sugar.

# Wet and Dry Fish

## HERRING

*How to Fry a Herring* in the right way is not common knowledge out of Scotland. For one thing the herring has to be fresh. Herring not newly taken from the sea makes excellent manure. The newly taken fish, as good as a salmon in its way, should at once be cleaned and dried, sprinkled with pepper and salt, and tossed in the coarsest oatmeal till thickly coated on each side. Have dripping in a frying-pan smoking hot, put in the herrings and brown them on each side, allowing five minutes a side. Drain on paper, and serve with thin slices of lemon and sprigs of parlsey. To each two herrings allow an ounce of oatmeal and the same of dripping. If the bones bother you in the eating, bone, split and flatten each fish before treating it as above. Plain boiled herring have to be even fresher than those that are fried, and they must come straight out of

Loch Fyne. These, boiled in their skins, have such a look of smooth well-being that they are known as "Glasgow Magistrates". But it is said that Glasgow magistrates no longer look as happy as a boiled, fresh Loch Fyne herring.

## SALMON

*To Boil a Salmon* is the best way of cooking it, though there are a dozen other ways that are a good second-best. If possible the fish should be boiled whole, well covered with well salted spring water. It ought *never* to be skinned beforehand, and the cleaning and scaling must be done with the utmost circumspection so that there is no unnecessary cutting. Cooking should be gentle, and about ten minutes to the pound allowed, but this will vary according to each fish and its fresh-ness. Scum should be removed during the cooking. The moment it is taken from the boiling water, and drained, it should lie on a napkin and be covered with several folds. The noble way to serve a fish that is nobly fresh (and accordingly, as Meg Dods has it, "crisp, curdy, and creamy"), is with no other sauce but a tureenful of the plain liquor in which it was boiled. When carving, help each person to a slice of the thick (from the shoulders and back) and a slice of the thin (from the side and the belly). Epicures know that the thin is the better. Salmon that is no longer quite fresh may profitably be boiled with some horse-radish and served with mustard sauce. When mere cuts are to be boiled the water should be warm to start with, and a squeeze of lemon will help to keep the flesh firm.

*Smoking*, *Kippering* and *Pickling Salmon* are mostly pro-cesses demanding time, space and practice, but there is one good and easy way of pickling, should you have more fish than you can use fresh, which will keep the precious stuff for you for a year.

Cut the fresh fish in pieces, boil, skin and bone

them, and wrap them in a dry napkin till the next day. Then put them in a deep crock and pour on two quarts of the best vinegar which has been boiled along with one quart of the liquor the fish was cooked in, one ounce of whole black pepper, half an ounce of allspice, and four blades of mace. The spiced vinegar must be quite cold when poured on to the salmon. Cover the whole surface with olive oil and leave it. If you can deposit your crock one summer in a friend's house, the contents will make an admirable *hors d'œuvre* for your next summer holiday in Scotland, provided always that your friend has been able to resist using it for breakfast or lunch meanwhile. We recommend this as a test of friendship.

## TROUT

If, whether by hand (guddling) or hook, you take any finger-length trout, try to cook them immediately by the side of the stream, by lighting a fire and laying them, cleaned and split, on hot flat stones. It is to be hoped that you have brought some butter with you. If not you must eat yout trout without, and this would be a pity. They are sweet, but they soon go soft. If you take them home (and it is always hard to throw the smallest fish back) remember that they make excellent stock for the boiling or *sauté*-ing of their larger brothers. If not so very small they will be improved in flavour if slightly salted and left to lie overnight. Next day wipe them, sprinkle again with salt and a little pepper, dip in milk and roll in coarse oatmeal. Cook very quickly in smoking hot lard, browning them on both sides, and serve with lemon and butter. Another way is to split them on the under side (always leaving the skin on) and to egg and breadcrumb both sides before baking or frying. A truly large trout should be boiled slowly in a stock made from heads and fins, with some vegetables added, and served *tout simple* with nothing but brown bread and butter, a parsley garnishing, and some of the strained stock in a separate vessel. Cold potted trout, made by taking the flesh, while still warm, from the cooked fish, putting it in a buttered pie-dish, seasoned, and running melted butter over the whole, is good and useful.

## WHITE SEA FISH

Allowing for a few distinguishing features, and a few dishes which are Scotch more by name than by nature, the preparation of white fish for the table in Scotland is not so national as to call for a list of recipes here. On the other hand, we are "pre-eminent in the glory" of fish that is dried or otherwise preserved for the breakfast table, as was admitted by Thomas Love Peacock's Rev. Dr. Folliott, who, as you will remember, said that this was our single "eximious virtue", and that he was "content to learn nothing from us but the art and science of fish for breakfast".

## WIND-BLOWN FISH

To wind-blow is the easiest procedure for the amateur, who can hardly compete with trade methods in smoking, kippering or salting. It is also useful for the amateur deep-sea fisherman whose catch is apt to be mixed and to consist chiefly of small fishes, such as whiting, youthful haddocks, sillocks (immature saith), cuddies and so forth. If these are to be kept for one day with profit they should be cleaned and skinned as soon after catching as may be, and the eyes taken out. They are then covered with salt, shaken free of it without delay or wiping, and hung up in bunches (by threading a string through the eyeholes) in a current of air. This can be indoors or out, but must not be in the sun, conditions which Scotland generously provides. To cook, roll lightly in flour, broil gently over a slow fire

and serve either dry or with a piece of fresh butter
rubbed over each. Whiting, be it noted, should be
hung up with the skin on and broiled without being
rubbed with flour. Or it may be boiled or brandered
and eaten with melted butter. This is a fish that needs
careful handling if its full delicacy is to be tasted and its
shape preserved.

The other way is to skin none of the kinds of fish, but
to clean, wash in salt water, and hang up in the
moving air where no sun will get them. They are left
until quite hard and used as wanted, *uncooked*, as a
relish with baps, barley bannocks or oatcakes.

The celebrated "rizzared haddock" should lie for
twelve hours in the salt, which should be well rubbed
along the sides of the bone of each split fish after cleaning. These are hung up in the wind in pairs by their tails.
Good-sized haddock should be chosen for this, and the
heads must be cut off. Proper large haddocks should
be smoked (though the small ones, known as "smokies",
are excellent too). For smoking allow them to lie all
night in the salt, and when they have hung in the wind
for a few hours, smoke them, over a peat or sawdust fire,
hanging in the chimney. If your chimney is not suitable, set an old cask, open at both ends, over some
burning peat or sawdust with a red-hot iron in the
middle and sticks or metal rods across the top for the
fish to hang from. Equable heat kept going for twelve
hours will turn them to the required bright yellow
colour. If you want to remove the skin before boiling
or broiling, hold the fish to the fire so that the skin
gets hot and then smack the fish sharply with the
palm of the hand, when the skin can easily be pulled
off. When boiling always have some milk in the water,
and serve with lots of butter. Of all these varieties
of dried and smoked fish, A. Soyer writes that they
are "the most light, wholesome and delicious food
that could possibly be served for breakfast". So
now you know.

## CROPADEU

Cropadeu is a haddock's liver well seasoned, enclosed in a dumpling made from oatmeal and water, and boiled in a cloth. The liver dissolves succulently in the oatmeal paste.

## PARTAN PIE

Pick the meat out of the claws and body of a crab or lobster; clean the shell, and replace the meat, having seasoned it with salt, white pepper and nutmeg; add dabs of fresh butter and some bread crumbs, and half a glass of vinegar beat up and heated with a little made mustard. Brown under the grill. Salad oil can be used instead of butter and the vinegar can be omitted for those who dislike sharpness.

## LIMPET STOVIES

To gather limpets at low tide successfully, you must knock them off sharply with the first blow. They are quick learners, and if you fail with your first blow they will resist your second. Luckily there are always heaps more uninstructed ones and they learn only by experience. When you have acquired two quarts, bring to the boil in water, remove them from the shells, and take out the eyes and the sandy trail. Take three times their quantity of peeled potatoes, and put layer about in a large pot, beginning with the potatoes and seasoning with pepper and a very little salt. Add two cupfuls of the liquor they were scalded in, and break up half a pound of butter over the top. Cover all with a cloth well rolled in round the edges, bring to the boil, and then simmer for at least an hour. If you remember to bring potatoes to the beach, have a three-legged pot, and can make a fire, there can be no better dish for a seaside picnic. Limpets are liverish if eaten in June. At other times they are not merely tasty, nourishing and easy to digest, but the liquor is prescribed for nursing mothers and for infants.

## Seaweed Dishes

Seaweeds have the great advantage over fungi in that none of them are positively poisonous, so that if you are on the Scottish shore with nothing to eat about you and you don't like wilks or limpets, you may safely nibble a bit of seaweed and thus keep hunger at bay, or firth. But you will be thirsty. Our edible seaweeds include *Carrageen* or *Sea-moss*; *Tangle* or *Redware* (Eng. *Sea-girdle*); *Henware* or *Honeyware* (Eng. Bladderlock); *Sloke* (Eng. Laver); and *Dulse*. *Sea-tangle* and *Dulse* can be eaten raw, the latter being reckoned as both "loosning" and "very good for the sight". To cook *Dulse*, wash carefully and simmer in fresh water till tender. Strain, cut up small, heat through in a pan with butter, add pepper and salt, and offer it to those who really love you. They are the only people, yourself excepted, who are likely to eat it. Tell them that when thus prepared, especially if eaten with the juice, it is more "loosning" than when in its raw state. Another thing to do with it is to roll it on a stone with a red-hot poker till it turns green. It is then kept dry to eat as a relish with potatoes. *Sloke*, in 1703, "restored to his former state of health a young man who had lost his Appetite, and taken Pills to no purpose", and for all you know it may do the same to you if you are in the same way. If your trouble is rather lack of money than of health, "they say that if a little butter be added to it, one might live many years on this alone, without Bread, or any other Food, and at the same time, undergo any laborious exercise". It should be washed to remove the salt and sand, steeped for a few hours in cold water to which a little bicarbonate of soda has been added, and stewed in milk, with beating to make it tender. This is part of the laborious exercise connected with it. Juice and weed together form the dark green soup that is so good for you. *Carrageen*, after being washed, is allowed to bleach and dry on a cloth out of doors for some days and is then kept in bags in the kitchen. It is made into a jelly by adding a heaped tablespoonful to a quart of milk and simmering till the milk thickens, when it is strained and cooled. It can be flavoured with cinnamon or lemon, and is served with cream. It is good for chest troubles, containing, as it does, iodine and sulphur. By adding twice the quantity of milk or water it can be made into a drink.

## Game

Game shall here be confined to grouse and venison. But in passing we may remind you that pheasant and partridge should be well done, wild duck and solan goose rather underdone, and grouse not more than just done. Also grouse should be hung in its feathers for anything from three to ten days, according to its age, the weather, and your taste.

## GROUSE

Youth in a grouse is indicated by rounded spurs, pointed wings, and soft down on the breast and under the wings. The younger the bird the less long must you hang it. Old grouse are not fit for cooking till the feathers pull easily from the "apron". When ready to cook, pluck carefully to avoid breaking the skin. When roasting "high" birds, put a piece of bread in the breast during the cooking and throw it away before serving. Never wash grouse, but wipe inside and out with a damp cloth after drawing. Young birds should be roasted, old ones braised or made into a pie.

*To Roast.*—Stuff with cranberries, red whortleberries, or butter into which pepper, salt and lemon juice have been worked. Wrap in rashers of fat bacon, cover with grease-proof paper, and put in a hot oven, lowering the heat almost at once. Baste often. They will take from twenty-five to thirty-five minutes, during which time you should pound up the livers with butter, salt and cayenne, and spread the paste on pieces of toast each large enough to hold a bird. Ten minutes before serving, unwrap the grouse; flour and brown them. The perfect roasted grouse should be neither dry nor wet, but it should glisten. No gravy should be served in the dish with it, and fried oatmeal makes a better accompaniment than bread crumbs. You may put what you please in the sauce-boat, but there ought to be a glass of rowan or cranberry jelly or of pickled peaches to hand round with it.

*To Braise.*—Having cleaned, trussed and seasoned, fry lightly in bacon fat till brown. Put in a stew-pan on a bed of sliced seasoned vegetables with a *bouquet garni* and enough water to cover the vegetables. (Use stock if you like, but it must not be highly flavoured.) Cover with buttered paper and a close lid and simmer gently for two hours or more. Strain the gravy from the vegetables and serve separately, thickened if necessary, with cornflour. Present your grouse at table on liver toast as if it were a young bird and with the same accompaniments. Somebody has to eat the old ones.

# VENISON

Somebody must eat venison too, as it is always getting killed and is little used for any other purposes. Hence chunks of it are often sent, regardless of postage, to poor relations, just to get rid of the stuff. Besides it always *sounds* all right. If really well cooked it really isn't so bad as when cooked otherwise. If an old buck, braise the chunk as you do grouse, but add two or three cloves and some prunes and a glass of port wine, simmer for three or four hours and do not try to pass it off as a young thing. You won't succeed.

To roast, cover it all over with a firm suet paste and greased paper, tie this up with tape, and cook in a fair oven from three to four hours. Undo it, season with salted and peppered flour, baste with melted butter and brown quickly. It will be greatly improved if some gravy (made from the stock of its trimmings or from mutton stock, to which you have added a teaspoonful of walnut catsup, a glass of port wine or a little lemon juice) is poured over it. Rowan or other sharp-flavoured jelly should be offered with it. Some people will eat more jelly than meat.

Or, of course, you may make a pasty, stewing pieces of venison (none of them measuring more than a couple of inches) in stock to which half a pint of port wine, a *bouquet garni*, and some allspice, pepper, mace, bayleaf and salt have been added, first having fried two or three chopped onions in the pan in half a pound of fresh butter. When the result has cooled, bake it in pastry, either in one dish or in separate turn-overs. We are not sure but that this classic manner is not the best, after all, for the disposal of the flesh of both red and roe deer. The skins make good bedside mats, and hard wearing gloves can also be furnished from them, but stag-killers seldom remember to send this part of the kill to those who could do with a bedside mat or a pair of hard-wearing gloves.

## Scotch Collops

Except that oatmeal is often used instead of flour in stuffing, the cooking of most butcher meats in Scotland follows the known modes. Collops, however, whether of mutton or beef, are special to the country, or, at least, better than elsewhere. We make them thus.

Remove from 1lb. of raw beef or steak all the skin and gristle, and all but a little of the fat. If the mincing is done at home, return any juice that comes from the meat, as this should make the finished dish sufficiently moist without addition of water or stock. If bought already minced, have a couple of tablespoonfuls of pure gravy run from roast beef to add later, but do not use stock. Choose rather plain water if the beef gravy is not handy. Put the mince into a buttered stew-pan, and whilst cooking, beat well with a thick spoon or pestle, and stir, to prevent knots from forming. When the pink colour has disappeared, but not before, add salt, pepper and a whole peeled raw onion. Put the lid on, draw to side of the fire, or turn the gas very low, and allow to simmer without boiling for twenty to thirty minutes, stirring now and then. Or it may be cooked in a covered stone jar in the oven. At the end of the half-hour, add a small handful of bread-crumbs oatmeal or barley, and some people will like a flavouring of mushroom catsup. When the whole has cooked for five minutes longer, serve surrounded by mashed potatoes or garnish with triangles of toast and slices of hard-boiled egg. Hare, venison, veal or mutton can be used the same way, but these should be further flavoured with a teaspoonful of *fines herbes*. The onion should always be taken out before the meat is served.

## Haggis, White Puddings and Black Puddings

These are so finicky to make and so easy and good to buy in Scotland, that we shall leave the stout spirits who insist upon making them at home to consult cookery books or the blacksmith's wife. Enough to say here that if you want to eat a white pudding at its best, give it a few minutes in the oven or under the grill after boiling. And use up what is left over by frying it in slices next morning along with the breakfast bacon. White puddings, or "mealies", as they are called, are served at their best with beef collops, minced carrots and onions and mashed potatoes.

## Cheese and Egg Dishes

*Scots Rabbit*, *Scots Woodcock* and *Scots Eggs* have all attained to international fame.

### SCOTS RABBIT

The Rabbit is best made from the distinctive Scottish, Dunlop or Gouda cheeses, although you can fall back at second best on a good Cheshire or mellow Stilton. Remove the crust from a slice of bread about half-an-inch thick. Toast lightly on both sides and butter on one. Grate your cheese, putting a little butter with it if it is not fat, and cook in a cheese toaster with a glassful of strong brown-stout porter (or beer) a teaspoonful of made mustard and some finely ground pepper. Stir till all is mixed and soft, spread on the toast, and brown under the grill before serving.

### SCOTS WOODCOCK

For the Woodcock spread thinner pieces of buttered toast with anchovy paste and keep them hot. Melt two tablespoonfuls of butter in a saucepan, put in three tablespoonfuls of cream and the raw yolks of three eggs, and stir together over the fire till the mixture is creamy. Do not boil. Add at the last a dash of cayenne and a little chopped parsley. Heap on the toast and serve piping hot.

### SCOTS EGGS

Scots Eggs are first boiled hard, then peeled and dipped in raw beaten egg and coated with a forcemeat of chopped ham, anchovy, bread crumbs and mixed spices that has been well beaten. Fry in deep clarified fat and serve with a gravy sauce in a separate dish.

## COTTAGE CHEESE EGGS

Cottage Cheese Eggs, in addition is a handy dish to serve when you are in a hurry and have some dry scraps of cheese (mixed sorts can all be put together) to use up. Slice thinly but do not grate the cheese, put it in a saucepan with a very little butter and enough water to moisten while it melts, add a shake of red pepper and a little Worcester sauce. Let the cheese stew very gently, adding, if you like, a tablespoonful of beer. When quite soft and liquid break in a fresh egg for each person and stir vigorously as for buttered eggs till the eggs are incorporated and lightly cooked. Serve piled on slices of buttered toast.

## Meal and Milk Meats

Of these Porridge is the prince. Unhappily visitors have been known to visit Scotland in search of porridge, and to return having found nothing but varieties of patent oats. This is to be regretted by the Scotch, if not necessarily by the visitor, who, perhaps upon tasting the true stuff, would have found it an overrated dish. Porridge, however, is well worth trying once, and some people like it so much that they will go on with it.

## PORRIDGE

There is only one right way of making Porridge. Use a handful of best Midlothian oatmeal, a breakfast-cupful of spring water and a small saltspoonful of salt for each person. Bring the water to the boil. The moment it boils let the meal fall into it in a steady rain from one hand while you stir with the other. Go on stirring till all is smooth, then simmer gently with the

lid on for about half an hour. Do not add the salt until
the meal has been cooking for ten minutes. Ladle
straight into separate bowls and serve with separate
mugs of cold milk or cream, into which each spoonful
of the hot porridge is dipped on its way to the mouth.
Sugar and hot milk are alike abominations, but butter,
or even syrup is permitted in some all-Scotch homes.

Before leaving oatmeal it may be noted that coarse
oatmeal which has been soaked in water with a little
salt overnight, makes, uncooked, a breakfast cereal as
good as any done up in cardboard, if the water is
drained off and a little cream or a good cupful of milk
served with it. Also a refreshing and stimulating drink
for a hot day is made by pouring a tumblerful of
water on a tablespoonful of oatmeal, stirring it,
leaving it to settle, and drinking the water. (See
*Travelling*).

## OATMEAL BROSE

Oatmeal Brose is a quickly made form of porridge
that needs no cooking. Put into a bowl two handfuls of
the coarsest oatmeal and press it down firmly. Add
salt and a good nut of butter. Pour in boiling water,
enough to cover the meal, and stir it up roughly with
the shank of a spoon (preferably a horn one) or a
wooden spurtle, allowing it to form knots. It should be
supped with butter-milk, but cream or milk can be
used instead.

## CROWDIES

The traditional Crowdie or Furag, which was the
universal breakfast dish when Scotland stood where it
did, was made by pouring cold spring water or fresh
butter-milk into finely ground oatmeal, stirring all the
time and making the meal as thin as a pancake batter.
Then you ate it, usually standing up as there was work
to be done immediately afterwards.

Crowdie Mowdie is prepared the night before by

putting into a jar a handful of oatmeal, a saltspoonful of salt and a breakfast-cupful of milk for each person, stirring well and covering. In the morning the jar is put into hot water and steamed for two hours or longer. It is, in fact, a sort of milk porridge.

*Butter-Crowdie* is made with coarse oatmeal (toasted), salt or sugar to taste, and butter fresh from the churn well beaten into the meal. Cream-Crowdie, a festival dish, is the same, but made with whipped cream instead of the butter. It should be frothy and light and will taste of nuts.

*Highland Crowdie* is a delicious form of curdled milk. To two parts of ordinary curds (Anglice *junket*) made by adding a tablespoonful of rennet to warmed new milk and then letting it stand till cold, add one part of fresh butter. Work them well together, adding salt, and press into a basin. Turn out next day, when it will cut in slices like a cream cheese. Take care that you strain off all the green whey from the milk curds before you add the butter. The whey by itself is good as a summer drink, but must be taken while fresh.

## HATTIT KIT

Warm slightly two quarts of fresh buttermilk, and add to it one pint of milk fresh from the cow. (If the fresh milk is already cool, the buttermilk must be warmed the more.) Mix well and leave all day. In the evening add another pint of new milk and mix again. It should now be firm and gather a "hat". Remove this firm top drain it in a hair sieve, and put it in a mould for half an hour. Turn out, strew with sugar and powdered nutmeg or cinnamon, and serve with thick cream. Hattit Kit is supposed to be made in the course of two milkings after a butter-making, each lot of new milk being milked straight into the vessel from the cow.

## RU'GLEN AND CORSTORPHINE CREAMS

There is a culinary controversy as to whether the Glasgow or the Edinburgh suburb, then villages, invented this milk dish, but as the two recipes vary slightly, we give both without deciding to which belongs the credit of precedence. For Ru'glen Cream put some sour milk into an earthenware jar or jug, stand it in a pan of boiling water, and leave it till the milk thickens and separates from the whey. Strain through a sieve or muslin so as to remove the whey. Beat the sour milk with a wooden spoon till the particles are well broken up, and add some double cream and sugar to taste. For Corstorphine Cream stand new milk in a jar in a warm place till it goes into a natural curd. To a quart of this add a pint of new milk, mixing well and leave for a whole day or night, after which add another pint of new milk, mixing again. After another twelve hours beat up the whole with moist sugar and serve with cream.

Both of these are, of course, the Scottish versions of the German *Dickmilch* and of the sour mare's milk of the Cossacks, now so widely known as *Yagurt*, which gave the clue to Metchnikoff. They are quite as conducive to health and long life as the German or the Russian varieties.

## Scones, Cakes and Sweets

### ROLLS

The floury oval roll with a navel on one side, which is called a "bap", is the best of all rolls for a sandwich and is a Scotch invention. We advise, however, that you should order them at a good baker's to be sent fresh-made and still hot next morning in time for breakfast. Of the many kinds of girdle scones we give only the simplest, but there is none better.

Sieve a pound of flour into a basin, add a teaspoonful of carbonate of soda, another of cream of tartar, and half a one of salt. If you want the scones rich, you can rub in two ounces of butter, but this is a mistake. Add, stirring, with a knife, enough buttermilk or thick, sour milk to make a very soft dough. Turn out on a floured board, divide in four, and flatten with as little kneading as possible, into round scones, about half an inch thick. Cut each of these in quarters, flour and put on a hot girdle, (tested by sprinkling with a little flour which should not brown at once there). Let them bake for about five minutes each side, when they should be slightly browned and well risen. You can tell when they are done by the edges being dry or by inserting a knife and drawing it out without dough sticking to it. Serve hot with butter, jam, honey . . .

## POTATO SCONES

Of the many good scones, including dropped ones, that are made on a girdle, these are the best for what is known as a "hungry tea"—a meal to be carefully distinguished from a "high" one. Mash half a lb. of boiled potatoes adding, if needed, a pinch of salt. Work in as much flour as it will take (about two ounces) and add half a gill of milk to make a stiff dough. Roll out as thinly as you can on a floured board. Cut into triangles or rounds and prick all over with a fork. Bake on a hot girdle for five minutes each side, turning with a knife. The bubbles ought to be brown. Butter immediately and generously and roll up before putting them on a hot plate.

## OATCAKES

Oatcakes take much skill and practice in the making, and there are many different varieties. We recommend that they should be bought if you do not know already how to make them, or if your hostess or landlady is too lazy to do it.

*Girdles.*—Girdles ought never to be washed. Clean the surface when hot with coarse salt and a piece of paper, afterwards dusting with a cloth. For scones, bannocks and oatcakes the girdle should be dry and slightly floured: for crumpets, pancakes and dropped scones (all made with batter) it should be greased.

## SHORTBREADS

Of these too there are several kinds, none of them easy to make for the first time, so they had best be bought. But if you must try, the Ayrshire way is the easiest. Sieve four ounces of flour and four ounces of rice flour together into a basin, mix, and work in with the fingers four ounces of best fresh butter. Add four ounces of castor sugar and bind the lot with the beaten yolk of an egg and two tablespoonfuls of cream. Roll out as thin as you want it, prick with a fork and cut into shapes. Bake on greased paper in a steady oven for fifteen minutes when it should be golden brown. Do not turn. Cool on a wire sieve and keep in an airtight tin. When you have made your first batch you will see why shortbread is rather expensive to buy.

## SWEETMEATS

Rock is far more difficult to make than Shortbread, as "pulling" is part of the process. If you are not a good puller, you should buy your rock in the same shops that sell the best shortbreads. But you might like to try Butter Scotch and Helensburgh Toffee, which are easier and almost as nice as the shop-bought. For the first, dissolve over gentle heat a pound of brown sugar in an enamelled saucepan, add four ounces of well-beaten butter and stir together until it has boiled long enough to harden when dropped into cold water. Add some essence of lemon or a quarter-ounce of powdered ginger dissolved in a spoonful of water. Beat for some minutes with a fork, pour on to a buttered dish, and while it cools score into squares. These are easily broken off when cold. For the second stir two pounds of loaf sugar, four ounces of salt butter, a teacupful of water and a tin of condensed milk together in a thick pan for forty-five minutes, when you will feel you have earned the Victoria Cross. But perhaps the toffee will be thought worth it by other people. At the end of the forty-five minutes (no, you are not yet finished) add a teaspoonful of vanilla and go on stirring *off* the fire for one minute longer. You will have learned to stir by that time. Pour into a buttered tin, dot with walnuts if you have them and any strength left. When cool cut into squares.

## A SILLABUB

Sweet puddings are not special to Scotland, but a beautiful sillabub, which professes to be native, is made by whipping a pint of thick cream with half a pint of white wine and the juice and grated rind of one lemon with some sugar to a stiff froth, skimming off the top as you whip. It may be prepared an hour or two before dinner.

# DRINKING

Until far into the eighteenth century we were largely a nation of wine-drinkers. Joseph Taylor, who visited us in 1707 and did not think much of us, observes that one of the few good things in Scotland was "the excellent wine in every place at 15d. per Quart, which tho' 'tis so cheap, I am satisfied will mightily contribute to the impoverishment of the Scotch, if they continue to drink the same quantity they do now, because they pay ready money for it, and have but few Commodities to make a return". Lord Cockburn speaks of having "heard Henry Mackenzie and other old people say that when a cargo of claret came to Leith the common way of proclaiming its arrival was by sending a hogshead of it through the town on a cart, with a horn; and that anybody who wanted a sample, or a drink under pretence of a sample, had only to go to the cart with a jug, which, without much nicety about its size, was filled for a sixpence".

Those happy days came to an end when Parliament imposed prohibitive duties on French wines.

> Firm and erect the Caledonian stood.
> Old was his mutton and his claret good.
> "Let him drink port", an English statesman cried—
> He drank the poison, and his spirit died.

The epigram is not quite accurate. Epigrams seldom are. We never took to port, but rather gave up drinking wine and did our best with our own beer and whisky.

## BEER

The Scots, unlike the English, make no boast of their brewing. They have no need; for, as a Spanish poet said of good wine, "it is its own best testimonial". That the great English beers are supreme of their kind is indisputable, but on the other hand there is an unconscionable amount of bad beer in England, and by bad we mean inherently bad. In this sense there is no bad beer in Scotland, though you may get beer that has been ill kept or ill drawn, and you may get no beer at all at the moment when you most want it. The great English brewers recognise the uniform quality of Scotch beer and take their Scotch trade seriously. Hence the bottled Bass or Allsop you drink, when you can get it, in Glasgow or Edinburgh is a more heartening drink than any contained in bottles bearing the same labels in London or Manchester. How else could they compete with our MacEwans, our Ushers and our Youngers? Edinburgh and Alloa provide the bulk of our native beers of the true mouth-gripping and gullet-soothing properties, and to Dal-

keith belongs the invention of green beer, which addi-
tionally soothes the eye. Glasgow manufactures a
special light Lager of which even Germans speak
with a reverence verging upon awe, not unmixed with
envy. But there is no home market for it. If you want
to taste it you must ship yourself somewhere east of
Suez. At the other end of the scale there is what
represents the "yill" or "tippenny" of our ancestors,
the so-called "sweet" or "Scotch" ale. It is a noble
liquor, ideal for cold weather, especially when mulled.
But remember that it is the same drink that Willie
brewed and Rab and Allan came to pree, and is
therefore not to be trifled with. According to Edward
Burt, who was nothing if not critical of Scotland, "this
drink is of itself apt to give a diarrhoea, and therefore,
when the natives drink plentifully of it, they interlace
it with brandy or whisky". The accusation is malicious.
All kinds of ale and beer are laxative, which is a good
thing, and Scottish brews have their fair share of the
general merit. Admittedly the practice of lacing them
with strong waters is an ancient, but it is not an honourable one. It is bad for the beer, disgraceful to the
whisky and ruinous to the drinker's stomach and
nervous system. It is a mode of drinking suitable only
for navvies, ironmoulders and Carlylean heroes.

## WHISKY

And now, *paulo majora canamus*, or touching the
drinking of whisky. At home no Scotsman with any
self-respect will drink any of the "proprietary whiskies"
so-called. We do not suggest that they are unwhole-
some: they are in fact perfectly safe and, when well
diluted with soda-water, not unpalatable beverages,
which one may without shame drink south of the
Tweed, where it is usually impossible to get anything
better. All that is wrong with them is that they are not
whisky. Their only title to the name is a legal fiction

which a well-meaning but ill-informed legislature has seen fit to impose on the public. True whisky is made from malt by means of a pot-still, whereas, most of the whiskies of commerce are patent-still spirit made from grain blended with a little pot-still to mitigate its flavour. Patent still stuff is legitimately used for blending, and practically all blended whiskies contain more or less; but no blend in which the pot-still does not predominate deserves to be called whisky. The best blends, however, are pure malt. The pity is that for some reason they have never been popular and are in consequence scarce. But if you really would know the glory of Scotch whisky, get by prayer or price a "single" unblended Islay, Campbeltown or Highland. "I have never yet", says Mr Neil Gunn, "met any blend of all malts or of malt and patent that had the individuality and distinction of a perfect sample of "single whisky". These classic whiskies are so numerous that Mr Aeneas Macdonald in his admirable little book, *Whisky*, gives a rhymed guide to them as an aid to memory. He has been kind enough to give us permission to reproduce it: [1]

## RHYMED GUIDE

### To the Highland, Islay and Campbeltown Malt Whiskies of Scotland

Name we first the brands that rule in
Islay in the Western seas:
Bruichladdich, Lagavulin,
Bunnahabain and Laphroaig,
Once I (lucky fellow!) fell in
With a man who had Port Ellen!

[1] While we do not share Mr Macdonald's low opinion of what he calls "crude doggerel", it is only fair to record his note that this is "the work of a Sassenach poetaster" who has "taken some liberties with Celtic pronunciation which may excite the anger or derision of the Gael".

Though, indeed, as good as these
Is Bowmore or Caol Ila,
Celtic witch and arch-beguiler,
Ard Beg, Malt Mill. And I shall
Surely drink more Lochindaal.

Last port seen by westering sail
'Twixt the tempest and the Gael,
Campbeltown in long Kintyre
Mothers there a son of fire,
Deepest-voiced of all the choir.
Solemnly we name this Hector
Of the West, this giant nectar:
Benmore, Scotia, and Rieclachan,
Kinloch, Springside, Hazelburn,
Glenside, Springbank, and Lochruan,
Lochhead. Finally, to spurn
Weaklings drunk and cowards sober.
Summon we great Dalintober.

Children of the Highland hills,
Product of the Highland stills,
Now's no hour to ponder faults,
Toy with test-tubes, sniff at malts,
Open-chested must we sing:
Away with care—the drink's the thing!
Fearing neither sir nor madam,
Praise we Dufftown and Glencadam.
Wanderer over hill and moor,
Weary, welcomes Edradour,
Purchasing new strength to loin
With Glendronach or Glengoyne,
Glenlochie, or ripe Strath Dee,
Cragganmore and Benachie.
Pious priest at mass or matin
'Mid the murmur of his Latin,
Thinks of Mortlach or Tomatin,
Sinning so, but is there any

Sin in dreaming of Balvenie,
Brackla, Millburn or Glenfiddich,
Cardow, Banff, or Teaninich?
Sailor after months of sailing,
Fishing, yachting, cruising, whaling,
Hears the joyous cry of "land oh!"
Thirsts at once for choice Knockando.
Let the magistracy glower,
Let the law put forth its power,
*He* will drink the good Inchgower,
Tamdhu, Parkmore, Aberlour,
And damnation to the funny
Tribes of ocean in Dalwhinnie,—
Drink until the stars go out.
Not for us such deep-sea bout.
Quite tipplers in our class
Are content with Glenfarclas,
Nor does fancy with us soar
Far beyond sound Convalmore,
Oban, Colburn or Dalmore,
With mayhap a straying wish
Towards Glen Elgin or Clyne Lish.
Hopeful nephew bound to see
Wealthy and repulsive aunt
(Shadows of a legacy)
Should equip him with Glen Grant,
He will find the interview
Smoother sailing on Knockdhu,
When debate grows overheated,
Chairs thrown down and men unseated,
To restore both law and order
Bring in Dlaas Dhu, Glen Cawdor,
Speyburn, Longmorn, or Strathmill.
Quick the tempest will be still
And sweet reason reign again
With the flow of Dailuaine.
If an angel unawares
Your domestic table shares,

You will not be wrong to give it
Tumblers of the real Glenlivet!
Serious poets, short of rhymes
As we all may be at times,—
For *ars longa, vita brevis*—
Woo the muse with good Ben Nevis,
Though the wench will come no less
For Glengarrioch or Stromness,
Scapa or fine Highland Park,
Lighteners of Orcadian dark.
Men will talk most brilliant bosh
On a diet of Ferintosh,
Argue, with emphatic oaths,
Black is yellow on Glenrothes,
Prove that four and four make nine
If encouraged by Glenfyne,
And, in paradoxic fury,
Square the circle with Glenurie,
Converts have been made, they say,
To some quite grotesque belief
By Strath Isla and Glenspey
And Glenturret (made in Crieff).
Cunning preachers rope the sullen
Heathen folk in with Glendullan.
In melee or collieshangie
Glentauchers or Glenmorangie
Timid mortals will inspire
With a high heroic ire,
Though their sudden fits of wrath'll
Quickly pass before Blair Atholl.
Leaders of the hopeless charge
Rallying for one assault more,
Should have come equipped with large
Flasks of Pulteney or of Aultmore
Or at least another score
Liquors veterans will think good:
Isla, Ben Romach, Glen Mohr,
Balmenach, Glenburgie, Linkwood,

North Port, Angus-reared at Brechin,
Aberfeldy or Ballechin.
While the vanquished in the fray,
Fleeing to the nearest bar,
Counsel take with Auchenblae,
Comfort seek in Lochnagar,
And, when human courage fails,
Stronachie the foe assails.
Scholar, drinking with a lout,
Knocked his boon companion out,
Bawling egotistically, "Shall an
Imbecile enjoy Macallan?
Craigellachie and Imperial
Are designed for souls aetherial!"
Sad that academic rage
Should pollute my peaceful page;
Class and faction I abhor on
Towiemore or Ord-Glenoran;
Ragged cap and top-hat glossy
Meet as equals on Glenlossie,
Bury hatchets in a hurry
In Glenugie or Glenmoray,
Talisker or Milton-Duff
(Damned be he cries, "Hold, enough!")
Rounding off at last the story
(Highland section) put we Finis
With Glen Albyn, Tobermory,
Glenglassauch, and Benrinnes.

## NOTES

If you would truly enjoy whisky, lay to heart these
simple precepts:

1. Failing a "single" whisky from a classic still—
and unless you are in its native district you may find
such hard to come by—get a good blend. That is not
difficult. Every good-class wine merchant in Scotland
has one. Take your choice and stick to it.

2. Have nothing to do with a whisky that has not a cast-iron guarantee of being at least five years old. About ten years of age whisky reaches perfection. After fifteen it deteriorates.

3. Don't be misled by the description "liqueur whisky". There is, strictly speaking, no such thing. The term is used to suggest, without actually saying so, that the whisky in question is above ordinary strength. It may be, or on the other hand it may not. If you must have a Scottish liqueur there is Drambuie, which some people prefer to Benedictine.

4. On no account contaminate good whisky with soda or any other mineral water. If you must dilute it, plain water—spring water if possible—is best, as Pindar observes.

5. Lastly, don't let your appreciation get the better of your discretion. It is often said that good whisky never did anybody any harm, but the statement requires some qualification. *Est modus in rebus*, or, to quote a bit of wisdom overheard in an Angus tavern: "Moderation, sir, aye moderation is my rule. Nine or ten is reasonable refreshment, but aifter that it's apt to degenerate intae drinkin'."

## Compounded Whisky Drinks

There are many helpful compounds in which whisky is the principal ingredient. The most celebrated of these is, of course,

### ATHOLE BROSE

The many ways of making it are all good for those who like it, but you can be content with this way.

Put a pound of dripped honey in a basin and add enough cold water to dissolve it (about a teacupful). Stir with a silver spoon, and when the water and the honey are well mixed, add gradually one and a half pints of whisky. Stir briskly till a froth begins to rise. Bottle and keep tightly corked. If liked, the old fashion may be followed of pouring the liquor over a little oatmeal from which it is afterwards strained.

## TODDY

Thoroughly warm a tumbler and a glass jug or bowl. Sugar to taste a glassful of boiling water and pour into the jug. When the sugar is quite dissolved put in half a glass of whisky and stir with a silver spoon. Then add more boiling water, and finally another half glass of whisky. Thin slices of lemon can be added, but the chief points are warm vessels, and mixing by putting in the water and whisky turn about.

## AULD MAN'S MILK

This is a good morning draught if you are heroic or depraved enough to want such a thing. Beat separately the yolks and whites of half a dozen eggs. Put to the yolks sugar, a quart of milk and half a pint of whisky. Next add the whites and stir gently. Flavour with nutmeg or lemon. (Rum or brandy may be used instead of whisky.)

## HIGHLAND CORDIAL

For Highland Cordial you must mix a pint of white currants, a bottle of whisky, some thin lemon peel, a teaspoonful of essence of ginger. Allow the mixture to stand for forty-eight hours, after which you strain it, add a pound of loaf sugar and again leave it alone for another day. Bottle and cork. It will be fit to drink in about three months.

## HIGHLAND BITTERS

Cut up

$1\frac{3}{4}$ oz. gentian root
$\frac{1}{2}$ oz. orange peel

382

and bruise in a mortar with

> 1 oz of coriander seed
> $\frac{1}{2}$ oz. of cloves
> $\frac{1}{4}$ oz of cinnamon stick.

Put in an earthenware jar and empty two bottles of whisky over it. Keep the jar closely covered from the air for a fortnight, then strain and bottle. This makes a warming short dram after a day's exposure to the elements. It also goes well in the knapsack for emergencies. But it ought to be kept for emergencies when taken out-of-doors. A little goes a long way down.

## HET PINT

Grate a nutmeg into two quarts of mild ale brought to the boil. To a little cold ale add sugar and three well-beaten eggs. Mix slowly to the hot ale. Add half a pint of whisky and bring the whole to boil again. Pour briskly from one vessel to the other till smooth and bright. If you are rich enough to follow the Old Style you should use light wine and brandy instead of ale and whisky.

## CALEDONIAN LIQUOR

One ounce of oil of cinnamon is dropped on $2\frac{1}{2}$ pounds of bruised loaf sugar, a gallon of good whisky is added, and when the sugar has dissolved the liquor is filtered and bottled.

To these whisky compounds we add two recipes for rum punch—one old and one new.

## GLASGOW PUNCH

For a poetical description we refer you to Lockhart's "Lament for Captain Paton" which is among our "Lucky Numbers" further back. But prose is more serviceable, viz:

To each tumblerful of punch allow one tablespoonful of icing-sugar, one lemon, one wineglassful of rum and about three-quarters of a tumbler of water. Dissolve the sugar with a little water in the punch-bowl, strain the lemon juice into this, add the water and mix thoroughly. In the just mixing of the sherbet, as this liquor is called, lies the secret of success. Now add the rum. Should limes be available, use less lemon, and after the rum is added, cut the limes and run each section round the inside rim of the bowl, squeezing in enough of the juice to flavour the whole without making it too acid.

## P.E.N. PUNCH

[Mr W. G. Burn-Murdoch's recipe, which has been greatly appreciated by foreigners, Sassenachs, etc., visiting his hospitable house on festive occasions.]

Rub the rinds of five lemons with lump sugar, using half a pound of the sugar. Put the lemony sugar in a bowl, add a bottle of old rum, then the strained juice of the lemons, and mix well. Put in a piece of cinnamon stick, and pour on the boiling water, stirring all the time.

By way of a worthy conclusion we give a noble recipe for

## THE HOGMANAY WASSAIL BOWL

Simmer the following spices in a teacupful of water—

| | |
|---|---|
| Mace | Nutmeg |
| Cloves | Ginger |
| Cardamums | Coriander seed |
| Cinnamon | |

allowing for each bottle of wine 10 grains of mace, 46 grains of cloves, 37 grains of cardamums, 28 grains of cinnamon, 12 grains of nutmeg, 48 grains of ginger and 49 grains of coriander seed.

Add the mixed spices to two, four or six bottles of port, sherry or madeira, allowing $1\frac{1}{2}$ pounds of loaf sugar (pounded) for 4 bottles, and set all on the fire in a clean bright saucepan; meanwhile have the yolks of 12 and the whites of 6 fresh eggs well whisked up separately and put in the wassail bowl. When the spiced, sugared wine is warm, take out one teacupful at a time till you have a third and add it to the eggs. Add the remaining two-thirds when it comes to the boil, but without letting it actually boil, pouring it in very gradually and whipping all the time to get a good froth, partly mixed through but mainly on the top. When all the wine is in, toss in 12 fine, soft-roasted apples. Send the whole up hot with a ladle.

# NON-HUMAN NATIVES

*The bum-clock humm'd wi' lazy drone,*
*The kye stood rowtin' i' the loan;*
*When up they gat, and shook their lugs,*
*Rejoiced they werena men but dugs.*

BURNS

# NON-HUMAN NATIVES

HERE Scotland holds her own. She stands as well as ever she did—in some ways better—as regards birds, beasts, flowers and semi-precious stones, not to mention gold. A considerable portion of this native stock, animate and inanimate, is peculiar to her. In no other British rivers can you hopefully seek for non-synthetic pearls, in no other British trees for wild-cats, caper-cailzies or ospreys, in no other British rocks for topazes filled with whisky-coloured fire.

## FLOWERS

We have most of the English species and are famous for our gardens and gardeners. On the whole our cottage gardens are better than those in the South. For one thing we have peculiarities of climate which, by retarding certain early blooms, enable these to appear at the same time as later ones. Thus spring and summer flowers may be seen, both at their best, side by side in Scotland. For example, if you have the good luck to visit Dryburgh Abbey in June, you may easily see lilacs, laburnums, hawthorns (called "flourish"), wisterias, rhododendrons and roses, all blooming in rivalry, while the ground beneath them is starred with spring flowers, such as hyacinths and daffodils that have not yet begun to look tired.

As for wild flowers, we have far fewer cowslips, this being a comparatively rare field-flower in Scotland. But our wild hyacinths—as we properly name the "bluebell" of England—are at least as good and as profuse as any elsewhere, and our true bluebells, which the English call harebells, are better, bigger and far more plentiful. So are our wild (Anglice, "dog") roses. Those who wish to see one of the floral sights of a lifetime will go to the Leadhills district of Lanarkshire in summer when the wild pansies are out. They carpet the soil there so closely, thickly and gaily that they must be seen to be believed. And even then you will rub your eyes, wondering if you have seen aright. The Hebridean Islands, too, are covered with wild flowers in June, and the lovely plant which we call sea-pinks and the English "thrift" multiplies its clumps on many of our coasts, both in the West and in the East. Our whins are more thickly covered with gold, which looks the brighter for its background of brilliant heather. Our brooms are excellent. The rowan is a common tree. The laburnum loves us.

We make a feature of alpine plants, even of arctic ones (these last being confined to the heights of Ben Nevis and Ben Lawers), of cryptogamic plants (mosses), of lichens and of fungi. Among the arctics are the rare saxifrages—*Rivularis*, *Cernua* and *Moalis*; among the alpines, *Pingincula alpina* is to be found in Skye, and both in Skye and in Coll the rare American genus, *Erioaulon septangulare*, while Arran boasts the unique *Pyrus aria* var. *fennica*, not elsewhere extant in Britain. Mosses are particularly rich in the West, where the in-running sea-lochs, the land bogs and the moderation of sunshine create favourable conditions to which there is no parallel except on the coasts of Norway, The Greater Cumbrae, which measures scarcely more than four miles in length by less than two in breadth, has a greater variety of different species than will be discovered in any other district of like extent in Scotland, perhaps out of Scotland. Continental botanists come to us for the sake of our *Hepaticae*. We have many and rare lichens, some of them used in the dyeing of tweeds and tartans. We yield the palm to none in fungi, edible or poisonous. In one small stretch—the Cadder Wilderness—about four miles from Glasgow—700 to 800 species of fungi have been gathered. On the other hand, tropical plants exist in Rothesay Bay. Collectors are advised to look about them carefully when strolling the purlieus of ruined castles and monastic institutions, as there they are likely to find plants "of dubious nativity" which, long since, came from overseas and have acclimatised themselves. An example is the *Nepeta cataria* that is naturalised under the walls of Craignethan Castle.

## MINERALS

We refrain from encouraging tourists to extract our gold. The process absorbs more energy than results are likely to justify. There have been visitors, however, who have dredged good-sized pearls from the larger rivers, particularly from the Teith and the Spey, enough to make themselves a necklace. These river pearls are imperfect in shape and clouded in colour, but are not without their charm. Throughout Perthshire and in most of the mountainous regions it is hardly possible to hunt for half an hour with a hammer without finding amethysts, cairngorms (topaz), agates, onyxes and other crystals and quartzes which can be cut and used for jewellery. The cutting of "pebbles", which used to be a notable industry, is now, unhappily, almost wholly discontinued. But English cutters are delighted to undertake the work of preparing and setting Scotch stones for people who pay. A word of warning here. Make sure, if you send your stones to an English cutter, that you get the same stones back in your brooch or cuff-links and not some scrap of ready-mounted English or foreign cornelian. The trick is a common one. Naturally, a factory having numbers of set stones in stock, finds it easier and more profitable to send you one of these than to make the best of your own finds. Do not permit it. The old Scottish cutter would have scorned such commercial subterfuges. Be warned, and stipulate from the first that the submitted estimate is to be for your own crystals and for no others, even if the others may look better.

Polished fragments of Scotch marbles and granites make good paper-weights and have an association value if you find them yourself. Garnets are found in considerable number and size along the Fife coast. So, on several coasts, is amber. And if you should come across a dead whale, there is no harm in looking to see if it has any ambergris about it. If there is, and you can secure it, the perfumers will pay well for it per ounce. It is found in the intestines of a spermaceti whale who has suffered from biliousness, and is a grey, fatty substance with ruddy, marble-like veins running through it, and it smells very pleasantly. Sometimes it is to be seen without the whale, either on the shore or floating on the sea, where, presumably, the mammal has thrown off its bilious attack. If you see a dead whale, inquire first if it is a spermaceti one, as otherwise investigation is certainly useless. We are bound to add that investigation of a spermaceti whale is very nearly certainly useless. It is certainly troublesome.

## BIRDS

From golden eagles downwards, we have birds, common and rare, land and sea birds, in greater variety than you will find in any other part of Britain. We have, in addition to almost all the familiar kinds known in England, such fowls as ptarmigan, ospreys, falcons (jer and orange-legged), hawks (merlin, hobby, ash-coloured, long-tailed blue), owls (golden, fern and horned), harriers (marsh and hen), ravens, goshawks, hooded crows, white-tailed sea-eagles, whaups or tilli-whillies, capercailzies, bristle-cocks and withery-weeps —in all some 539 species. If you are found red-handed with a dead grouse, partridge or pheasant and asked to explain yourself, say you took it to be a tilliwhillie or a withery-weep. You may pull this off if you look the part. Again, you may not even if you do.

The nightingale is the only bird found in England which we cannot produce. Persons have asserted from time to time that they have heard the song of a nightingale in Scotland, but on each occasion the performer has been found to be merely a skilful imitator. Once, indeed, for a few months we had a few genuine specimens, but they never stayed long enough to know what singing was. We owe their brief dumb presence to Sir John Sinclair, Scotland's first President of the Board of Agriculture. Sir John, determined to remedy, if he could, our defect in respect of nightingales, procured as many eggs as the London dealers could steal from English nests for him and post to the North wrapped in cotton-wool at a shilling apiece. At the same time he employed men in Scotland to prepare for their immediate reception by robbing the nests of robin redbreasts of a single egg for which a nightingale's was substituted. The robin, as cuckoos and other practical ornithologists are aware, is a diligent and conscientious parent who annually diminishes his waist-line by rearing several broods in succession. The Scottish robins and the English dealers and eggs all played their parts loyally up to a point. The Southern birds hatched out and were seen flying about as if unaware of the trick that Sir John and his little brother conspirators had played on them. Sir John slept well, and dreamed of what Thackeray has called the *jugulating* that would sound the following season in Scottish airs. But when September came, every nightingale, without notifying the Board or so much as bidding their foster-parents *au revoir*, left the shores of Scotland. Not one returned. No Scottish poet, accordingly, has been able to hearken to a nightingale on his native heath except over the wireless. Those early Scottish *makars*, such as Dunbar and Henryson, who speak with familiarity of the bird, were either lying or plagiarising, or they heard the song when they were abroad, which they mostly were.

## REPTILES AND WILD BEASTS

Unlike the Irish, we have our fair share of adders and they bite as badly as if not worse than the English ones. But we have no other snakes, and no lizards. Our loch monsters are famous, especially during the silly season. Some of these turn out to be seals, which are notoriously intelligent and dramatic. Seals abound and are very musical, as Mrs Kennedy-Fraser and other folk-lore experts have discovered by eavesdropping behind rocks. We are waiting for a broadcast of a Hebridean seal. You are allowed to shoot seals, but the natives will not approve the practice and you can do nothing with the creature's carcase. His flesh makes considerably worse eating than venison and his skin is useless to the furrier, which things are evidences of his sagacity.

There used to be wolves in Scotland, but they have died long since. There are, further, no polecats and no martens left, although a hundred years ago they sported by the hundred. But the wild-cat, which, unlike the polecat, is a real cat, after verging on extinction, is looking up again, even in regions like Rothiemurchus, where it was thought to have wholly died out. Be careful, if you see one, not to attempt to stroke it. It does not purr under the human hand. One is said to have killed a knight in full armour, and even if yours did not kill you it might damage you. Whatever may be the truth of the story about the knight and the cat, a Scotch wild-cat has been seen within living memory to fight victoriously with an eagle, and you know what eagles are. Or perhaps you don't. One was seen by a walker lately. It was roosting on a decayed cabbage-stalk and looked depressed.

Deer, of which some people think there are too many in Scotland, can be a great nuisance to cross-country walkers, who slip about and foul their shoes among the droppings of a herd which they may not so much as have the satisfaction of seeing. This is particularly exasperating to those who neither possess shootings nor enjoy venison when shot by other people. Other vermin, for which nobody takes shootings, are plentiful, such as badgers, otters, stoats and weasels, foxes, rabbits and hares. One may see scores of hares at one time, blue and brown, and, of course, white ones in winter. Although in parts of Scotland the fox is hunted in the conventional English fashion, there is no prejudice against shooting or trapping him, so there will be no disgrace in your obtaining a brush as a trophy, no matter how you may come by it. Remember that foxes are bad for grouse.

Besides the true wild-cat, wild and semi-wild farm cats are common. These, having gone native, object to being stroked almost as much as the true ones, so do not venture it. Remember the motto of the Mackintoshes—"Touch not a cat but a glove".

# DOGS

Besides a quantity of intelligent and not so intelligent mongrels, dogs of several distinctive breeds are to be found in Scotland. All are tame, most are sporting, and some are of practical use as workers. Each breed can boast a world-wide reputation.

King among them is the *Collie* or *sheep-dog* (collie means sheep). The cleverest of these is the original small Shetland collie, which is curly-haired and dark. For centuries he has been the beloved and profitable friend of shepherds throughout the British Isles. He can work a flock of sheep unaided and has been known to herd a batch of straying chicks back to their mother without injuring one hair of their fluff. His more showy cousin, through, it is said, intermarriage with the fox, has been developed into a creature of remarkable beauty in its purest state, while retaining its utilitarian charms, especially when permitted the forfeiture of some of its purity in favour of brains *versus* breeding. Originally black, tan and white, he is now more popular as sable or sable and white, with a fine long nose, a narrow head, an eloquent feather tail and a heavy, splendid coat. His eyes, dark and "speaking", are set obliquely, his ears are expressive, his ruff Elizabethan. There is a feather on each foreleg but none on the hind legs below the hock. Over-bred show specimens apart, he deserves all the best that has ever been said of him as an affectionate, hard-working animal whose youthful exuberance of spirits is rivalled as he grows older by his ability to follow the workings of the human mind as expressed in his master's face, voice and ways of whistling, and his willingness to gratify human wishes. The reputation of the collie for treachery is not well founded. He can usually be guaranteed to bite only interfering strangers, who are here reminded that the practising sheep-dog which trots at the heels of every shepherd is a busy creature who likes to be left in peace while resting. Also he is frequently of an age at which idiosyncrasies ought to be studied if harmony is to be maintained. There are smooth and rough collies, sometimes both kinds in one litter. The smooth variety has often a merle or marbled colour. A dozen clubs devote exclusive attention to his breed. Single specimens have been sold for £1300. His work at a sheep-dog trial is one of the things best worth seeing in Scotland.

All our other breeds are terriers, and of all the Scotch terriers the real original is the *Cairn* or *Highland terrier*. This in spite of his existence not having been recognised by the Kennel Club until 1910. His ideal weight is about 14 lb., his fundamental quality "gameness". There are no limits to his courage and tenacity, but he evinces an ineradicable inclination to poach, and also to kill his prey, be it tame poultry or wild rabbits. He may be red, sandy, grey, brindled or nearly black, but he is most fancied in a creamy buff with a dark mask. He is shaggy, strong and compactly built, and his movements are free. He has wide-apart dark hazel eyes in his small foxy head, which has, however, breadth across the skull. His eyebrows are shaggy and there is an indentation between them. His muzzle is powerful but not heavy, and he is neither overshot nor undershot. His ears are small and pointed but not too closely set, his tail short and not feathery. It should never curl over his back. His lady, when blonde with a dark mask, is one of the beauties of the canine world.

The *Scottish terrier*, often called the *Scottie*, used to be known as the *Aberdeen*. He thrives and is a favourite in every country to which he has been taken. Hardihood, loyalty and a capacity to enter with zest into the life of his owner are his outstanding virtues. For some reason he is most fancied in a black coat, of which the chief distinction is that this is worse in quality than any other colour of coat in which he can be had. He weighs from 17 to 21 lb. and has powerful hind-quarters, a deep chest and straight forelegs. His head need not be very large, but should be fairly long, with a flat skull, a large nose and a medium-sized muscular neck. He is prick-eared and has dark brown eyes.

The *Skye* is one of the oldest breeds, but is quite out of fashion to-day. Having been popular, however, in the days of Queen Victoria, who greatly fancied them, Skyes may yet return to favour. The main cause of their decline was an exaggerated breeding for length of coat which, normally, should not be more than $5\frac{1}{2}$ inches. This interfered with his original function as a destroyer of foxes, badgers and otters, besides making his toilette a nuisance. This was a great shame, as by nature he has no nonsense about him and is always ready for hard sport. He can be dark or light blue, grey or fawn with black points. His body is long and low and straight, with broad shoulders, a long neck, and short, straight legs without dew claws. He is smothered in a thick, double coat of hair, which veils his forehead and eyes, and falls in locks round ears which can be dropping or upstanding. Drop-ears belong to the original type. Prick-ears should be small. He ought to hold his feathery tail either low or level with his back. His forehead is wide, eyes hazel or dark brown, close-set, nose black, head long, with strong jaws and teeth closing level.

The *Clydesdale* or *Paisley terrier*, a variety of the Skye, is also seen too seldom nowadays. He got his name through being bred by the Paisley weavers, who were also great bird fanciers and snarers. Characteristic is the silky coat, which some aver is of Spanish origin. It can be light blue or silver, but dark blue was the most prized.

The *West Highland terrier* was originally no more than a white Cairn (*q.v.*), and such are still quite common and much loved. But a new type has been bred and finds more favour. He has a straight coat of 2½ inches and a straight tail without bushiness. Strongly built, straight in the back, with a deep chest and back ribs and powerful quarters, the West Highlander stands on muscular legs. His eyes are widely set and dark hazel, his muzzle tapering and not too long, his nose, roof of mouth and pads black. His mouth should be neither overshot nor undershot. Dogs weigh from 14 to 18 lb., bitches from 12 to 16.

The *Dandie Dinmont*, once known as a *Border terrier*, is a near relation to the Bedlington of Northumbria, but he is short-legged and long-bodied instead of long-legged and short-bodied. He acquired his name and a widespread vogue by figuring in *Guy Mannering* and is of Teviotdale breed. He may be either blue or yellow (a "pepper" or a "mustard") and is very strong and flexible, with straight, short and immensely muscular forelegs, and a short curved tail that is full of gaiety and held high. His head is strong and large with awe-inspiring jaw muscles and a well-domed forehead crowned with a remarkably light and silky top-knot. His muzzle is tapered and his teeth exceptionally large and competent. His eyes, wide apart, are a lustrous dark hazel, his ears pendulous, low on the skull and set far back and well apart. His coat should be about 2 inches and his weight anything from 14 to 24 lbs. That he is no longer modish distresses neither him nor his devoted owners.

To sum up, Scotland is the best place in the world to see a man about a dog. And when you have got the dog, there are almost none among the other natives here mentioned whom he may not be taught to retrieve or kill for you. If you have the patience you could probably train him to fish for pearls or salmon or to run up trees after wild cats. As for subterranean work, he will not be daunted by the very hole of Pluto, and he always manages to get back, usually with something in his mouth. We have no hesitation in recommending every manifestation of the Scotch dog.

# KIRKS AND CORBIE STEPS

*"Ah, it's a brave kirk—nane o' yere whigmaleeries and curliewurlies and open-steek hems about it—a' solid, weel-jointed mason-wark, that will stand as lang as the warld, keep hands and gunpowther aff it."*

SCOTT

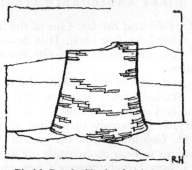

Pictish Broch, Shetlands (*circa* 3rd
century A.D.)

# KIRKS AND CORBIE STEPS

## ARCHITECTURE IN OUTLINE

THE earliest type of building you are likely to meet
with in Scotland is the *broch*, an open, round and
tapering tower superbly built of stone slab walls 16 ft.
thick, originally about 40 ft. in height, enclosing a
circular space about 40 ft. in diameter. No windows
pierce the walls, only a small door, while within the
walls are built galleries, cells and stairs, and a hearth
and a well occupied the centre space. Many *brochs*
exist in the north and west of Scotland, dating mostly
from the first to the fifth centuries A.D., and they were
used either as a defence against sea-raiders or as the
castles of a conquering aristocracy. They are stark
and solemn and have no parallel outside Scotland.

The arrival of Columba at Iona from Ireland in the
sixth century and his missionary successes among the
Picts on the Scottish mainland were the means of
establishing cultural relations between Ireland and
Scotland. The architectural consequences were,
briefly, the hermit's cell (to be seen at *Inchcolm*),
the carved Celtic cross, the square-ended plan for
churches and the tall round refuge towers to be seen

403

at *Abernethy* (Fife) and *Brechin*. One of the most perfect of Celtic crosses is in *Iona* itself. It is dedicated to St. Martin of Tours and stands opposite the west door of the Cathedral.

St. Margaret, who as wife of Malcolm Canmore was Queen of Scotland from 1070 to 1093, was grand-daughter of an English king and had been brought up in Hungary. It is scarcely surprising, therefore, that she, like St. Columba, was the means of bringing fresh influences to bear on Scottish life and architect-ure, and it was largely through her and her son, David I, that Romanesque or Norman architecture penetrated into Scotland. The Romanesque char-acteristics are the round arch, generally massive pro-portions, flat wooden ceilings and long narrow churches. The large Scottish churches of this time rank among the great ones of Europe. *Kirkwall Cathedral*, begun in 1137, is a noble building originally planned in the orthodox Norman manner with a central tower, transepts with eastern chapels, nave of seven bays, choir of three and a single eastern apse. The interior is very high for its width. *Dunfermline Abbey* church nave was the work of David I and is reminiscent of Kirkwall. (Note especially the two spirally fluted and two incised columns at the east end.) The west façade of *Jedburgh Abbey* is another im-portant and striking example of Norman work.

Several small Norman churches show the influence of the square-ended Celtic plan—*St. Oran's* at Iona, *Stobo* and *Aberdour* are all churches of this type that finds no similar expression outside Scotland. The more usual Norman plan, with an apse, can, of course, be seen at *Dalmeny Church* (which is superb) or at *Leuchars*.

Scots were (and are) very fond of sticking to certain features of building design long after they had been dropped elsewhere, and the round arch is an example of this eclectic conservatism; at the *Nunnery Chapel, Iona*

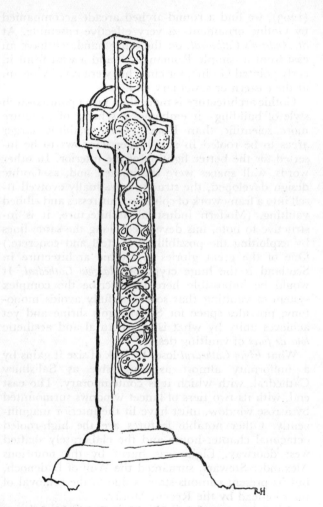

St. Martin's Cross, Isle of Iona (9th century A.D.)

(1203), we find a round-arched arcade accompanied by Gothic ornament—a very effective ensemble. At *St. Andrew's Cathedral*, on the other hand, we have an east front in simple Romanesque and a west front in early pointed Gothic, for churches were usually begun at the eastern or sanctuary end.

Gothic architecture is more than just a pointed-arch style of building—it embodies a scheme of structure more scientific than Romanesque, enabling larger areas to be roofed in and bigger windows to be inserted for the better lighting of the interior. In other words, wall spaces were diminished and, as Gothic design developed, the structure gradually evolved itself into a framework of columns, buttresses and ribbed vaulting. (Modern industrial architecture, it is instructive to note, has developed along the same lines by exploiting the possibilities of steel and concrete.) One of the great glories of Gothic architecture in Scotland is the huge crypt of *Glasgow Cathedral.* It would be impossible here to describe the complex system of vaulting that so successfully avoids monotony, provides space for St. Mungo's shrine and yet achieves unity by what is a structural and aesthetic *tour de force* of vaulting design.

What *Elgin Cathedral* loses by lack of size it gains by a uniformity almost as impressive as Salisbury Cathedral, with which it is contemporary. The east end, with its two tiers of lancet windows surmounted by a rose window, must have lit the interior magnificently. Other notable features are the high-roofed octagonal chapter-house and the elaborately shafted west doorway. Elgin was burnt by the notorious Alexander Stewart, surnamed the Wolf of Badenoch, but its present ruinous state is due to the removal of the roof-lead by the Regent Moray.

Other great early Gothic ruins in Scotland are *Arbroath Abbey* and *Dryburgh Abbey*.

From the simplicity of early Gothic with its lancet

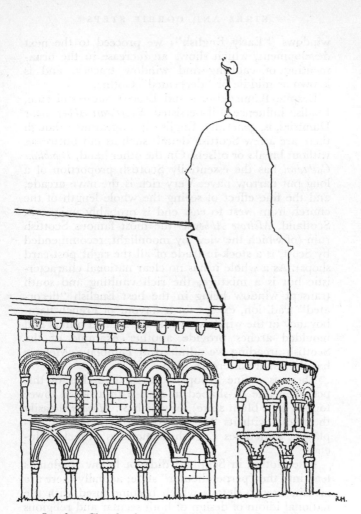

Leuchars Church; chancel and apse showing Romanesque
arcading (belfry in outline later addition).  12th century

windows ("Early English") we proceed to the next development, which shows an increase in the ornamenting of vaulting and window tracery, and is known as middle or "decorated" Gothic.

Despite Bannockburn and Bruce's successful rule, English influence still persisted. *Sweetheart Abbey*, near Dumfries, is, generally, English in appearance though there are a few Scottish details such as tall buttresses without breaks or offsets. On the other hand, *Dunblane Cathedral* has the essentially Scottish proportion of a long but narrow nave. Very rich is the nave arcade, and the fine effect of seeing the whole length of the church from west to east end is probably unique in Scotland. *Melrose Abbey* is the most famous Scottish ruin (of which the view by moonlight, recommended by Scott, is a stock-in-trade of all the right post-card shops). As a whole it has no clear national characteristic but is a mixture, the rich vaulting and south transept window being in the best English "decorated" tradition, except for a flavour of French flamboyancy in the windows, while the shafted pillars and moulded arches provide another example of the Scottish arcading we admired at Dunblane. Melrose has the usual Cistercian plan.

There is a fine group of parish churches of this period in Fife (T-shaped in plan with a broad tower topped by a blunt spire), of which *St. Monans* is easily the finest, with its "decorated" window tracery displaying sometimes English, sometimes French influence.

Late Gothic in Scotland did not follow England's lead into the "perpendicular" style; actually there are certain French details which become fused with the national idiom of design of both secular and religious buildings—the revival of apses and the use of flamboyant tracery in windows, and the corbelling out of turrets in secular buildings. Of the national features which developed about now are the naïve curvilinear

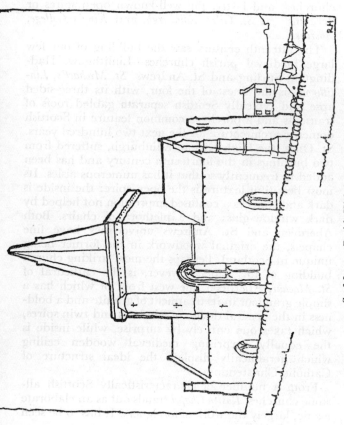

St. Monans Parish Kirk (14th century)

tracery, the stone slabbed roofing (to be seen at *Seton* and *Corstorphine*), the elaborate "Sacramental Houses" for the Elements, such as we see at *Kintore* and *Crichton* churches, and lastly, the well-known open spires or "crowns" at *St. Giles, Edinburgh*, and *King's College, Aberdeen*.

The fifteenth century saw the building of our few large medieval parish churches—Linlithgow, Haddington, Stirling and St. Andrews. *St. Michael's, Linlithgow*, is the finest of the four, with its three-sided apse and typically Scottish separate gabled roofs of transepts and a porch—a common feature in Scottish domestic architecture for the next two hundred years. St. Giles, the High Kirk of Edinburgh, suffered from two burnings in the fourteenth century and has been added to frequently so that it has numerous aisles. Its most beautiful feature is the open spire: the inside is dark and conveys a confused impression not helped by dark window-glass and a plethora of chairs. Both Aberdeen and St. Andrews universities have fine chapels, the original woodwork in the former being unique in Scotland. Perhaps the most striking church building of this time, however, is the cathedral of *St. Machar*, Aberdeen, the west front of which has a simple grandeur in its treatment of granite and a boldness in the general design of windows and twin spires, which takes one entirely by surprise, while inside is the equally surprising medieval wooden ceiling which heraldically displays the ideal structure of Catholic Christendom.

From a number of characteristically Scottish all-stone churches, *Roslin Chapel* stands out as an elaborate exotic, largely the work of foreigners. It has to be seen to be believed.

The earliest medieval secular buildings are thirteenth-century stone keeps (*Dunstaffnage* or *Inverlochy*), usually built with stone surrounds on promontories overlooking river or loch. During the fourteenth and

RH

St. Machar's Cathedral, Aberdeen (15th-16th centuries)

411

fifteenth centuries we see development from the simple peel tower such as *Neidpath* (Peebles) or *Newark*, to the more elaborate plan of such castles as *Tantallon*, *Spynie* and *Doune*. Usually these incorporated separate ranges for kitchens, visitors and chapel, grouped round a courtyard. Castles were not only fortresses, they served as local government centres.

Neidpath Castle on the Tweed (14th century)

The sixteenth century saw the building of palace-castles, such as *Linlithgow*, *Stirling* and *Falkland*, all of which demonstrate Scotland's early use of Renaissance detail (which arrived *via* France). The courtyard front of Falkland, with its medallions and double tier of ornamental columns, is typical of this group.

Simultaneously we have the development of Scots Baronial, wherein French features like the elaborately corbelled turret were welded with naïve ingenuity into the design of Scottish fortified houses, the lower storeys of which were left plain so that the elaborate upper floors and roof structure blossomed forth with the extraordinary profusion that characterises Castles *Fraser* and *Craigievar* in Aberdeenshire or *Amisfield* in

Falkland Palace, Renaissance detail (16th century)

*Dumfriesshire*. Allied with this evident vigour of essentially functional [1] design was a sure sense of proportion —for seldom, if ever, do we find a roof that seems "wrong" in shape.

[1] Functional: a style of building wherein convenience and the claims of structure dominate design, taking little heed of external symmetry.

413

Meanwhile the ordinary house took form and a few remaining examples reveal its naïve and varied charm. Perhaps the most interesting town houses are *Provand's Lordship*, Glasgow, *The Palace*, Culross, *Acheson House*, Edinburgh and *Argyll's Lodging*, Stirling, while by far the most impressive country mansion is *Traquair*, rambling yet shapely, its lines softened by the casual texture of harling. At no time before or since had

Amisfield Tower, Dumfriesshire (*circa* 1600)

Scottish domestic architecture such individuality, and though this wholesome tradition in effect died out in the seventeenth century, being killed by the later Renaissance, it persisted much longer in cottage and farm buildings: it was the native idiom.

Two buildings occur about this time which will strike the reader as out of the normal course. *Heriot's Hospital* and *Wintoun House* have generally a flavour foreign to the strongly national tendencies of contem-

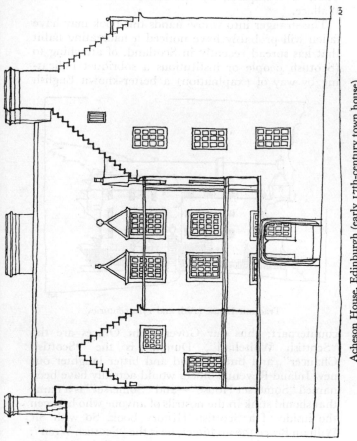

Acheson House, Edinburgh (early 17th-century town house)

porary architecture. Their details, notably the chimneys at Wintoun, are markedly English, and they were built, it transpires, by the same master of works, Wallace.

The stranger into whose hands this book may have fallen will probably have noticed a nauseating habit that has spread recently in Scotland, of attaching to (Scottish people or institutions a sobriquet indicating by way of exaplnation) a better-known English

Traquair House (16th and 17th centuries)

counterpart; thus our Government Offices are the "Scottish Whitehall", Dunbar is the "Scottish Chaucer", and but for loud and bitter laughter our new Inland Revenue offices would actually have been named "Somerset House"—and "Somerset" is a name that should stink in the nostrils of anyone who has seen the inside of a Scottish History book. So with Sir William Bruce the architect, he is the "Scottish Wren". Contemporary he certainly was, but little else. His most complete work is *Kinross House* and garden, his most famous the main court of *Holyroodhouse*. Both are refined and neither is the least English, but rather

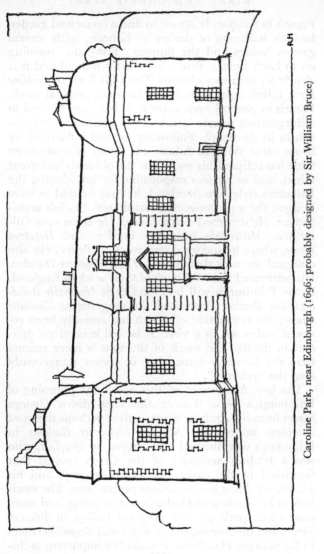

Caroline Park, near Edinburgh (1696; probably designed by Sir William Bruce)

French in flavour. It is rare to find a house and garden in such harmony of design as Kinross, with several garden houses and the famous "Fish-gate" opening on to Loch Leven. Bruce built it for himself and it is clearly an architect's house. The 1691 front of *Caroline Park*, Edinburgh, is probably his most original work. French in general appearance—it has been likened to a Burgundian manor-house—but unmistakeably Scottish in its sly detail. Following on and influenced by Bruce came William Adam, the father of sons whose fame has eclipsed his own. But the old man had great talent, and as he was responsible for introducing the Palladian style into Scotland, he may be said to have bridged the gulf between Scottish and English architecture. He designed *Yester House*, *The Drum* near Gilmerton, *Mellerstain* near the Border, and *Hopetoun House*, where he incorporated work by Bruce. He also designed the now demolished *Town House* at Dundee. His celebrated sons did most of their work in England, but in Edinburgh will be found their *University Buildings*, the *Register House* and the magnificent *Charlotte Square*, the north side of which has recently been restored and is worth a visit; it is well massed yet delicate in detail. The work of the sons is more refined than the father's—sometimes it comes dangerously near the "refaned".

The best monument of this age is the planning of Edinburgh's New Town; the view down George Street from St. Andrew Square gives perhaps the most complete impression. Adam's *University Building* in Edinburgh was finished and altered by Playfair, who was a leading architect of the Greek revival that flourished in the early nineteenth century, and his University dome is of excellent proportions. The vestibule of his *Academy* at Dollar is worth seeing, and more convenient perhaps, the *National Gallery* in Princes Street and the fine façade of *Royal* and *Regent* Terraces in Edinburgh. Hamilton was another important archi-

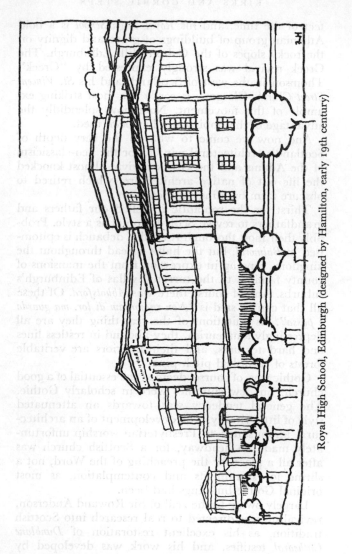

Royal High School, Edinburgh (designed by Hamilton, early 19th century)

tect of the time, and his *Royal High School* is a bold Athenian group of buildings of grace and dignity on the rocky slopes of the Calton Hill, Edinburgh. The Greek revival was strongly expressed by "Greek" Thomson in the west of Scotland, and his *St. Vincent Street Church*, Glasgow, is easily the most striking example of this movement. Note how splendidly the advantage of the sloping site has been used.

And now we come to what is the very depth of Scotland's architectural winter, for the neo-classicism of the Adams and the Greek revival almost knocked the life out of native architecture, which retired to obscure farm buildings and cottages.

Thirst for the romantic impelled our fathers and grandfathers to revive Scots Baronial as a style. Probably their most thorough revivalist debauch is epitomised in *Balmoral*, but the habit spread throughout the kingdom, ranging in expression from the mansions of county families to the turreted villas of Edinburgh's suburbs. And of course there was *Abbotsford*. Of these all that can be said is "*Non ragioniam di lor, ma guarda e passa*". As imitations of the real thing they are all depressingly amateurish, they abound in restless lines and hard textures, and their interiors are veritable forests of varnished pitch-pine.

Gothic was, of course, deemed the essential of a good church, but few churches were in scholarly Gothic. The general tendency was towards an attenuated style of little vitality. The development of an architectural idiom suited to Presbyterian worship unfortunately made no headway, for a Scottish church was after all a place for the preaching of the Word, not a shrine for sacraments and contemplation, as most original Gothic buildings had been.

Largely owing to the zeal of Sir Rowand Anderson, revivalism was directed to real research into Scottish tradition, as his excellent restoration of *Dunblane Cathedral* testifies, and his work was developed by

Sir Robert Lorimer, the architect of the *Scottish National War Memorial*. The Scottish tradition, not fully understood, it is true, became popular and Lorimer throve as a fashionable architect, the "Lutyens" —let us too commit the nauseating sin—of Scotland. And truly, few buildings can have caught the public

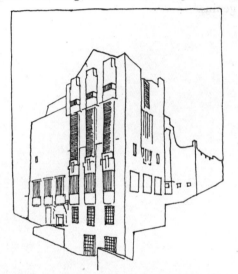

Glasgow School of Art, designed by Charles
Rennie Mackintosh, 1894

imagination as fully as Lorimer's war memorial, whatever we may think of it architecturally.

But the real hope of Scottish architecture does not lie with Lorimer or his followers. In 1894 a young architect, C. R. Mackintosh, suddenly produced his design for the *Glasgow School of Art*, a piece of pioneer modernism which has had more influence on modern European architecture than any other building of its time. Here are the seeds of modern "functional" architecture, and, if we have eyes to see, we shall realise how much Mackintosh owed to the sturdy functional tradition of sixteenth and seventeenth-century Scottish architecture. His houses at Helensburgh and Kilmacolm tell the same tale. But Mackintosh was a prophet in his own country and it is only now he is dead that we begin to give true recognition to his genius.

# TRAVELLING

TRAVELLING

Here's to budgets, bags and wallets!
Here's to all the wandering train!

BURNS

# TRAVELLING

## WARNINGS TO WALKERS

In Scotland the term walkers includes cyclists and motorists, as even these, if they wish to see Scotland, have often to get off or out and use their legs and their wits. When preparing to journey in Scotland by any other path than railway lines, the three grand things to keep in mind are the weather, the ground and the customs of the Scotch. In other words, prepare for cold, rain and mist, for rocks, bogs and innless roads, and for the fact that our natives, especially our Highlanders, while they are the soul of hospitality, are apt to take for granted the virtue of total abstinence in travellers. That is to say, your clothes, your carried refreshments, and your precautions against being caught out by fatigue or fog in remote spots, are all more important than if you were walking in England.

Take clothes first. No matter what month it may be, you cannot count on the kindness of the weather. This is especially true if you are climbing. In the Grampians even in July there are days when the south wind speedily masses rain-clouds along the range you have chosen. As often as not early morning sunshine is a bad sign for a day's outing, and east wind is no guarantee that it will not rain. You may be lucky and strike a fine spell in the North when all England is under rain. June and September are both likely months for this. But do not rely on it. Be prepared for the worst. For men there is no dress equal to the kilt for Scottish out-of-doors, especially for cross-country or path-walking in the high places. It guarantees warmth to the vital parts of the body when sitting or standing, is difficult to wet through, and leaves the limbs free. Heather was not made for trousers. The sporran also is convenient as an extra pocket. If you have no tartan of your own there is nothing against your wearing a tweed kilt, and you can have it waterproofed if you like. Women should wear a thickly pleated skirt—that is, pleated in the same generous fashion as a kilt. With the kilt goes a sweater or cardigan over a shirt for both sexes, and a jacket over the sweater, the extras to be discarded and carried in the pack when not required. If, at the same time, you can acquire, and learn how to wear without impeding yourself, a thin plaid, you are secure against the worst that Scotland can do. This also can be waterproofed while remaining soft and thin, and so will serve as a rug or a wrap as necessity dictates. Practise folding and draping it over one shoulder and across the breast, drawing one end through your waistbelt. It is a graceful garment and will not be in your way. The black-and-white "shepherd's plaid" of fine wool is recommended, but colours are a matter of taste. Remember that if you are stormstayed in the hills, a few folds of the plaid over your head will do more to keep you warm than a heavy overcoat. This reminder is necessary for the many who now walk hatless. Shoes, of course, should be pliant and soft as to the uppers, thick in the sole and thoroughly water-tight. But even the best shoes do not help you if you land in a bog.

When collecting your food and drink, remind yourself that "hunger-bunk" is a common affliction not only in making the Pass of Glencoe, and that if it is upon Glencoe your heart is set there are some fifty miles without a shop or a house available for refreshment between Crianlarich and Fort William. Remind yourself also that beers are few and far between, especially in the Highlands, and that at the end of a long day's walk, if you are not returning to your starting-point, you may easily find nothing but a cup

of tea and some cold potted-head. Impromptu or professional hosts will be found ready for all emergencies,
so that a recent walker writes with enthusiasm of the
courteous reception given in a Highland cottage to a
party of walkers who arrived stark naked, having lost
their clothes when fording a river. But your inner man
may not receive the same attention as that which is
forthcoming for your outer. The easiest and safest
extra foods to carry with you are slabs of chocolate
(these can now be had of unprecedented strength and
stimulating properties), coarse oatmeal and raisins.
For regular picnic use the best sandwich in the world,
and the most filling, is made by slitting baps, buttering
both inside pieces and closing them over a thick slice
of spiced bacon, which is a Scottish speciality of which
we are justly proud. A copious flask of whisky (*Talisker*, if you can get it) should be accompanied, says an
expert, by another, or even two smaller flasks of
different whisky, both to keep strictly for emergencies
and because that in your leading flask may turn out to
be bad. On no account let yourself encroach upon any
of the flasks early in the day, and be firm in preserving
inviolate those which are intended for accidents, until
an accident happens. Even the copious flask is intended
to come into play only towards the end of your day,
when that last, unlooked-for forced march presents
itself and a fillip is much needed.

## GENERAL HINTS

Take with you a compass, a whistle, an electric
torch, vaseline, sticking-plaster and, if you are climbing, an aneroid and an inch map with contours 100
yards apart.

The compass habit is a needful one to all who climb,
and even if many days pass without your having to use
it never discard it because of that. Even edges of mist

or the faintest "haar", combined with the difference between your right and left leg and your all-too-human convictions about directions, can play you tricks in the mountains that are as queer as any of Maskelyne and Devant's, but far more dangerous. Besides, if there are several of you, the compass decides arguments. When the air is clear, of course, you take your direction in using the compass by a feature of the landscape. When there is a mist, you send one of the party on ahead just as far as you can see him wave a handkerchief, when he serves as the feature. In either case the needle tells no lies however peculiar its pointing finger may seem to you. The whistle will turn out useful in a dozen ways, and it may save lives when the hold-up is serious and prolonged. You can go on taking turns at blowing a whistle long after voices would have given out. The uses of the aneroid will be obvious to all who are capable of profiting by them. Vaseline is only a little less useful than a whistle and will be pounced upon for many purposes unforeseen at starting. One often forgotten use of sticking-plaster is the prevention of an incipient blister. It will not cure the blister, but if applied in time it will keep it from developing or bursting. If you are aware before starting of a weak place in your heel or a faulty place in your shoe, some plaster between the two, smoothly stuck on to your skin when you are dressing, will obviate the painful reaction which is otherwise sure to take place after a few miles of trudging. And until you come to steep descents, which are far harder on the feet than ascents, you do not fully know what the weak points are. Also nails have a way of springing into active being when you have been through a bog or two. The inch map is an absolute necessity for the mildest mountaineering, and half-inch maps with contours 250 yards apart are perilous in the extreme. The electric torch is chiefly comforting, but may be actively useful as an adjunct to the whistle, particularly in cases of accident to a walker not surrounded by mist. It can be lashed to the end of a stick and waved.

Before setting out on an expedition from one point to another, always try to inform somebody at the starting-point as to your route and destination, and promise this same person (who should be possessed of some gumption) that you will send back word of your safe arrival within a reasonable interval. This will go some way towards safeguarding you against serious accidents, and serious accidents *can* happen in Scotland.

*Naismith's Formula* is a convenient means of calculating beforehand how long you must allow for covering any given distance. For refinements there is another formula furnished by Monkhouse in his *On Foot in North Wales*, but Naismith was a Scot and his formula is hard to beat for practical purposes. It is based on the factors of distance and height. The normal speed of walkers does not greatly vary, and the weight carried makes little difference, except, be it noted, during steep descents, when it adds considerably to the task of endurance and accordingly adds to the after-state of fatigue if you have much further to go on the level. For your calculation you allow an hour for every three miles and an extra half-hour for every 1000 feet you mean to climb. Take also into account storms, bogs, rests, sleeps, losing your way or going back on your tracks for something left behind. If you propose to cover twenty-two miles and to climb in the course of the day 6000 feet, you may reckon on spending $7\frac{1}{2}$ hours plus 3 hours $= 10\frac{1}{2}$ hours exclusive of your extras, *i.e.* on your feet. This enables you to send a message beforehand to your destination as well as leaving the information behind you.

Always remember that, while water in Scotland, for drinking or bathing, is mercifully plentiful and exquisitely fresh, the springs are often too cold for safety in drinking, and that icy water when you are hot and tired has the effect of spoiling your wind, while it may also upset your stomach. Therefore warm it in the sun or in your cupped hands before you drink. If you want a drink that will sustain as well as refresh you, put a little oatmeal in your horn tumbler and fill up with water, stirring well before you drink, and letting the oatmeal settle first. You can then eat the oatmeal as well if you like. It is nice stuff to chew and promotes saliva. Further, oatmeal with chocolate serves well as a meal if you are storm-stayed. If you have salt, water and a fire you can make it into porridge, or you can soak it in cold water and eat it afterwards, or you can fry trout rubbed in it on a stone, first cleaning and slitting the fish.

But this brings us to

## CAMPING,

about which you probably know a lot already if you are thinking of doing it. Perhaps, however, a few specially Scottish precautions and advices may be useful to you. Here are some.

A piece of wire-netting encircling the fire three-quarters of the way round, fixed upright like a little fence, is a help to camp cooking. You can fix sticks in it with various foods impaled on their ends. This keeps you from burning your hands and saves carrying many metal vessels. If you *do* burn yourself it is better to treat burns with very strong tea or with bicarbonate of soda than with oil. The wire-netting serves also for actual grilling when laid over a hot fire.

Always carry spare washers and a spanner if you use a Primus.

The lid of a saucepan reversed and put on the pot while something is cooking, or water being boiled, serves as an additional vessel for cooking such things as tomatoes or for warming up other foods. A good grill can be done on a clean spade or plate of iron, but there is now on the market a sort of corrugated iron pan which grills admirably on oil or a fire and can be used also as a frying-pan.

Midges, gnats and clegs, the first and last mentioned being particularly troublesome in Scotland, will not attack you readily if you have washed your face and hands and legs in water in which some Epsom salts have been dissolved. See that you do not wipe all traces of the salts off with the towel. Wearing fronds of bracken or pieces of bog-myrtle round the back of the hat and hanging down over the neck and shoulders helps to keep off both flies and strong sun. The sun can shine fiercely in Scotland at times.

When a thorn or deep splinter has run into the hand or foot and is extracted, do not use iodine, but rather apply first for a time a wet compress of bread and water or of hot water or milk. This helps to draw out any dirt or poison there may be far under the skin, while iodine affects only the top and trouble sometimes results. Iodine should always be carried, but it should, in the above-mentioned cases, be applied after the poultice. Iodine is good for most insect bites, but bicarbonate of soda is even more effective, being strongly antacid. A small packet takes up little room and will come in useful in many ways, including treatment for sunburn.

Those who suffer from cramp should always carry a needle somewhere. In the severest attacks a quick prick with the point of the needle will give sufficient shock to the adjoining nerves to allay the onslaught. Swimmers frequently carry a needle concealed in the cap where it is protected from the water.

To catch a crab on the shore without letting it bite you, seize it by the shell of its back using your thumb and third finger, arching the forefinger, the third finger and the little finger as high up in the air as possible. There is then no possibility of your getting hurt if you do not lose your head, and in this way you may convey your catch from pool to pot and eat him fresh.

> Celestial Tea—a fountain that can cure
> The ills of passion, and can free the fair
> From frowns and sighs from disappointment earned.
> To her, ye fair, in adoration bow!

So wrote Robert Fergusson when tea was something of a novelty in Scotland. The Scotch are now, if anything, more perfervid tea-drinkers than the English. But it is not everybody that knows how to make what is the best cup of this best of hot drinks in a hostel or on a camp-fire, using only a single vessel to do it. The method, patronised by Scottish navvies, is simplicity itself and has the additional virtue of economising with the tea, as only half the amount is required to obtain the same strength as you get by using a tea-pot and kettle. In a pot, saucepan or tin put as much cold water as you will want for your drink and scatter over the surface half the amount of tea you would measure out in the usual way. Bring the water to the boil but do not let it boil for even an instant when it does come to the boil. Take it off the fire and stir it once. The tea will go to the bottom and you can pour the clear golden liquid straight into the cups. It should not taste in the slightest degree stewed. The same procedure makes admirable coffee.

## TO MAKE A PEAT FIRE

In some parts of Scotland, as in Orkney, where there is practically no wood and coal is out of the question by reason of its expense, peat is the only fuel, and a fire of peat once started is not allowed to go out overnight. True stories are told of married couples who, having lighted their peat fire on the cottage hearth the day of their marriage, have never let it go out throughout a long married life. In the ordinary way, however, peat may be used either as an adjunct to a

coal fire, or with wood, or simply to keep a fire that
has been started with wood and coal going all night
in a smothered fashion so that it needs only stirring,
blowing up and additional fuel first thing in the morning. For this last purpose damp peats are the best,
but for starting a peat fire the turves must be absolutely
dry. The ideal hearth for a peat fire is a plain flat stone,
and the kindling is done with paper and chips or dry
heather roots and small dry shavings of peat until all
has caught, when larger pieces of peat are added.
Once the fire is going it is kept in by the process known
as "smooring" (Gaelic, *smalhadh*), which is a symbolic
ceremony. The embers are spread out evenly on the
hearth and formed into a circle, which is divided into
three equal sections leaving a small boss in the middle.
A peat is then laid between each section, each peat
touching the boss, which forms the common centre.
The first peat is laid down in the name of the God of
Life, the second in the name of the God of Peace, the
third in the name of the God of Grace. The whole is
then covered with ashes so that every particle of fire
is hidden and subdued without actually being put out,
this being done in the name of the Three of Light.
The central heap, which remains slightly higher than
the rest, is called "Tualla an Tri" or the Hearth of the
Three. When all is accomplished the smoorer closes his
or her eyes, stretches out the right hand, and speaks
aloud a smooring prayer similar to the kindling prayer
found in our *Lucky Numbers* which is appropriate to
blowing up the fire in the morning. The southern habit
of throwing stray peats on a coal fire is no doubt cheerful, but it is a shameful waste of good peat.

## BOG-MYRTLE CANDLES

If you should happen to be near a really good bog
in May or June, when the bog-myrtle is in bud, you
can make bog-myrtle candles. Like all such under-

takings, it *is* an undertaking, but it may amuse you to try it. The candles are guaranteed to burn (with what the books of words call "a soft light") and, whilst doing so, they smell of the plant from which they are derived. Can one smell fairer than this?

Pick a bucketful of the buds, choosing those that are red and tight, and keeping them as free from grass and moss as you can. Pour over them two bucketfuls of boiling, well-salted water, bruise and stir well for ten minutes, strain the liquid through butter-muslin, and leave it to cool. When cold it will be covered by a layer of wax. Take this and use, either alone or mixed with an equal quantity of white paraffin wax, for your candle-making. Home-made candles, as you probably know, are made by melting the wax or tallow and repeatedly dipping into it the cotton wicks, letting each coating cool before the next is added, until your candle seems to you to be thick enough, when you stop. There will be no mistaking your bog-myrtle candle for the commercial kind, even when it is finished. For one thing, there's the scent.

An ordinary bucketful of buds should produce enough bog-wax to make two candles. With paraffin wax added they should produce four. But if it is birthday candles you want, you might be able to deck an almost adult birthday cake from the same amount. And, of course, for the modest, there are tapers.

## HOW TO MAKE A HEATHER BED

From Beltane (May 1st, O.S.) to Samhuinn or Hallowe'en (October 31st, O.S.) the Highland herds, accompanying their cattle to their summer pastures on the hills, used to sleep in sheilings or rough huts. They took trouble in making their heather bed on which they lay all the nights of these six months, and campers and others may like to know precisely how they made them. Heather is a better substance than bracken for a mattress, although, where bracken is more plentiful than heather, it is not bad. Bracken is best stuffed into a strong mattress-case and shaken up now and again. Heather needs considerably more manipulation, but when properly used makes a far springier and more enduring couch. Strictly speaking it requires a framework of logs, or a partial framework composed of two logs lashed to an angle at one end and having the other ends braced against a wall in the corner of a shed or room. Inside this frame the heather-stalks—all about 9 inches long and chosen from the springiest you can find—should be packed as thick and close as it will stand, as if growing out of the floor, but slanting slightly toward the *head* of the bed. If a permanent bed of heather is wanted in a cottage or country house, a good plan is to rip the old spring out of a wooden bed-frame. The heather can then be renewed every six months or so. When cutting the heather see that it has as little root as possible, and dry it thoroughly in the sun before making your bed. The heather bed is yielding as well as springy. It retains a pleasant fragrance for a long time. And it has the reputation for giving refreshing slumbers, soothing the nerves and restoring the vigour to aching limbs.

## HOSTEL MODES AND MANNERS

Those who make or intend to make use of the Scottish Youth Hostels are here reminded that the Hostel is a new institution which is of most ancient origin. Its uses commend themselves to all travellers who walk or cycle through the country with slender purses, but such travellers ought not to forget that more delicate manners and a greater exercise of courtesy are demanded of hostel dwellers than of those who attend house parties in rich houses. Cadgers and borrowers can spoil a week-end for other holiday-makers, who, perhaps, have been saving and scraping through many months of toil for their single outing of the year. Turns have to be taken in washing and cooking. Outfits should be complete. Solitary foot-passengers should be careful not to attach themselves, without the most pressing invitation, to carefully selected parties. Already a body of legend is growing up of high-heeled and improvident walkers who throw themselves unmercifully on the mercies of others who have taken more trouble to think things out beforehand. If you have nothing but weaknesses to offer to the general store, don't offer them. But if you can sing or cook, throw your shyness to the winds and go ahead. You may make the friends of a lifetime. A thorough examination knowledge of this book should go a long way towards making you popular. And here are three small items by which you may begin to show your worth:

*Cold Porridge.*—Never throw it away. Carry with you a penny packet of mixed herbs and of dried, chopped parsley (if you cannot get fresh, which is better). Stiffen the cold porridge with bread crumbs and season it with salt, pepper and herbs. Spread it thickly on thin rashers of bacon for yourself or anybody upon whom your fancy is fixed. Roll up the bacon and tie it with a thread. Fry the rolled bacon and serve either with fried eggs or on toast or bread fried in bacon fat. See that you serve it very hot. You will be made welcome after this and may be asked to sing of an evening.

*Green Dumplings.*—If you cannot sing, you can add to the evening stew a few Green Dumplings—that is, if your trip takes place at the time of the year when things are covered with their first budding greenness. The dumplings are made in the ordinary way with suet and flour seasoned with pepper and salt, but they are green with some of everything that grows in spring freshness, which you gather unobtrusively during the day. Pick the green buds of hawthorn, the succulent tips of nettles, grass, and other green things, remembering that in this condition nothing is poisonous, include dandelion leaves, daisy stems, shoots of young corn and turnip-tops or anything that tastes sweet and harmless. Wash them and chop them fine. Work them into your dough till it is green through and through. For soups make small dumplings not more than an inch across: for stews and meats make them larger so that they can be cut up. They go with anything, are delicious and play the part of a salad in wholesomeness.

*Sausages.*—Without them the hostel could not exist, and the Scotch sausage is the best in the world. Never suffer them to be pricked with a fork before you fry them. Instead dredge them lightly with flour and then rub them smooth. Always put a small piece of butter or dripping in a clean pan before you put the sausages on the fire. Fry them slowly, shaking every now and then and turning till equally done all round. The green dumplings eat well with them and serve instead of potatoes.

THE HOSTEL PILLOW.—Users of hostels are supposed to carry with them their own plate, mug, knife, fork and spoon. Also their own sheet sewed together to form a bag into which they insinuate their persons for sleeping. Blankets and other bedding is provided. But the pillows are hard and, being stuffed with straw, sometimes prickly. A bathing-dress of the regulation swimming-suit kind is not only useful for bathing in, but, when drawn over the hostel pillow, makes a comforting extra pillow-case. If you do not believe this, or if you are too fastidious to resort to it, you will be well advised to carry a pillow-case in your rucksack. You will further do well to carry your own towels, together with a couple of dish-cloths and some soap-flakes with which to wash both. If you are one of those who cannot walk more than twelve miles in a day without suffering, do not be persuaded into joining walkers who propose a twenty-mile walk. Even the green dumplings will not then save you from general execration.

But perhaps you know more about camping and about hostels than we do, in which event you can defiantly chant the following song by A. S. Wallace to any tune you like—if you can get it to fit.

## HOME AGAIN

Yes, I used the extra overcoat you sent,
    And for blankets I'd enough to make me smother,
But I didn't need the oilskin *in* the tent—
        *Oh*, no, mother!

Yes, it's true I had no change of underwear,
    But I borrowed some from Jimmy Thomson's brother,
He was staying in a cottage quite near there—
        *Oh*, yes, mother!

No, we really never worried at the storm;
    In the evenings? Well—er—we read to one another,
Or conversed on—University reform—
        *Oh*, yes, mother!

Yes, we've all enjoyed the camping very well;
    It's a finer life, I think, than any other.
What? It's cheaper to put up at an hotel?
        Oh, *no*, mother!

# BOILS, BLAINS, BRUISES AND
BLIGHTS

*But after all, gentlemen, these modern advances in the noble science and art that you have so laboriously studied these five years and more, what are they but addenda? Great and admirable as they are, the wise physician will treat them with no more respect than they deserve, but will continue to rely on what is, in the last resort, his sheet-anchor—the "vis medicatrix Naturæ".*

Medical Graduation Address,
Glasgow University
(early 20th century)

# BOILS, BLAINS, BRUISES AND BLIGHTS

## CHAPTER ONE

FROM no spot in Scotland, so far as we know, is a doctor more than twenty miles away. Borne in a second-hand car, sustained by the Everlasting Arms, he will hurry to your aid before his telephone bell has stopped trembling.

It would be wicked and cruel to him and to you if, by putting at your disposal this porridge of useful tips and hints, we led you to believe yourself an adept in the least of his mysteries.

On the other hand we are not his tout and we feel free to warn you against certain ways of being ill in Scotland, and to tell you what to do in circumstances which might find you despairing and dithering. Not that it isn't pleasanter and cheaper to be ill in Scotland than anywhere else. A Case of the Itch (or Scottish Fiddle) was once cured in Buckie for five shillings, which included quite a large pot of Unguentum Sulphuris. The Case had previously spent seven hundred pounds on being treated (by vaccines and whatnot) by a series of London Knights and Baronets. He was naturally delighted at having secured so good a bargain.

Even Benefit of Surgery (as it is called) can be had in any of the cities of Scotland for the price of a suit of clothes; and you may recover from your mutilation in a Nursing Home, which is much cheaper and more comfortable than a Station Hotel. You must, however, choose your Surgeon cleverly, throw yourself on his mercy, and claim Scottish, Jewish or Irish ancestry.

*How to Choose a Surgeon.*—The car outside his door

must have cost less than £300. His house must be decorated by the etchings of D. Y. Cameron. He must be ill-dressed. He must talk very little, and what he does say must be in his native accent. If he greets you in any sort of genteel hybrid dialect, pretend that you have come to sell him an encyclopedia. He must not, however, be dirty.

*How to Behave in a Scottish Nursing Home.*—You must complain continually, otherwise you will be disregarded. You must not try to be popular. You will not succeed. You must keep a note of extras against the time when you will get your Bill.

*Appendicitis.*—Appendicitis is *vieux jeu*, but still very popular. If you wish to test our information about Scottish Surgeons, you can't do better than appendicitis. It shows itself as a horrible, great pain in the lower right-hand side of the belly, and if you get it you must not temporise with castor oil but get into a town at once.

*The Inside.*—And this brings us to consider the Inside generally. Scottish hotel food is often filthy, and farmhouse food is good but heavy. The laxative best suited to your personality should be used, at the beginning of your visit, with some freedom.

## CHAPTER TWO

Most illnesses or accidents incurred by you will be due to your own folly. For example, a great part of Scotland consists of mountain and moorland. These areas look very charming and can be seen best from a well-laid road. If you are foolhardy enough to attempt a cross-country walk, or scramble, you will lay yourself open to all manner of traumata, some of which we shall describe. But kindly note this. The passage following is not intended for people who take to moor and mountain animated by the lust for blood. To those who take bloody engines to moor and mountain, moor and mountain are at liberty to do what they like so far as we are concerned. But we have great pity on those who cross the wilderness at the urge of simple vanity and folly. Foolish and vain indeed they are; for Scotland is full of the most beautiful golf-courses, tennis-courts and American bars. In these, the safety of the customer is always considered. They are free from the dangers that beset the adventurer in peat-hag and escarpment. They appear to hold inexhaustible stores of interest. Man, however, being what he is, it is possible that you may wish to boast of having trod the heather like one of the Covenant (or like one of the '45). Here is our help, freely.

*You May be Bitten* by the *Pelias berus* or common adder. If you are a child, this monster's attack may prove fatal. You must at once knot a handkerchief round the bitten limb, as far from the bite and as near to the heart as possible. You must thrust a fountain-pen into the knot and, using this instrument as a handle, screw the bandage as tight as it will go. You may keep the bandage in position for twenty minutes, but no longer. After that you may loosen it for a little and then tighten it again. You must cut into the wound bravely and deeply with your penknife, making a gaping cross with the deepest two of your cuts, and you must squeeze the blood and juice forcibly from it. You must then dry it and burn the raw surfaces with a hot cigarette or with the crystals of permanganate of potash. You must then dress the wound with a wet dressing of water made pink with your permanganate and make as quickly as possible for bed, hot bottles and hot drinks. It is very unlikely that you will be bitten by a snake in Scotland, but if you are, these are the acts you should perform.

On the other hand, you are certain to be bitten by insects and principally by the Cleg, or *Haematopota pluvialis*, and by the beautiful little bar-winged Midge.

The cleg is a greyish-brown horsefly and the only defence against him is divine philosophy, for he bites through the thickest stockings. The only defence against the midge is flight or extreme drunkenness. He has made the Scottish gloaming unbearable on the West Coast.

## CHAPTER THREE

*Bone and joint injuries* sustained in crossing the moors require a separate chapter to themselves. The proper defence against them is what is known as the Heather Step. Poachers, shepherds, and gamekeepers acquire this at or about the third generation. If you haven't mastered this manœuvre it is likely that you will suffer from sprain either of the knee or of the ankle. If this happens, take off both boots and stockings and carefully compare one limb with the other. If the deformity of the injured limb can be accounted for by swelling alone, the condition is probably a sprain. You may bandage it tightly with strips of shirt, sling the limb from your belt and hop home. If there is an obvious fracture, you had better, other things being equal, stay where you are. After you have limped, crawled or been carried home, a doctor will tell you whether or no it is a simple sprain after all. If he is convinced that it is a sprain he will probably tell you to rest it. Do not obey him but be nobly up and doing as soon as you can put foot to ground.

*If you tumble off a mountain*, all you need remember is that a broad, tight bandage round the chest minimises the pain of broken ribs; that to pull the shoulder back and the elbow up and forwards and to fix the arm so is probably the best thing to do for a broken collar-bone; that the chest is an excellent splint for a broken arm and the opposite leg for a broken leg.

There are other precautions to be taken; terrors to be encountered; remedies to be applied. We shall refer to them in the next chapter.

# CHAPTER FOUR

Before you set out, cram your pockets with chocolate. It is possible, however weather-wise and direction-instinctive you may be, to spend many hours against your will on the Highland moors, and hunger and exhaustion are bad travelling companions. They will be your chief enemies. You will have others.

*The Highland Bull* does not, as a rule, belie his benevolent appearance. Artists sit and paint him for hours. If you put a little ravine between you and the most testy Highland bull, you will be quite safe.

For some years past the Scottish Uplands have been peopled by murderers fleeing from justice. We are told that all but the fiercest can be appeased by the offer of a bar of chocolate and a ten-shilling note. Failing this, a few seconds' steady pressure over the carotid tubercle—to be found an inch or so below the angle of the jaw—will produce unconsciousness in the desperado. During this you may make off.

The walking-stick, or *cromach* as one of Scotland's most dreadful lyricists insists on calling it, may be used effectively if you remember to thrust at the bellyband instead of striking at the head.

*Savage dogs* may be driven off with shouts and stones.

*Eagles* and *wild-cats* are likely to attack only the youngest of our readers.

# CHAPTER FIVE

*The procedure at Burns Nichts* may engage our attention for a little.

According to Marian MacNeill, the late Meg Dods constructed a haggis as follows: "Clean a sheep's pluck thoroughly. Make incisions in the heart and liver to allow the blood to flow out and parboil the whole, letting the windpipe lie over the side of the pot to permit the discharge of impurities; the water may be

445

changed after a few minutes' boiling for fresh water. A half hour's boiling will be sufficient; but throw back half of the liver to boil till it will grate easily; take the heart, the half of the liver, and part of the lights, trimming away all skins and black-looking parts, and mince them together. Mince also a pound of good beef-suet and four or more onions. Grate the other half of the liver. Have a dozen of small onions peeled and scalded in two waters, to mix with this mince. Have ready some finely-ground oatmeal toasted slowly before the fire for hours, till it is of a light-brown colour and perfectly dry. Less than two cupfuls of meal will do for this quantity of meat. Spread the mince on a board and strew the meal lightly over it, with a high seasoning of pepper, salt and a little cayenne first well mixed. Have a haggis bag (*i.e.* a sheep's paunch) . . ." And so on.

This displays the haggis (correctly) in a very formidable light. The English make tremendous fun of the haggis, as they do of ghosts, the French and the Germans, of everything, indeed, that they have cause to fear. They have cause to fear the haggis.

It is the *pièce de résistance* of the Burns dinner, and it is washed down by "nips" of neat whisky and accompanied by mashed potatoes.

After the dinner, a large number of very bad speeches are made. There is often one good speech. It is made by a clergyman. The Scottish clergy are invariably cultivated and eloquent men, for their cloth is not particularly respected and they are elected to their livings by the votes of dour sermon-tasters.

*The Clergyman's speech* is usually directed towards making the life of Burns fit for home consumption. A laudable object.

Be that as it may, unless the Burns Night happens to be a Temperance Burns Night (which it may well be), you will be forced to drink a great deal of whisky. If you are foolish enough to yield, take before retiring ten grains of aspirin; or arrange that it shall be administered to you.

There is little more to be said about Burns Nights.

## CHAPTER SIX

One must try, in a compendium like this, to visualise every possible accident or illness that might befall a stranger, howked out of his environment and dumped in Scotland without the benefit of that slow and complete growth of immune bodies which makes it possible for a native to survive. But, honestly, we can think of nothing that could happen to you in Scotland that might not happen to you, equally, in England, if we except being refused the use of a boat on the Lord's Day.

Even about the *weather* there is nothing characteristic. This is strange when one recalls a curious phenomenon observable by anybody in a train crossing the Border. We refer to the well-known fact that the air north of Gretna ceases to be yellow and becomes suddenly blue. It is a kind of blue that is seen concentrated between pine boles in Scottish woods and is the colour, we are told, of the garments of the Blessed in Paradise. It is a blue that cleanses the eyes and through them the mind and all the inward parts. We can confidently recommend it.

*The Scots Mist*, on the other hand, is in no way peculiar to Scotland. It enshrouds the Khyber Pass, where we once saw it lending dignity to the ugly Arms of a Scottish Regiment, carved out and painted on the rock.

## CHAPTER SEVEN

From *ailments of the Psyche*, peculiar to the place, you will not be immune. The most prevalent is *Accidie*, the *nostroyenya* of the Russians. It is endemic among the Celts and is infectious. Savages usually have some herb

which is sovran for the principal indigenous disease.
But herbage is rare on the Highland farm, and chew-
ing heather roots is, at best, a palliative. The Celt
chooses, rather, the homeopathic method of brooding
on the workings of his imaginary imagination. Try this
if you are attacked in the country. If you are attacked
in a town, think of Wigan.

## CHAPTER EIGHT

We are conscious that this is in no way the work we
had planned. It is inaccurate. It is vague. It is in
every way insufficient. But, by Heaven, it is pawky
and full of whimsy!

448

# RIGHTS AND WRONGS

*It's a kittle bitch, the Law.*
OLD SAW.

# RIGHTS AND WRONGS

## A Legal Notebook for the Holiday

### EXORDIUM

THE "week-ender" need not concern himself with the
more abstruse aspects of the law. For him let *plagium*,
and, still more, *wadset*, remain a closed book. He is a
holiday-maker, and his pursuit of pleasure or leisure
must be assumed to be innocent and free from dole.
While every citizen is presumed to know the law, the
inadvertent lawbreaker may expect leniency if he has
transgressed one of the innumerable statutory rules
and regulations which pour out from the Stationery
Office each year.

### *ITER*—THE JOURNEY

Though air, light and running water are free and
belong to no one, in the words of the ancient Civil Law,
it is regrettable, but true, that one cannot step from
one's house without impinging upon what is the
property of another person. Though the public have
a right of passage along public roads the property in
the road may belong to the person through whose
lands it passes. While it is true that local authorities
have duties to keep roads in repair, the traveller has no
right of action against the authority for an imperfect
road or for not immediately clearing the road of snow,
unless, indeed, negligence be proved. The public have
only a right of passage which extends over the whole
road. Though there be a footpath a foot-passenger is
entitled to walk on any part of the road, if he walks
with due care. Let it never be forgotten that the negli-

gent use of an admitted right may both deprive the negligent one of any recourse against another by whom he may be hurt, and may also expose him to liability for another's hurt. A private road, which is generally so marked, can only be used by the owner of the road, his servants or his guests, or those with whom he has business. If what appears to be of the nature of a private road, but is not so marked, be the only available *via* for the traveller, let him take it but at his own risk. It may be a private road to which the public have access; and in this case remember that all users of the road, including the owner, are bound to use the same care in driving thereon as if they were on a public road and, further, that the provisions of the Road Traffic Act apply to the owner of the road as much as to the public. The public have no legal right of access, of course, to a private road, but their presence may be tolerated or at least not expressly prohibited. Should the gate to the road be shut, let the traveller beware and be gone, for his presence on the road would then be trespass if he has no reasonable excuse for being there.

## TRESPASS

This word was introduced into our law from England, but may now be taken to mean any "temporary intrusion, entering, or being upon, the lands of another without his consent". It is founded upon an exclusive right of property, which yields, however, where public interest or necessity requires that access be allowed, *e.g.* for extinguishing a fire, pursuing a criminal, or destroying dangerous or noxious animals. Let not the traveller, however, pursue the wily rabbit, however noxious, on theoretical grounds, in another's lands. Where there has been trespass, the proprietor's only remedy is an action of interdict, and the only penalty to which the trespasser is liable (apart from destruction of property or other malicious mischief) is the expense of the action of interdict. If, however, decree has been granted against the trespasser and he repeats the offence, he will be liable to penalties for breach of interdict. Therefore, if innocently trespassing, hand your card to the person prohibiting your passage and make your way to safer ground. Should this person use violence to you unnecessarily, he will be liable therefor in an action of damages. Spring guns are illegal in unenclosed grounds and probably even in enclosed grounds save for this one purpose, the protection of a dwelling-house between sunset and sunrise. The provisions of the Road Traffic Act, 1930, and the Highway Code—which applies to all users of the road and which the beneficence of Parliament has made available to you—should be studied before journeying on the roads of this country. It is, however, worthy of mention that the leaving of vehicles in dangerous positions is punishable.

## RIGHTS OF WAY

The way must run in a definite and ascertained track from one "public place" to another. What the term "public place" means is a question of some difficulty, but let us say that it is "a place to which the public resort for some definite and intelligible purpose". The seashore is not necessarily such a place. The proprietor of the ground through which the right of way passes may erect gates, etc., for the protection of his own property, so long as these do not interfere with the public use. Rights of way have had in the past to be stoutly contended for, and an example of the resentment felt at encroachments on public rights is to be found in the following remarks made by Lord Cockburn, with regard to his youth, about the year 1794.

"When I was a boy nearly the whole vicinity of

Edinburgh was open. Beyond the Causeway it was almost Highland. Corstorphine Hill, Craiglockhart Hill, the Pentland Hills, the seaside from Leith to Queensferry, the riverside from Penicuik by Roslin and Hawthornden to Lasswade, the valley of Habbie's Howe and innumerable other places, now closed and fast closing, were all free. Much of this was the indulgence of private owners certainly, but much more of it was because, by the long usage of an unenclosed and very ill-ploughed country, the people had acquired prescriptive rights. But when improvement began ways were taken in, the obstructed blustered; but law was dear and the owner was constantly on the spot to enlarge and defend his usurpations. Scotland has very few individuals with heavy purses and dogged obstinacy to stand up, as in England, for their rights. The interest of the gentry was in favour of private property and all public agitation or resistance was discouraged. The Scotch are not gregarious in their pleasures. Each Justice protected his brother, knowing that he would shortly require a job for himself. Thus everything was favourable to the way-thief, and the poor were laughed at. The public was gradually mantrapped off everything beyond the high road. This Society [*i.e.* the predecessor of the Scottish Rights of Way Society, Limited, Edinburgh] may still do some good, but it is about fifty years too late. The true thing to humanise the people, and *save property*, is to have a footpath through every field. The alleged mischievousness of the Scotch, *when they are trusted* and have an interest in preserving what they are allowed to enjoy, all my experience induces me to deny. . . ."

In conclusion, it is wise, before presuming that there is a right of way, to ascertain the facts from a responsible source. The Scottish Rights of Way Society have caused boards, with relevant notices, to be erected in certain localities.

# PARKING

The general law is that a vehicle may not be left on a public road longer than is necessary to take up or put down passengers or goods. This law has never been rigorously enforced everywhere—otherwise modern vehicular traffic would become impossible—but the law is by no means in desuetude. The fact is that the traveller must ascertain as best he can, before he travels, what are the local rules as to reasonable grounds for interference by the police. In some localities latitude is allowed. Diagonal parking may be prohibited or allowed at the discretion of the local authority, which is now empowered to make authorised parking places, where again sweet confusion exists; for in some no lights may be left on a car, in others, at certain times, lights must be lit. The same irrational disorder applies to rules as to locking of cars. There is but one advice. Seek out the necessary information and in every place leave the vehicle—whatever its type may be—in such a position that it cannot cause danger to reasonable users of the road. The infringement of rules and regulations—particularly local ones—cannot always be guarded against. Act, however, as a reasonable and careful traveller, and your punishment will be negligible.

# TRAIN TRAVEL

The contract between the traveller and the railway company is determined by the company's regulations and bills. The terms of these regulations, etc., are embodied, by reference, in the ordinary railway ticket. It therefore behoves the traveller to make himself acquainted with them. The issue of a ticket is no guarantee that any particular train will run, or that, if the passenger is abnormal in size or any other way, a safe access to a railway carriage is a certainty.

As in other spheres of activity the passenger can have recourse to negligence on the company's part, as a ground of liability, though this may be difficult to prove. The railway company does not guarantee immunity from accident, only reasonable care. Expense incurred by passengers, consequent on breach of contract, may be recovered to the extent of what is reasonable in the circumstances. If you put luggage in your compartment, the company are not liable as common carriers but only for negligence. The porter who labels your luggage is an agent of the company. Luggage deposited is in a different category. A railway company's obligations as regards passengers and luggage are determined both by statute and by common law.

## WIFE AND CHILDREN

Should the traveller be coupled in wedlock, and have issue, note these points. Should a wife be injured by the negligence of her husband she cannot sue him for damages. A child, on the other hand, may recover damages against its parent, if injured by the parent's negligence and *vice versa*. Your wife may pledge your credit up to a reasonable amount but no further. What is reasonable is a matter of fact. You may be living beyond your means; if so you should not indulge in week-ends without adequate control of the spending partner. This may be considered to be impossible. Further, you must keep your younger children under control. Let this not deter you from a week-end. A reasonable control is, as elsewhere in the realm of liability, a safeguard. Until majority of the child the parent has a duty of control, not well-defined but subject to reasonable construction. It is the ambition of some children to light fires. Let these be under control. By the Trespass (Scotland) Act, 1865, lighting a fire on or near any private or public road or enclosed or cultivated ground, or camping on private property is punishable by fine or imprisonment, unless the consent of the owner or occupier is first obtained.

# FISHING

Fish caught become at common law the property of him who catches them, with the exception of whales of a large size, over six-power draught. This applies even to salmon fishing, which is *inter regalia*. The catching of the fish may, however, be punishable under statute, or under common law, and, under statute, the fish and the thing in which they are contained may be confiscated. The container may be a cart (including a motor vehicle) and it, along with a package containing the fish, may also be confiscated if the fishing was illegal. (There are special rules for whale fishing.) As regards normal waters care is necessary before fishing. Sea-fishing within the three-mile limit is free to any subject of the realm, and may be exercised in any way not prohibited by statute. Outside the limit, international law or custom prevails. He who first harpoons a whale will, if he retains a hold, be entitled to the mammal. It is, however, difficult to get access to the sea except through somebody else's property. This is a matter for inquiry beforehand. Though the public may have a right to navigate tidal, or even non-tidal navigable waters, this does not include a right to moor boats on private ground, and you land at your own risk. You may travel by boat up a navigable river and enter a loch from which it flows and yet find yourself in trouble. The sea, from the three-mile limit to low-water mark, belongs to the Crown. The foreshore is vested in the Crown or in those to whom the Crown has conveyed it. It is not *inter regalia*, but the Crown has, in addition to right of property, a responsibility, in connection therewith, as guardian of the public uses of navigation and fishing. While the public may use the sea for navigation or fishing this confers no right to *approach* the sea save by access open to all, and confers no right of wharfage. With regard to rivers, the right of fishing may be vested in someone other than the ostensible proprietor. If so, notices usually warn one of the fact. There is no public right of fishing, other than sea fishing.

## FLYING

The old lawyers, who dreamed not of flying, laid it down that the owner of land owns everything within his boundaries, *a coelo usque ad centrum*. Legislation has, however, empowered those flying aircraft to invade the property of private persons, and, while telegraph or telephone lines may cross the middle air above your property only by your leave, upon payment of compensation, aircraft may fly through the middle air, subject only to statutory provisions, national and international, and the liability to make good damage where it is caused to other persons' property through negligence. Questions of liability between colliding aircraft are determined by maritime precedent; damage to persons and property carried by aircraft are determined by statute, but the question of liability towards persons and property on the surface of the earth is a difficult one. Damages for trespass over your property are not recoverable. Damages for injury done to you or your property by an aircraft in flight, taking off, or landing, are recoverable, and negligence need not be proved. The danger of flying is an apparent one and he who flies must, like the owner of the wild animal, abide by the consequences. Should the accident be due to your negligence, although on the surface of the earth, you cannot recover damages.

## HIRE OF THE MEANS OF LOCOMOTION

This does not include hire of *services* such as are involved in train, bus or aeroplane travel where the traveller hires the services of those exploiting these means of locomotion for commercial ends, but is intended to cover the hire of a horse, a bicycle, a motor car, an aeroplane, or any other form of vehicle. The hirer guarantees only a reasonably suitable form of locomotion, and if it is unsatisfactory the hirer has no remedy short of alleging negligence. Circumstances alter cases, and one who proposed a lightweight motor bicycle as suitable for a 24-stone passenger might well be held to have taken the risk. If the hirer chooses the particular vehicle or animal he takes the risk of unsuitability. The hirer is liable for damage only if he puts the thing to an unreasonable use. In hiring a motor vehicle remember that it is illegal to drive with indifferent brakes and worn tyres.

## DRINK AND INNS

The requirements of the traveller cannot be estimated in advance, but it is as well to remember that, by the Tippling Acts, no person can recover at law a debt due for spirituous liquor, or upon a security given therefor, unless the debt was incurred *bona fide, at one time*, to the amount of £1 at least. This does not apply to lodgers at an inn. The hours during which liquor may be obtained in different places are set forth in various handbooks. Remember that if resident in an hotel you may not stand your guests drinks after licensing hours. Local authorities may introduce their own variations in the licensing hours for inns, public houses and clubs, and these are approved by the Sheriff, so far as each establishment is concerned, within the limits set down by the local authorities. The consumption of liquor within licensed premises, but without the permitted hours, is illegal, although the liquor may have been ordered within those hours. Liquor may be supplied at any time to a *bona fide* traveller. The distance travelled by the *bona fide* traveller, before he seeks his refreshment, is immaterial in Scotland, provided he may be said to have materially begun his journey. The person supplying liquor is entitled to satisfy himself, by legitimate means, as to *bona fides*.

## HIRE OF LODGINGS

When booking rooms at an inn remember that in such a contract, where the amount to be paid is not fixed, it is, in the event of dispute, to be settled at a reasonable amount; and further, that when rooms are booked and are thereafter cancelled by the traveller, his liability therefor may be likewise cancelled by consent of the prospective landlord. This cancellation of liability depends on commercial usage. Some landlords insist on a deposit beforehand, when rooms are booked. If the cancellation by the traveller is based on a well-founded objection to the rooms, as being unreasonable accommodation, the traveller may cancel with a clear purse; but it must be said that reasonable accommodation is a question of fact.

## NUDITY

Indecent exposure of the person is an offence and, in certain circumstances, a crime—if the place is a public one and it is stated in the charge that the lieges were annoyed in a particular way. This mode of behaviour is best performed in private. Wear a bathing-suit of proportions suitable to the customs of the locality. The point about the offence is that annoyance must be caused to someone. Whether it is reasonable to be annoyed is a question of fact. It is not advisable to be annoyed by means of binoculars.

# PERORATION

Finally, remember *Lex semper intendit quod convenit rationi*: the intendment of a law is always in accordance with reason, *e.g.* if everybody did that sort of thing what would the world come to?

# APPENDIX

## THE TOURIST'S MATRIMONIAL GUIDE THROUGH SCOTLAND

[As marriage is not in any proper point of view a desirable week-end activity, we have not discussed it in the foregoing notes; but lest we should be charged with omitting all reference to the most celebrated peculiarity of our legal institutions we subjoin the admirable statement of the law by Lord Neaves.]

Ye tourists, who Scotland would enter,
　　The summer and autumn to pass,
I'll tell you how far you may venture
　　To flirt with your lad or your lass;
How close you may come upon marriage,
　　Still keeping the wind of the law,
And not, by some foolish miscarriage,
　　Get woo'd and married an' a'.

　　　　*Woo'd and married an' a',*
　　　　*Married and woo'd an' a';*
　　　　*And not by some foolish miscarriage*
　　　　*Get woo'd and married and a'.*

This maxim itself might content ye,
　　The marriage is made—by consent,
Provided it's done *de praesenti*,
　　And marriage is really what's meant.
Suppose that young Jocky or Jenny
　　Say "We two are husband and wife",

461

The witnesses needn't be many—
   They're instantly buckled for life.

    *Woo'd and married an' a',*
    *Married and woo'd an' a';*
    *It isn't with us a hard thing*
    *To get woo'd and married an' a'.*

If people are drunk or delirious,
   The marriage of course will be bad,
Of if they're not sober and serious,
   But acting a play or charade.
It's bad if it's only a cover
   For cloaking a scandal or sin,
And talking a landlady over
   To let the folks lodge at her inn.

    *Woo'd and married an' a',*
    *Married and woo'd an' a';*
    *It isn't the mere use of words*
    *Makes you woo'd and married an' a'.*

You'd better keep clear of love-letters
   Or write them with caution and care;
For, faith they may fasten your fetters,
   If wearing a conjugal air.
Unless you're a knowing old stager,
   'Tis here you'll most likely be lost;
As a certain much-talked-about Major
   Had very near found to his cost.

    *Woo'd and married an' a'*
    *Married and woo'd an' a';*
    *They are perilous things pen and ink,*
    *To get woo'd and married an' a'.*

I ought now to tell the unwary
   That into the noose they'll be led,
By giving a promise to marry,
   And acting as if they were wed.

But if, when the promise you're plighting,
  To keep it you think you'd be loath,
Just see that it isn't in writing,
  And then it must come to your oath.

> *Woo'd and married an' a'*
> *Married and woo'd an' a';*
> *I've shown you a dodge to avoid*
> *Being woo'd and married an' a'.*

A third way of tying the tether,
  Which sometimes may happen to suit,
Is living a good while together,
  And getting a married repute,
But you who are here as a stranger,
  And don't mean to stay with us long,
Are little exposed to that danger;
  So here I may finish my song.

> *Woo'd and married an' a',*
> *Married and woo'd an' a';*
> *You're taught now to seek or to shun*
> *Being woo'd and married an' a'.*

# THE CALEDONIAN CALENDAR

*The days gang by wi' tentless speed*
BURNS

# THE CALEDONIAN CALENDAR

THE Scots are, broadly speaking, a Celtic people with a strong Scandinavian leaven, and their festivals derive from both sources.

In ancient Europe there were two methods of dividing the year. The non-Celtic peoples divided it in accordance with the solstices and the equinoxes, their two chief festivals being held at Midsummer and at Midwinter or Yule, as our Scandinavian forebears called it. The Celtic peoples, on the other hand, divided it in accordance with the entry of the seasons, their principal festivals being at Beltane (May 1st) and Hallowmas (November 1st), or, more strictly, Hallowe'en. This division of the year was natural to a people at a pastoral stage of development, for at Beltane the cattle went out to their summer pastures and at Hallowmas they returned to the fold. (The two systems were not mutually exclusive, the non-Celtic nations, for example, kept Walpurgis Night, and there was a ritual gathering of the mistletoe by the Druids, or Celtic priests, at the time of the summer and winter solstices.) The minor Celtic festivals were St. Bride's Day and Lammas, which fell on February 1st and August 1st respectively. "At four termes in the zeir," we read in the old records, "viz., Alhalowmas, Candilmas, Beltan, and Lambmes"; and though the dates have been slightly dislocated by the reform of the Calendar, the Scottish Quarter Days still follow the ancient division of the Celtic peoples, while in England they follow the non-Celtic usage.

The principal festivals in modern Scotland are Beltane, now merged with Midsummer, which is celebrated principally in the Common Ridings of the Border burghs; Hallowe'en, which is the great children's festival throughout the country; and Yule, which, owing to prejudices of the Kirk, does not now mean Christmas but "the hinner end" of the old Yule, embracing Hogmanay and Ne'er Day. Auld Handsel Monday, the "boxing-day" of the domestic servant and the farm labourer, is now virtually extinct.

## ST. BRIDE'S DAY

The Festival of Spring. Originally dedicated to a Celtic goddess of that name, later re-dedicated to St. Bride of Kildare. Bride ruled from Candlemas to Hallowmas. The winter quarter, from Hallowmas to Candlemas, was presided over by the Cailleach, or Auld Wife, who raised the winter storms.

In the Hebrides, on St. Bride's Eve, the girls of the townland tied a sheaf of corn in the semblance of a woman, decked it with shells, crystals, and the first spring flowers, and carried it from house to house, singing their processional song, *Bride Bhoideach, Beauteous Bride*. Oblations of cakes, cheese, etc., were made, and with these the girls repaired to a house agreed upon and made a feast, at which the lads joined them, the figure of Bride being set up in their midst.

In every house Bride's bed was prepared, in which the sheaf was ceremoniously laid and left till dawn, with a wand of birch, broom or other sacred wood beside her.

The sheaf represents the spirit of vegetation, and in various parts of Scotland Bride still reappears at the Kirn, or Harvest Home, as "The Maiden"—the last sheaf cut in the harvest field—which is decorated with ribbons, brought home in procession and hung up prominently at the Harvest Supper. When cut after Hallowe'en the sheaf is known as the *cailleach* or clyack.

Candlemas and Fastern's E'en have both affiliations

468

with the pagan festival of Bride. Until recent years, Candlemas was a general school holiday. A Candlemas King and Queen were crowned, cakes and sweets were distributed, in the afternoon "the ba' " was played, and in the evening there was "the Candlemas Bleeze" —usually a whin-bush set ablaze—which is a relic of the sacred bonfire of the Druids.

On Fastern's E'en the matrimonial brose (containing a ring) is eaten, the sauty bannocks ceremonially prepared and a bit put by "to dream on", and fortunes are spaed, usually by dropping the white of an egg into a wine-glassful of water and studying the shape it assumes.

## BELTANE AND HALLOWE'EN

Druidism, which was still the official religion of Scotland in the sixth century, was a form of sun-worship peculiar to the Celtic peoples. At Beltane and Hallowe'en, on the hill-tops, the Druids lit great bon-fires in honour of the sun and performed curious rites for protection and purification, and to promote fertility in man, beast and field. The Beltane fires were lit at dawn, the Hallowe'en fires at dusk. Arthur's Seat, in Edinburgh; Tinto Tap, near Lanark; and Kinnoull Hill, near Perth, are among the many traditional sites. Though the two festivals had many features in common, they differed a good deal in character. By Beltane, the seed had already been committed to the ground; by Hallowmas, the crops were already "inned". The one was in essence a Day of Supplication for a good harvest, and the other a Harvest Thanks-giving.

On Hallowe'en, too, the spirits of the departed were believed to revisit their old homes. It was the last day of the Celtic year and the whole other-world was upset. The fairies were "out" and all sorts of uncanny creatures were released for the night. Witches and

469

warlocks cleaved the air on broom-sticks or galloped along the road on tabby-cats transformed into coal-black steeds, and it was dangerous to go out after dark, unless protected by fire lit at the sacred flame. It was a season of omens and auguries, and glimpses of the future could be obtained, especially by those who had "The Sight".

In the young folk's festival of to-day many of the old divination rites survive as parlour games—Burning the Nuts, The Three Luggies and The Hidden Charms. "Dookin' for Aipples" is in all probability an ancient Druidic rite symbolising the passing through water to Avalon, apple-land, the land of the immortals. We are told that Thomas the Rhymer and the Fairy Queen, on their way to Elfland, "waded through rivers abune the knee".

> Syne they cam' on to a gairden grene,
> An' she pu'd an aipple frae a tree.
> "Tak' this for thy wages, True Thomas;
> It will gie thee tongue that can never lee."

The hazel-nut used in the divination rites symbolises "the magic tree that wizards loved" as the source of all wisdom, the grotesque masks of the guisers represent the uncanny creatures of the other-world who are supposed to be at large on this night; whilst the bonfires, the turnip lanterns and the "can'le in a custock" are the last traces of the fire-rites with which our forefathers worshipped the Unknown God, whom they believed to be enthroned in the hub of the sun's golden wheel.

The Beltane and Hallowe'en bonfires have blazed across the centuries in an unbroken chain, up to our own time, but they have gradually descended from the hill-tops to the village knoll. There are plenty of people still alive who have rolled their Beltane bannocks down some Highland hill, but it is in the Border burghs that the "Feast of Summer Come Again" is best commemorated. The bonfires appear to have died out; but the distribution of oak-leaves (the sacred tree of the Druids) at Hawick and the visit to the Moat at dawn are relics of the days of Druidism.

Until Scotland became industrialised, Yule was the one recognised holiday season in the year. The full celebration lasted from Yule E'en to Twelfth Night, but servants and labourers usually had to content themselves with "the hinner end". All routine work was discarded; the whole house was cleaned and polished, and all sorts of gudebread prepared. Short-bread and Black Bun remain the *pièces de résistance* on the Hogmanay dresser or sideboard. The Yule Ale was brewed in advance, and the Yule bread proper baked on Yule E'en between sunset and dawn—originally in honour of the Nativity. On Yule morning, every-body, gentle and simple, breakfasted on Yule Brose, which was made with rich stock instead of water. Those who could not afford a goose for dinner had a slice from the Yule Mart. During the Daft Days (as the period of jollity was called) the guisers were out. The White Boys of Yule, as they were called, were quite different from the Hallowe'en Guisers. They went about in white shirts, tall paper caps, false beards and masks—all but one of their number, who wore black—and performed their play, *The Goloshins*. The Yule Boys are the Scottish equivalent of the English Mummers.

## HOGMANAY

Hogmanay, or New Year's Eve, and its ritual call for no description. It shows no signs of falling into decay. There is, however, a regrettable laxity in the way that "first-footing" is carried out nowadays. For real luck the "first-foot" must be a dark man, who is a *bona fide* visitor and not merely one of the company who is sent outside just before midnight in order to

come in again on the last stroke. And New Year toast
should be given in these traditional terms:

> Weel may ye a' be,
> Ill may ye ne'er see,
> Here's to the King
> An' the gude companie.

The ancient Scandinavian fire-rites, other than the
burning of the Yule-log, have very nearly died out.
The most notable survivals are the Burning of the
Clavie at Burghead, and the magnificent pageant of
Up-helly-a (the Norse Uphalieday) in Lerwick.

## National Festivals

Jan.    1. Ne'er Day (New Year's Day).
        – Auld Handsel Monday (First Monday of
           the New Year, O.S.).
        6. Uphalieday (Twelfth Night). The Daft
           Days end.
       25. Burns Night.
Feb.    1. St. Bride's Day, or Candlemas E'en.
        2. Candlemas (Scottish Quarter Day).
       14. St. Valentine's Day.
March   – Fastern's E'en (Shrove Tuesday) (mov-
           able).
April  11. Gowkin' Day (All Fool's Day).
        – Pasch (Easter) (movable).
May     1. Beltane.
       15. Whitsun (approx. Old Beltane) (Scottish
           Quarter Day).
June    9. St. Columba's Day.
       23. Midsummer Eve.
       24. Midsummer. The Battle of Bannock-
           burn.
Aug.    1. Lammas (Scottish Quarter Day).
Sept.  29. Michaelmas.

Oct.    31. Hallowe'en.
Nov      1. Hallowmas.
        11. Martinmas (Old Hallowe'en) (Scottish
            Quarter Day).
        30. Anermas, or St. Andrew's Day.
Dec.    25. Yule. The Daft Days begin.
        31. Hogmanay.

## Principal Local Festivals

### YULE

Jan.           Burghead    The Burning of the
                           Clavie
               Lerwick     Up-helly-a

### CANDLEMAS

Feb.           Jedburgh    The Candlemas Ba'
               St. Andrews Kate Kennedy Day

### BELTANE-MIDSUMMER

June           Peebles     Beltane Festival
               Hawick      Common Riding
               Galashiels      „
               Selkirk         „
               Lanark      Lanimer Day
               Dumfries    Guid Nychburris Day
(third week)   Linlithgow  Common Riding
               Kilbarchan  Lilias Day
July           Lauder      Common Riding
               Musselburgh     „
(last week)    Langholm        „

## LAMMAS

| | |
|---|---|
| Aug. | St. Andrews Lammas Fair |
| | Kirkwall      ,, |
| Sept. (second week) | Annan     Common Riding |

## HALLOWMAS

| | |
|---|---|
| Nov. | Edinburgh   Hallowfair |

# THE SCOTS REGIMENTS AND THEIR TARTANS

*Our sodger buddies look'd braw, look'd braw*
LADY NAIRNE

# THE SCOTS REGIMENTS AND
# THEIR TARTANS

BESIDES the Scots Guards and the Scots Greys, Scotland contributes ten regiments of the line to the British Army, five of them in trews and five of them in the kilt. Although these regiments are under the British War Office with its headquarters in Whitehall, their idiosyncrasies have been preserved more faithfully than many Scots institutions, and much more than the idiosyncrasies of the majority of English regiments of the line. Thus in a time of khaki-ed standardisation, the Scots regiments have maintained their tartans, and jealously guard many peculiarities, of which very few Scotsmen know anything, although they can learn a great deal in the wonderful Scottish National Naval and Military Museum in Edinburgh Castle, which is under the curatorship of the learned Major Mackay Scobie.

As regards the tartans worn by the various corps, it would, in Major Mackay Scobie's words, be well to describe them as "now known". The Seaforths and the Highland Light Infantry wear the red-and-white striped tartan, the groundwork of which is the same as the Black Watch, which may be primarily associated with these corps and not with the "Clan Mackenzie". Indeed, it seems as if *their* patterns had become a clan one, and not the reverse. In any case, they are regimental setts, the tartan having been invented in 1794. The same is true of the tartans of the Gordons, the Argyll and Sutherlands, and the Camerons. The Gordon was first and foremost a regimental sett for the Fencibles of 1793, and later, for the ducal family.

The Camerons have their own regimental pattern, now described as Cameron of Erracht.

Similarly, the Royal Scots Fusiliers wear the military pattern tartan, as also did all Lowland regiments at first when dressed in semi-Highland uniform in 1881, except the Scots Guards and the Scottish Rifles, both of whom opposed it.

Pipers of various corps wear the old "music" tartan —that is, Royal Stewart—but the Royal Scots Fusiliers wear Erskine, granted in 1928. The tendency, indeed, is to emphasise the early history of the Scots regiments, and especially their connection with the families which raised several of them.

The accompanying tables show at a glance the chief differences in the uniforms of the various regiments.

| Old Nos. | Kilted Regiments | Tartan | Sporran |
|---|---|---|---|
| 42nd and 73rd | Black Watch (1725) | Black Watch (29 piped pleats) | White and 5 short black tassels |
| 72nd and 78th | Seaforths (1778 and 1793) | Regimental or Mackenzie (32 box pleats and 2 side) | White and 2 long black tassels |
| 79th | Camerons (1793) | Regimental, or "Erracht Cameron". (24 box pleats for men: 28 side pleats for officers) | Black and 2 long white tassels |
| 75th and 92nd | Gordons (1787 and 1794) | Regimental or "Gordon" (29 to 31 side pleats) | White and 2 long black tassels |
| 91st and 93rd | Argyll and Sutherlands (1794 and 1799-1800) | Regimental (27 to 29 box-pleats) | Black and 6 short white tassels |

| Old Nos. | TREWSED REGIMENTS | TARTAN | HEADGEAR | FACINGS |
|---|---|---|---|---|
| 1st | Royal Scots (Lothian Regiment) (1633) | Hunting Stewart | Kilmarnock | Blue |
| 21st | Royal Scots Fusiliers (1678) | Military or Scots Fusiliers | Bearskin cap | Blue |
| 26th and 90th | Cameronians (Scottish Rifles) (1688 and 1794) | Douglas | Chako | Green |
| 25th | K.O. Scottish Borderers (1689) | Leslie | Kilmarnock | Blue |
| 71st and 74th | Highland Light Infantry (1777 and 1787) | Regimental or Mackenzie | Chako (diced) | Buff |
| | Scots Guards | Royal Stewart (Pipers only) | Feather bonnet | Blue |

479

# THE HOLIDAY FRIEND

R

*By the delicious warmness of the mouth,*
*And rowing eyes that smiling tell the truth,*
*I guess, my lassie, that as well as I,*
*You're made for love; and why should ye deny?*
ALLAN RAMSAY

# THE HOLIDAY FRIEND

## A Note on the Establishing of Social Contacts

THE matrix or prime condition of a holiday is the abatement of labour. Energy is thereby released for other and more genial purposes, whether actual of the body or speculative of the mind, which for the greater part of the year, in the greater proportion of mankind, is spent in the quotidian offices of a mercantile, professional or industrial occupation. In the perdurable words of the Bishop, that is, a vacation provides both *time* and *inclination*. It is true that people who are brutish by nature, or in whom the felicities of curiosity and imagination have been starved by the mechanical circumstance of their environment, will squander this happy increment on the golf-links or the tennis-courts; and the muscular explosions that propel a volley or a forehand drive, as also the mental exertion required to equate windage and the parabolic drift of a slice, will sensibly hinder their perception of the aphrodisiac quality of leisure. Yet this quality cannot be disputed, and whatever may be said for the use of Arabian skink, eringoe root, the durian, the brains of sparrows, civet and nux vomica, it seems probable that the exploratory instinct and happy fantasy of love will find in idleness a more healthy nourishment than in any of these reputed specifics; and while there is a sufficiency of young men and women, their nature not yet perverted by athleticism, who have the virtue to perceive and the grace to admit the aggravation of amativity that should in all cases accompany a holiday—but especially in the months of July and August and September—it is clearly desirable that knowledge of

the preparatory strategy and preliminary tactics of a
love-affair should be more generally diffused. For in
spite of the growing easiness of manners and the
diminishment of formality there are still many who
find difficulty in accosting a stranger without em-
barrassment—which is more ruinous to love than great
ugliness or a sour breath—and of these many, some,
could they but cross with courtesy and determination
the frontiers of non-acquaintance, would make gentle,
trustworthy and pleasing companions.

How, then—with what passport, that is, or recog-
nisable yet decent countersign—should these frontiers
be approached?

With discretion, in the first place. Let there be some
period of diligent yet concealed reconnaissance during
which the active or approaching party may assure
himself that the objective is truly desirable and not
patently beyond his reach; that it is not ineradicably
habituated to nourishment and entertainment out-
with his financial resources; that it is not surrounded
by lovers already too strongly entrenched to be dis-
lodged within the duration of a summer holiday; that
it is not indissolubly joined to an ailing parent or a
bespectacled friend.

Having satisfied himself on these points, the approaching party should behave with fortitude and
resolution: but fortitude in a mask of gaiety, resolution
in a garment of ease. Let him smile, but not lickerishly
or with too gaping an aspect. Let him speak clearly,
but on some trivial subject, for many young women,
though agreeable to all the senses, have no more in-
tellect than a pullet, and like a pullet from a thunder-
ing blue charabanc will flee squawking from any
word upon the *impasse* in Ethiopia, the harmonic resources of Hindemith, or the incoherence of the
*Zeitgeist*. As introductory gambits or forcing bids for a
sentimental friendship, topics such as these have only
a limited appeal; they may serve in Bloomsbury, but

in Arran or Dunoon a comment on the weather is more generally acceptable, while a well-timed reference to sea-bathing or ballroom-dancing will establish a reputation, not easily shaken, for fluency and *savoir vivre*.

In the manner of the suitor—as he has now become —there should be apparent a courteous inclination to humour and amuse the object of his suit. To a strong and primitive nature this may be tedious, but a modern holiday resort is generally too populous to permit the more urgent approach of Solutré and the mammoth-hunters. A self-doubting and timorous mind, on the other hand, will be tempted to exaggerate its complaisance, and show anxiety to please: a fault more mischievous than the ash-plant. A safe course between violent Scylla and fawning Charybdis may be found in some small and seemingly careless display of generosity, such as the purchase of wine or sweetmeats. Mr Norman Douglas has said that chocolate is "of no value as an endearment, an incentive working not upon body but upon mind; it generates, in those who relish it, a complacent and yielding disposition". Mr Nash, the American poet, debating as rival allies the cocoa-bean and the grape, has clearly observed, and in a memorable poem succinctly described, their social values:

> Candy
> Is dandy;
> But liquor
> Is quicker.

But celerity in coming to the goal of desire will not be over-estimated save by the fool, the vulgarian and the base disciple of efficiency. The wise man, the gentle and the ingenious, will rather recall with favour the pleasant verses of Ben Jonson's friend, Sir John Roe, who sang:

> Dear love, continue nice and chaste,
> For if you yield, you do me wrong;

Let duller wits to love's end haste,
I have enough to woo thee long.

And yet to woo by wit, for the long fourteen days of holiday, one-only chance-got littoral acquaintance, might muscle-bind invention, or dehydrate it, make it sinewy and dry; do not emulate the limpet, that is doomed by lack of vision to fidelity, and grows in time so weary of faithfulness it will change its sex. Rather recall the virtuosity of that musician who, playing but one tune, could play it to perfection on thirty-seven different instruments.

Now a word against the belief that exposure of the limbs, so prevalent on the sea-shore, inevitably provokes a mutual amiability: *summa ars est artem celare*, said the Romans, and their decision, that *ars*—in particular *summa ars*, which implies a certain prominence—should be artfully concealed or clad, deserves a wider recognition than it has lately received. Even the all-comely, the smooth-symmetrical young woman who too liberally exposes herself is either a fool or unfortunate: a fool if, of her own volition, she puts all her goods in the shop-window; unfortunate if the company she keeps is so dull that womanhood, for its Bœotian gaze, must be spelt out in all its alphabet. Where manhood is not yet debased, her littlest smile should be a sufficient invitation, and the well-contrived *œillade* the very duplication of Lord Nelson's flags at Trafalgar.

---

Jenny said to Jocky, gin ye winna tell,
Ye shall be the lad, I'll be the lass mysel';
Ye're a bonny lad, and I'm a lassie free;
Ye're welcomer to tak' me than to let me be.
*Allan Ramsay*

# TO THE
# STRANGER WITHIN OUR GATES

*God send ye mair sense and me mair siller.*
OLD SAW

# TO THE
# STRANGER WITHIN OUR GATES

THAT there may be no misunderstanding or offence,
let it be said at once that the following remarks are not
intended for that growing section of Scotland's population, the English who are settled among us. These are
not "strangers", but, in the Scottish phrase, "in-
comers". All such are advised not to read this section,
and that for two reasons. In the first place, applied to
them, our admonitions would be an impertinence.
Secondly, ardent as is the native Scot's love and admiration for Scotland, it is lukewarm compared with
that of the English incomer, who is so inordinately
sensitive to the slightest breath of criticism of the land
of his adoption that he might even discern satire in our
blameless words. And this is but natural. Abuse Scotland to a Scot, and he may tolerate it, even acquiesce
in it—he is, as Dr. Johnson pointed out, not responsible for the accident of his birth: but venture even to
criticise Scotland to an English incomer and you
disable his judgment, and invalidate his taste, than
which nothing is less forgivable. There are said to be
in the remote North congregations so careful for the
purity of public worship that they glue up the leaves
of the pulpit Bible containing the Paraphrases lest any
strange minister should offer to employ the abominations in praise of God. The English incomer ought to
do likewise with these pages of *The Scots Week-End*.
They are not meant for him, but for those who are
truly strangers within our gates, who come to Scotland
for a little while, chiefly to play there rather than to
pray, and go away again, sometimes to speak well of
us as hosts and play-providers, sometimes ill; sometimes to return, sometimes not.

And now, stranger, having stated what you are not, let us consider more precisely what you are. You are of every colour, race and culture. When you are not a British subject you are most probably an American; but in the great majority of cases you can and do call yourself an Englishman. This means, *inter alia*, that you find it difficult, when you find it worth while trying at all, to pronounce a pure vowel, and that your aspirates are not all they might be. (Excuse us, Sir or Madam, but you do, and they are not.) And to make up for this you sometimes slip in a consonant. You have, even in your own high places, been known to refer to your admirable legal system as the *lore* of England.

But let these things pass. It is nothing to the purpose to classify you according to your pigmentation, your allegiance or your particular way of mispronouncing a noble language. What matters here is your motive in coming among us, and on this principle you belong to one or other of two categories—you are either a "sportsman" or a "tourist". If you are the former we could address you at some length and with even more vigour of expression. In either event it is improbable that you will pay any attention to our strictures. We submit them, however, in brief, neither for your sakes nor our own, but for that which is dearer than either to every Scotsman—the principle of the thing.

By a "sportsman" we understand (*a*) a wealthy English tradesman or (*b*) an American trust magnate or (*c*) a Levantine money-broker or (*d*) the parasite, male or female, of any of these, who comes to Scotland because it abounds in beautiful and edible wild creatures that can be "preserved", that is to say, encouraged to breed in order that they may be slaughtered by him (or her), not because he (or she) is hungry, but because it is such good fun. We abstain from cavilling here at a liking for blood-sports—it is a taste that has been shared by many estimable men in all ages—but if you come to Scotland to pursue them, there are one or two things we wish you would bear in mind.

In the first place, remember that so that you, the stranger, may have your pleasure (for which, praise God, you are made to pay through the nose) huge tracts, amounting to several millions of acres, that once supported men and cattle have been laid waste, and that for the most part these wastes are rigorously policed by your hirelings. Without your permission we set foot on our native heaths at our peril. This we can understand, for it is essential that the game you pay for should not be disturbed in multiplying; but you, in return, must understand that we resent as unnecessary our being stopped on the King's highway by your gamekeepers and impertinently questioned. In Scotland we have long been taught that "he that ruleth his spirit is better than he that taketh a city", or, as Horace has it, *Animus, nisi paret, imperat*. Whether this in all circumstances is a good thing for us is perhaps debatable. There can be no question that in these circumstances it is a good thing for you, ensuring, as it does, that your throat remains unslit. Consider this, and do not assume that because you do not belong to Scotland therefore Scotland belongs to you. Putting aside the bad logic, such an assumption is in the worst taste.

Does this studiously moderate statement of the position sound somewhat harsh? Are you really, belying your behaviour, a good fellow at heart, whose *gaucherie* is merely a result of your lack of imagination? If so we ask you to find some means of letting us see it.

There is a story—perhaps it ought to rank with our Celtic legends—that once upon a time an English clergyman of means, who was also a Christian, acquired a small sporting estate in our Highlands. So attached was he to the place, the people and their ways, that he not only became an elder in the local parish church, but even sat for several years as a member of the General Assembly. (How he squared accounts with his bishop is not told.) We do not suggest that you should follow thus far the example of this man of God. Not everybody finds the atmosphere of a kirk-session congenial. But there are limits in the same direction that you might reach without harming yourselves or us. We admit the possibility that, unlike our clergyman, you do not like us. There have been some of us who have not liked you. Or, not disliking us, you may feel that you lack spiritual contacts with us. There was an old Scot who wrote that "there is nocht twa nations undir the firmament that are mair contrar and different fra utheris nor is Inglis men and Scottis men", and some good English writers have said the same. In either circumstances you have no choice but to keep aloof from us, even while you occupy our ground. If you feel a foreigner, by all means be a foreigner in Scotland. But let us point out that even this implies an acceptance on your part of the customary obligation of a foreigner to walk delicately among his hosts. You cannot, Sir or Madam, both eat our oatcake and have it.

At this point we can hear some of you protest: "But I *do* like you Scotch! How can you think otherwise? Don't I turn up in force at every Highland Gathering of the season to see you throwing the hammer and tossing the caber and hear the pibroch sounding, sounding? Splendid chap the Highlander—finest on earth—so handsome, brawny, courteous, dignified and all that."

While we submit to your good opinion we should value it more if we could think that you knew what you were talking about. The Highlanders who are still suffered to inhabit their glens represent less than a quarter of the population of Scotland, and even them you do not know by sight. The only Highlanders with whom you are on speaking terms are the handful you employ as gamekeepers, and you are far from knowing what these think of you. So, to be frank, are we. For your Highlander's private opinions are as abstruse and unfathomable as your cat's, though possibly, as far as you are concerned, much the same. That is to say, it is improbable that he loves you, but he recognises that you provide him with a semi-gentlemanly livelihood that does not feel too like work. He has many virtues, but industry is not one of them. Neither is candour. On the other hand, he may claim to be the only man who can be a complete sycophant without forfeiting his dignity.

At this point, stranger, we ought to beg your pardon. We have been talking too much on the assumption that you are a sportsman, whereas the odds are a hundred to one that you are nothing of the sort, but belong to the tribe of very welcome guests who cheerfully bear with our weather, our licensing laws, our Sabbaths and our funny or infuriating little ways, all because Scotland is still a home of wild beauty.

The weather, let us point out, we cannot help: it is, like the beauty, as God made it. But seeing He has made it what it is, you may find it unreasonable that we should compel you to go hungry and thirsty on Sunday to His Glory, especially as we don't do it ourselves. We are prepared to admit that on a superficial view your objection is plausible. But it is a deeply-rooted conviction of ours, and, being such, its rightness may not be doubted, that on Sunday, eating and drinking ought to be done only in the home. You may urge that you have not got a home up yonder. We are sorry, but that is your misfortune, not our fault. Having homes, of which we not infrequently tire during the passage of the Sabbath, we ourselves have only to nip into our car and run up to (say) Gleneagles for a round of golf and a good binge afterwards. The notion that we are bigots is a vulgar error. We make exceptions—but only for ourselves.

As all this is intended for your greater guidance; and for warning that shall include some measure of encouragement, in spite of discouraging appearances, we ask rather your thanks than your pardon for ending with a short series (no longer than the Ten Commandments) of "Don'ts" for all who are citizens of the British Commonwealth or of the United States of America:

1. *Don't*, if you are English, keep telling us how much better educated we are than your own countrymen. You ought to know that it is not true. We do. At the same time . . .

2. *Don't* pretend that you can't pronounce the guttural aspirates of our place names. You can say *loch* if you like to try once or twice, and it sounds better than *lock*.

3. *Don't*, on the other hand, fancy that we shall admire as just your pronunciation if you say that you play "goff" when you mean that you play golf. Books which tell you that the *l* is silent are incorrect. In the Scots vernacular it is vocalised, so that the game becomes *gowf*. But you are not required or expected to speak the Scots vernacular.

4. *Don't* say Dúnlop or Kínloch or (worst of all) Cárnegie, for Dunlóp, Kinlóch and Carnégie. Your education ought to instruct you that these *duns*, *kins*, *cars*, etc., are no more than common descriptive prefixes and never the significant part of the name. Not that our place-names are not tricky. The Glasgow water supply comes from a loch of which the name does not rhyme with "latrine", however much you may be tempted to think so. And the London bus-conductor who bids his Scottish fare alight at Eljin Avenue is misinformed.

5. *Don't* claim acquaintance or anything else with So-and-So "or any of that ilk", still worse "any of

his ilk". No such thing as an ilk exists or ever did exist. "Of that ilk" means "of the same". It is an idiom used when a laird's territorial designation is the same as his surname. Thus it is permissible, as we sometimes use, to speak of "Macleod of that ilk". But it will be safer for you to stick to "Macleod of Macleod".

6. *Don't* refer to our places of worship as "kirks". We may sometimes speak of our Establishment as the Kirk, because it is our native word. But to you it is the Church of Scotland.

7. *Don't*, if you mention our national bard, call him Bobby Burns. He never answered to that name in life, nor do we call him by it since his death. Besides you don't catch us saying Bill Shakespeare or Alf Tennyson.

8. *Don't* permit yourself the use of the word *pawky*, not, at least, when you are striving to select one of the few Scots words for which there is no exact English equivalent. *Pawky* means neither more nor less than sly. It is, therefore, uncomplimentary rather than otherwise. It conveys nothing, we trust, that is specifically Scottish, either in regard to humour or to character.

9. *Don't* confuse or identify a sporran with a filibeg. You may wear the filibeg without the sporran, but you had better not try to wear the sporran without the filibeg. The police object.

10. *Don't* let our bad example or anybody else's well-meant precept persuade you that you must never call us and ours "Scotch", but always "Scottish" or "Scots". This is a recent piece of pedantry. Like most pedantry it is born of ignorance and nourished on snobbery. It has no authority in usage that can properly be called Scotch, Scottish, Scots or good English. "Scotch" is the normal form throughout Britain, and Sir Walter Scott, when he was writing English, correctly designated

himself a Scotchman. Pedantry has so far prevailed that the Scotch Office has had to become the Scottish Office, but we have not yet attained to Scots whisky, butter-Scots or hop-Scottish.

If in addition you can remember that a gigot (locally pronounced jiggot) is a leg of mutton and an ashet (*assiette*) the dish upon which it is served, you should get through Scotland as comfortably and creditably as can be expected.

# ENVOI

Fairweill thairfoir my hairt adew
fairweill and have gudnicht.
God graunt that we doe never rew
bot to have chosin richt.

# INDEX OF AUTHORS

# INDEX OF SONGS

THE END